CU00842654

BURNS AND TRADITION

BURNS AND TRADITION

Mary Ellen Brown

University of Illinois Press
Urbana and Chicago

First published in the United States of America
by the University of Illinois Press

Printed and bound in Hong Kong

This book is printed on acid-free paper.

Library of Congress Cataloging in Publication Data

Brown, Mary Ellen, 1939—
    Burns and tradition.

    Bibliography: p.
    Includes index.
    1. Burns, Robert, 1759–1796–Knowledge–Folklore,
mythology.   2. Burns, Robert, 1759–1796–Appreciation–
Scotland.   3. Oral tradition–Scotland.   4. Folklore–
Scotland.   5. Scotland in literature.   I. Title.
PR4342.F6B76   1984   821′.6   83–10311
ISBN 0–252–01102–3

For PERRIN and TORRENCE

Contents

List of Plates

Preface and Acknowledgements

Robert Burns was born on 25 January 1759 in the small village of Alloway on the southwestern coast of Scotland, not far from the town of Ayr. The first child of a middle-aged father, Burns was born into a rural, agricultural environment; his father was a gardener at the time of Burns' birth, but subsequently leased successively and unsuccessfully several farms, always attempting to be more independent and prosperous and hoping to avoid hiring out his children in service to others. William Burnes, for so he spelled his name, was particularly concerned that his son be educated, for education was essential for religious participation and the resulting good life. Together with neighbouring parents he engaged a teacher; and when that arrangement ended, he continued his son's education himself after the long, shared working hours which subsistence required of them both. Several weeks of study in slack summer seasons completed Burns' formal education. Informally, he read all available books – mostly English and Scottish literature and history – and sought to improve his mind by joining with male contemporaries in a debating society, formed in 1780 in Tarbolton. Free-masonry also expanded his horizons and provided an important social outlet. The writing of poems and songs gave Burns an additional mental activity and set him apart from the majority whose lives were hard and agriculturally dominated. When his father died, a victim of that hard life, leaving Burns and his brother Gilbert as heads of the family, Burns was twenty-five.

Free from his father's constant direction and supervision, Burns entered into a series of relationships with women which resulted in his fathering their children. The pregnancy of Jean Armour, one of the beauties of the small town of Mauchline, near the farm of Mossgiel Burns and Gilbert had rented, precipitated several important events in Burns' life and might be identified as the catalyst for a series of occurrences that have led to Burns' worldwide recognition today.

Although it is impossible to discover the exact relationship of the various events one to another, the following seems plausible: Jean's parents forbad her marriage to Burns because he was not considered good enough; in fact they encouraged her to destroy the written, signed, but unofficial, marriage agreement with Burns which was legally acceptable at the time. Burns' acknowledgement of his role in Jean's predicament led him to be publicly rebuked as a fornicator by the Presbyterian Church which was, in the eighteenth century, a powerful and effective instrument of social control. His father's death, the religious, public rebuke, and his dissatisfaction with farming led him to contemplate emigration to Jamaica in hopes of improving the quality of his life in a milieu where his past hardships and transgressions would not be public knowledge. Such a move must have seemed radical and the possibility of a return to Scotland remote: it occurred to him to leave behind a record, a monument to his existence, in the form of the poems and songs he had been writing probably since his teenage years – as had others in his immediate and extended cultural environment – and circulating orally and in manuscript form to his friends and neighbours. In 1786 a selection of his work, paid for by prior subscription, was published in Kilmarnock. The reception was favourable. When a copy of this collection, *Poems, Chiefly in the Scottish Dialect*, found its way to Edinburgh and was praised, word was indirectly sent to Burns that he should come to the capital city and arrange for a second edition. This positive response to his literary endeavours beyond his local environment altered Burns' plans to emigrate, if indeed they had ever been serious, and gave momentary direction to his life. He did not marry Jean, though periodically he returned to her with much the same result, until two years later, after his Edinburgh sojourn. But one might conclude that her first pregnancy initiated the publication of his work and by extension led to his recognition as a poet beyond the rural and local milieu.

From the very beginning, Burns was sceptical of the interest shown in himself and his poetry in Edinburgh; however, he was quick to capitalise on his reception, arranging for an Edinburgh edition only slightly expanded beyond the Kilmarnock volume. This edition, financed through subscription as the earlier volume had been, could boast as principal subscribers the *crème de la crème* of Edinburgh society – the Caledonian Hunt. This connection with high society, coupled with the intelligentsia's acclaim through the blind poet Thomas Blacklock, the novelist Henry Mackenzie, and others brought Burns into contact with an entirely different audience and order of persons when contrasted with his genuinely rural, small-town, agricultural origins. First things came first – his edition. When time permitted – as it certainly did in the evenings – he was in the beginning 'wined and dined' by the socially high and curious. When his novelty value wore off, he sought the company of a more egalitarian society, be it in the convivial clubs, like the Crochallan Fencibles or Cape Club, or in the back-street howffs where he met individuals less influential and renowned in that day. Fortuitously, he met James Johnson, the engraver, with whom he collaborated for the remainder of his life in publishing that monument to Scottish song, *The Scots Musical Museum.*

Financial uncertainties and professional potentialities must surely have bothered him throughout this time. Compared with his past, however, his stay in Edinburgh was virtually idyllic, and financial worries did not keep him from a life of relative leisure. His growing public recognition in Edinburgh and Scots-speaking Scotland enabled him to move freely and to receive generous hospitality. He took several trips – to the Highlands, to the Borders – meeting correspondents and the curious, and visiting well-known topographical spots celebrated earlier by others or destined to be immortalised later by him. Only once, for a day, did he cross over into England. His travels, as was his life, were undeniably Scottish. Burns remained in Edinburgh longer than necessary in the constant expectation of being paid by his publisher William Creech for the Edinburgh edition of his work; he needed the money to establish himself, either as a farmer, as a soldier, or as a government employee. He had hoped no doubt for a patronage job which would free him for writing. Although genuine chances of this never materialised, he was able to utilise all his influence and pressure to get his name on the excise list and receive the requisite training.

Finally he had to make a decision about the future course of his life. Offered a farm in Dumfriesshire by an admirer/well-wisher, supposedly at a reasonable rent, he decisively returned to the soil, wed – however belatedly – Jean Armour, and moved to Ellisland. His hesitancy to take up farming again was based on prior experience: he knew the demands of the life; he had seen his father fail repeatedly. His excise training must have provided mental solace and assurance of potential employment should agriculture fail. Whether Burns was a half-committed farmer or whether the land was inhospitable is unclear; farming did not go well. Gradually he began to work into an excise position, riding many miles a week in service to the Crown, simultaneously farming. The bare subsistence expectation and the hard physical labour involved finally contributed to his giving up the farm, moving to Dumfries, and taking up full-time excise work.

In the Ellisland and Dumfries days, he moved among persons of all social classes; his recognition as a poet made him a respectable and sought-after companion. His work was consuming. Finding time for work, socialising, and family responsibilities may well have overtaxed his health. Add to that his leisure-time writing, largely for the *Museum* and for another song collection, *A Select Collection of Original Scotish Airs for the Voice*, engineered by George Thomson, and his accomplishments appear prodigious. Despite intermittent and possibly radical treatment, Burns died on 21 July 1796; he was thirty-seven years-old. The fame, the recognition, the infamy, the stories – incipient during his life – began then to grow and develop.

Burns became and continues to be a figure in the Scottish legendary and customary tradition, which is predominantly oral and unofficial and passed on aurally and by observation and imitation. This cultural tradition directly affected his own life, providing the themes, the tunes, the style, the strategies, and the subject matter of many of his own creative works. The stuff of his poetry and songs was consonant with the world in which he lived: it drew deeply from the Scottish cultural tradition. It seems right therefore that some of his works share a place in the Scottish oral tradition with the kind of material that inspired them in the first place.

Tradition is a constant process across time and in time, linking past with present, thus ensuring continuity. It is also dynamic and ever-changing as culture and societal needs alter. One of the elusive but preserving cultural bases which bind people to one another, it unites individuals and refutes the isolation and insularity man as a social being fears. Burns belonged to the Scottish cultural tradition: it informed, both unconsciously and consciously, his own creative endeavours; he actively collected, edited, and annotated songs which were a part of the shared tradition because he felt they were important cultural documents. His knowledge of the oral poetic and song tradition was so deep and intimate that some of his own works entered the dynamic process of oral transmission. There is a beautiful balance here – what he used he gave back in kind. His relationship to the dynamic of Scottish oral tradition, however, does not end here: the force of his achievements and the distinctness of his personality encouraged the telling of stories about him – first from the personal perspective, later in a more distanced legendary form, and finally through jokes and anecdotes. These stories and his poems and songs have been incorporated into a widely celebrated calendar custom, with its own rituals and requirements. The relationships of Burns to tradition are many and reciprocal.

I did not know all of this when I first began my study of Burns: in fact, my initial contact with Burns was accidental: he turned out to be the probable editor/source of one version of a widely known ballad, 'Still Growing', whose history I was studying. That discovery raised further questions to be answered – questions about Burns' reliance on oral tradition in his own work generally and finally questions about his dual impact on Scottish literature and culture – through his poetry and songs and through the narratives and celebration which focus more on Burns the man than on his work.

In trying to answer these questions, to explain why, I have looked at many books and articles – scholarly and popular – on Burns. Without them this study could not have been made. Often they have touched tangentially on questions which interested me. But none of these works has dealt with the pattern of Burns and tradition as a whole, the topic of this book.

The sources for this study have been varied and have included printed works, manuscripts, archive material, questionnaires, and fieldwork. In the historical and critical chapters I am indebted both to previous scholarship and to primary sources relating to Burns. In studying tradition's use of Burns, I employed a variety of data-gathering techniques, with significant emphasis on fieldwork. During visits to Scotland – the summer of 1972, the school year 1973–4, and part of the summer of 1976 – I collected a variety of material on the contemporary Burns Suppers and many versions of current legend and anecdotal tradition. My early fieldwork focused on already identified tradition bearers. Later I used a more general and highly random interview technique to determine how Burns was viewed and what was known about him and his work. My aim was to gather data from as many sources as possible in order to document the complex relationships of Robert Burns and tradition. Since, however, tradition is on-going, changing, developing, there is in reality no end to the study; for Burns continues to be a figure of consequence – in legend, in custom, and in art.

My quest for answers brought me in touch with many people: I could never name them all or adequately repay their generosity, their various hospitalities, their welcome. What I discovered early on in this work was the calling card Burns offered me – the mention of my subject was frequently an instant 'open sesame' to people and places and traditional knowledge. My forays to Scotland assure me that in that corner of the world there is a measure of humanity, echoing as well as affirming Burns' own wish

> That Man to Man the warld o'er,
> Shall brothers be for a' that. —

My debts are many: some can never be paid. Without MacEdward Leach this book would never have been written; he introduced me to the study of folklore and particularly to the ballad; the latter led me circuitously to Burns and the lyric. But that was long ago. Between then and now, many have helped — through belief and scepticism: scholars, enthusiasts, colleagues, friends, chance acquaintances. To them all I am grateful — particularly to the countless Scots who so willingly gave of their time to aid my work.

I would especially mention the Scottish Burns Club, Edinburgh; the Edinburgh Ayrshire Association; the Edinburgh Burns Club; the Ninety Burns Club; the Happy Friends Old Age Pensioner Club, Church of Scotland, West Mayfield, all of whom graciously welcomed me to their meetings and activities; the members of the Burns Club of Atlanta, the Detroit Burns Club, and the Burns Club of St Louis for their willingness to answer a questionnaire; to Robert Dinwiddie & Co. Ltd, Dumfries; the British Library; the Edinburgh University Library; the National Library of Scotland; Indiana University Library for making their collections of materials available to me.

The Mitchell Library, Glasgow; the Scottish National Portrait Gallery; the Scotsman Publications Ltd; The Pierpont Morgan Library; The Librarian, Aberdeen University Library; Professor Bø Almqvist, Department of Irish Folklore, University College, Dublin; Professor John MacQueen, School of Scottish Studies, University of Edinburgh; Oxford University Press (for extracts from the Oxford English Texts edition, *The Poems and Songs of Robert Burns* edited by James Kinsley (3 vols), © Oxford University Press 1968); Macmillan Publishing Company (for extract from *Born to Win* by Woody Guthrie, edited by Robert Shelton. Copyright © The Guthrie Children's Trust Fund 1965) have kindly granted me permission to quote and print certain materials. Earlier versions of some sections of this book were published in *Scottish Studies*, *Studies in Scottish Literature*, *Journal of the Folklore Institute*, and *Arv*; the material is reprinted here in altered form with the permission of the respective editors.

My particular thanks go to colleagues and friends who have been party in one way or another to this work – listening, responding, suggesting: Bø Almqvist, Alexander and Jessie Bruce, Alan Bruford, Alexander Fenton, Hamish Henderson, G. Henderson Laing, Robert E. Lewis, Jean McCourt, Mary MacDonald, John MacQueen, Ailie Munro, Séamas O'Catháin, G. Ross Roy, Anthony Shipps, Sean O'Súilleabháin, G. Scott Wilson. I owe additional gratitude to David Buchan, Emily Lyle, and W. Edson Richmond who willingly took time from their own busy schedules to read and comment on portions of this work. Jane Burgoyne gave support, enthusiasm, and friendship, introducing me to many persons and groups, making aspects of my research not only easier but much pleasanter: her knowledge and encouragement both aided and sustained me. Thomas Crawford read and commented, advised and cajoled from long distance: his friendship and scholarly guidance have been of greater benefit than I could ever adequately express.

Finally, I would like to acknowledge the particularly generous support and encouragement of Indiana University, especially the office for Research and Graduate Development.

My debts are many; in some small measure, I hope that this work repays the interest, help, and encouragement I have received.

Edinburgh and Bloomington *M.E.B.*

1 The Early Period: Burns' Intuitive Use of Scottish Tradition

(That Bards are second-sighted is nae joke,
And ken the lingo of the sp'ritual folk;
Fays, Spunkies, Kelpies, a', they can explain them,
An ev'n the vera deils they brawly ken them.)
'The Brigs of Ayr, a Poem'

Robert Burns is remembered as much for his personality and character as for his poetry and songs. It is rather ironic that as an individual his roots in a peasant class are extolled, even emphasised; however, as a creative artist his debts to written, élite precedents are principally cited. Both are probably somewhat extreme positions: as an individual Burns both represented and transcended his class; as a poet and songwright he followed the example of earlier writers while being simultaneously influenced by the oral literary forms which flourished in the milieu of his birth.

The stress on Burns' literary sources is a natural and explicable one: those who study Burns as literary historians and critics see him and his work through the dimension of time and often in comparison with other written work – the tangible records of the artistic endeavours of the past; and he does seem to have been the culmination of the Scottish literary tradition and to have profited from exposure to English literature. Burns himself praised a number of his predecessors and tried, in as much as was possible, to read the best of past artistry and to keep abreast of current efforts. The primary matrix in which he lived, however, was not completely a literate one: much of the artistic communication he shared with his contemporaries was oral and aural; for the ballads and folksongs he absorbed from multiple hearings[1] and

1

the legends and other narratives which punctuated convivial convers-
ation were a more pervasive and typical – if, unfortunately, ephemeral –
part of the everyday world in which he lived than the poetry of Robert
Fergusson or Thomas Gray. In a famous biographical letter to Dr
Moore written after he had received acclaim as a poet, Burns described
the influences he had come under when he was a boy and specifically
mentions his mother and an old woman, loosely connected with the
family, who provided him with an early stock of songs, tales, legends,
beliefs, proverbs, and customs:

> In my infant and boyish days too, I owed much to an old Maid
> of my Mother's, remarkable for her ignorance, credulity and
> superstition. – She had, I suppose, the largest collection in the county
> of tales and songs concerning devils, ghosts, fairies, brownies,
> witches, warlocks, spunkies, kelpies, elf-candles, dead-lights, wraiths,
> apparitions, cantraips, giants, inchanted towers, dragons and other
> trumpery.[2]

The oral artistic creations, cumulatively built and recreated, passed on
from generation to generation, stable in general form but varied in
individual performance, were his birthright and a natural and universal
part of the general society in which he lived – where traditional custom,
belief, and practice dominated and overt creativity and innovation were
not sought. This traditionally oriented way of life and the oral artistic
communications it supported and sustained played a far more signifi-
cant role in shaping and determining the directions of Burns' artistry
than has been recognised.

Like all writers or creative artists, Burns was not an isolate; and he
cannot be realistically divorced from the milieu in which he lived. He was
a product of what had gone before and what was and his artistry often
lay in uniquely blending, juxtaposing, or representing this. He was a part
of a long tradition.[3] When T. S. Eliot suggests in 'Tradition and the
Individual Talent' that all artists are a part of a tradition and are
representatives of it, he is referring essentially to literary and élite
aesthetic traditions.[4] Any artist is, as well, a product of a cultural
tradition, and it is Burns' cultural tradition which has been slighted and
frequently overlooked in most serious studies of the man and his work.

The rural Ayrshire into which Burns was born might be described as a
modified peasant society: it was rurally based and dominated by
agriculture; its people were relatively homogeneous and shared a body

of knowledge, mostly oral; it was a society in many respects characterised by a preference for the old ways, for what had always been, the 'tried and true'. This society often provided the background and informing principle for Burns' writing; and the oral artistry found in such a society shaped the form, content, style, and process of much of his work. These traditional manifestations of culture – folkways or folklife and oral literature – might be broadly called *folklore*. And what follows is a documentation and illustration of the multiplicity of ways folklore affected Burns' art, exhibiting his debt to his own folkloric matrix and the traditional and repeated aspects of life, especially the oral artistic communications, which were a part of it.

This debt to his milieu and its artistry was largely unconscious and intuitive prior to 1786.[5] Edinburgh marked a transition to a far more aware and conscious artistry, to be discussed in Chapters 2 and 3, which was both antiquarian and national in inspiration. The poetry prior to Edinburgh deals primarily with folklife,[6] with description of the rural existence, resulting sometimes in frankly occasional pieces; and Burns makes his larger comments about life against this backdrop, which was his milieu and naturally became an important part of his creative view. While Hugh MacDiarmid faults Burns for this localism,[7] it was undoubtedly essential for the establishment of his poetic voice and rarely kept Burns from suggesting a more universally applicable principle or sentiment as well. The events of 1786 – the publication of the Kilmarnock edition and the visit to Edinburgh – precipitated a shift away from this local poetry which drew its inspiration from the region of the poet's birth.

Burns was not an oddity in writing poems and songs.[8] He knew other local poets who shared his predilection for rhyme and exchanged verse letters with several – notably John Lapraik. The existence and prestige of poets, representing relatively defined locales, sometimes mere rhymers or village versifiers, may have its roots in the Celtic past where poet or bard stood in close relationship to priest or chieftain, being responsible for memory of the past as well as celebration of the present. Such a tradition surely continues in the often puerile laureate effusions composed to mark the special events of the present. But long ago the poet held a central position close to the seat of power and celebrated high points of the life and yearly round of activity; he spoke for as well as against the status quo, was often under protection of chieftain or priest's office, and used well-established traditional forms and structures as vessels for a contemporary message. Burns too took the forms and structures of the past and developed them by using the present:

sometimes his pieces were frankly occasional and descriptive; in others
his satire and social criticism worked effectively as in the days of the
Celtic bards. But unlike the Celtic bard, Burns had no chieftain to
protect him, to sanction or approve his words.

Like the Celtic bard, Burns wrote for a local audience, which shared
his interest in the geographic area and in current events and issues. That
audience was known to him; it included his friends and his neighbours;
and as often as not he read or recited his productions aloud to them[9] or
circulated them in handwritten manuscripts. The audience he
addressed – their politics, ethos – no doubt affected what lines he added
or cut, amply illustrated in his lengthy correspondence with Mrs Dunlop
and the manuscript versions he frequently sent her. Such flexibility
reflects an attitude more akin to oral communication than to the
impersonality of the written literary world where the reading public is
only generally known and where the literary text is fixed and unchang-
ing. Burns' audience always retained a specific quality for him, even
when he was no longer a local, but more nearly a national, poet. The
principal edition of his work, the 1786 Kilmarnock edition, was
essentially aimed at a relatively local audience, though, to be sure, his
Preface looked beyond it. This concern with audience is characteristic of
oral communication; it reflects a need for immediate response, for give
and take. Burns' poetry and songs, like the traditional folksongs and
narratives, were passed on in a small, local, mostly homogeneous group.

If his audience was local and shared his world, that world found its
way into his creative work as an essential ingredient in facilitating
communication. He began with the common world, the familiar which
he knew and to which he – as are all outstanding writers – was
extraordinarily sensitive. He was not merely a describer, an ethno-
grapher; he selected and focused on aspects of the shared world as a base
from which to draw broader conclusions and generalisations about the
human condition. And in transferring reality to creative work, whether
destined for oral or written transmission, his own unique personality
and background – albeit shaped by the common tradition – contributed
to an equally individual perception of the world. Nonetheless his
depiction of the world held in common with his audience lay within the
recognisable parameters of general experience and formed the essential
understood background which often effectively drew the readers or
hearers of his work into the poem or song and provided them with a
basis for the response all artistic endeavours strive for if they are indeed
an effective means of communication. Burns wrote about what he knew
using familiar forms and familiar language as well as familiar content.

From a specific account of aspects of religious controversy rampant in Burns' day in 'The Ordination'[10] and in 'The Kirk of Scotland's Garland – a new Song' (no. 264) to a depiction of a gathering of three friends, including himself, in 'Willie brew'd a peck o' maut' (no. 268), Burns drew on his own environment for surface content. The obvious and identifiable are especially blatant in his frankly occasional and extemporary poems and songs, which, like 'At Roslin Inn' (no. 158), remark on the obvious and record an impression; they remain not as a great testimony to his poetic power, but as testimony to his spur-of-the-moment poetic ability.

The celebration of the immediate, often a shared experience, links Burns with both the earlier bardic and the later poet laureate traditions. Many of his occasional poems are said to have been off-the-cuff extemporaneous productions. Some were composed in writing and remain today incised in windows of various inns he frequented. Other works he created mentally, in memory, and later, after a long journey on horseback perhaps, put in writing.[11] The oral sound rather than the written text may well have controlled his composition.[12] His use of proverbs and sayings from oral tradition,[13] phrases from traditional songs,[14] not to mention the whole stanzas and refrains which provided the basic material for many of his songs suggests a compositional technique akin to oral formulaic composition.[15] Multiple versions of some of his works may also reflect a concept of artistic product which does not insist on fixity of text; such disregard for a definitive text links Burns to the world of traditional oral composition. In many ways, Burns was a kind of transition figure – an individual who straddled both the literate and the oral worlds, and his own method of composition reflected compositional approaches from both worlds.

He composed and wrote, of course, as all artists do – at least in part – in order to communicate, perhaps to influence. But he created as well to provide solace for himself: 'However as I hope my poor, country Muse, who, all rustic, akward [*sic*], and unpolished as she is, has more charms for me than any other of the pleasures of life beside – as I hope she will not then desert me, I may, even then, learn to be, if not happy, at least easy, and south a sang to sooth my misery. – '[16] And he created to relieve tension – as entertainment – as part of life. Creating, composing was for Burns, as for oral poets past and present, organically a part of the life he led:

> Leeze me on rhyme! it's ay a treasure,
> My chief, amaist my only pleasure,

> At hame, a-fiel, at wark or leisure,
> 　　The Muse, poor hizzie!
> Tho' rough an raploch be her measure,
> 　　She's seldom lazy.
>
> Haud tae the Muse, my dainty Davie:
> The warl' may play you [monie] a shavie;
> But for the Muse, she'll never leave ye,
> 　　Tho' e'er sae puir,
> Na, even tho' limpan wi' the spavie
> 　　Frae door tae door.
> 　　　　　　　　　(ll. 37–48, no. 101)

And the use of poetic and song form, recognisably distinct from daily discourse, allowed Burns to write of love for women whom he could not ordinarily so address and to write of subjects, especially bawdry, he might not discuss in polite conversation. The functions of his art were many.

Burns' focus in his early work on local topics, his frequent use of traditional material, his acceptance of the fluidity of texts, his stress on audience and the oral socialisation of his own works, and his articulated views on the function of composition – all suggest Burns' strong and largely intuitive ties to the traditional and partially oral matrix of late eighteenth-century Ayrshire. This is not meant to diminish his relationship with the literary world: he read; he felt a debt to Allan Ramsay, to Robert Fergusson and others – both Scottish and English. And it was through the creative medium – writing and related print – he shared with them that his work lives today. But the literary and literate world was superimposed on the traditional and oral world which formed the very basis of his being. It provided him with forms and structures, content and contexts on which to build. Scottish tradition and Scottish oral artistry were his birthright.

Burns utilised various aspects of the whole gamut of traditional life and art available to him. The content of his poems and songs overtly drew upon the repeated themes, made reference to known locale as well as to facets of the shared oral art; utilised phrases, lines and stanzas extant in the tradition; described custom, practice, belief, and milieu; and repeatedly used the structures and forms of the traditional oral artistry circulating in his milieu. Not only was the content and often the structure of his work drawn from the folkloric milieu, but his very medium of communicating – the Scots vernacular – and stylistic devices such as repetition and frequent use of refrain assert his cultural heritage. And in several works he replicates the traditional matrix for artistic communication. Scottish traditional life and especially its oral and artistic forms dominated Burns' own aesthetic perspective and formed, frequently, the unconscious basis for his creativity.

Burns' most obvious debt to the oral world of which he was part is at the level of overt content. His kinship with earlier poetry and song is illustrated by his use of themes, shared with his predecessors, whether their medium was oral or written. Earlier in the eighteenth century, the Jacobite theme had certainly had definite political overtones, but as restoration of an independent Scotland and a distinctly Scottish monarch became less and less a possibility, the Jacobite theme became the accepted vehicle for popular nationalistic expression, indulged in, through composition or participation, by persons who might not have supported the Jacobite risings of the first half of the century. This romantic Jacobitism had many adherents, Burns among them, and vague references to Bonnie Prince Charlie, especially to his absence and to the implications of his overseas' residence for Scotland, occur in Burns' songs, particularly when he draws on earlier Jacobite songs and phrases to provide a link with the established tradition — 'him that's far awa',[17] the White Cockade, the badge of the Stuarts,[18] 'Here's a Health to them that's awa'.[19] While nationalism appears in various guises in Burns' work as in 'The Vision' (no. 62) with its celebration of the power of poetry in proclaiming a Scottish nation, the theme is more often than not linked with Jacobite sentiment as in the 'Song —'

Tune—Captain Okean—

Slow

The small birds rejoice in the green leaves returning,
   The murmuring streamlet winds clear thro' the vale;
The primroses blow in the dews of the morning,
   And wild-scattered cowslips bedeck the green dale:
But what can give pleasure, or what can seem fair,
   When the lingering moments are numbered by Care?
No birds sweetly singing, nor flowers gayly springing,
   Can sooth the sad bosom of joyless Despair. –

The deed that I dared, could it merit their malice,
   A KING and a FATHER to place on his throne;
His right are these hills, and his right are these vallies,
   Where wild beasts find shelter but I can find none:
But 'tis not my sufferings, thus wretched, forlorn,
   My brave, gallant friends, 'tis your ruin I mourn;
Your faith proved so loyal in hot, bloody trial,
   Alas, can I make it no sweeter return!

                           (no. 220)[20]

Additionally, this song utilises another recurring theme – the contrast of the seasons and the moods they project and reflect.[21] Playing against this theme in 'Sonnet, on the Death of Robert Riddel, Esq. *of Glen Riddel, April 1794*', Burns speaks of the inappropriateness of spring to his mood in this comment:

No more, ye warblers of the wood, no more,
   Nor pour your descant, grating, on my soul:
   Thou young-eyed spring, gay in thy verdant stole,
More welcome were to me grim winter's wildest roar.

                     (ll. 1–4, no. 445)

Laments, too, were a form or kind of song Burns shared with his predecessors and contemporaries though he recognised their stereotyped nature when he wrote: 'These kind of subjects are much hackneyed; and besides, the wailings of the rhyming tribe over the ashes of the Great, are damnably suspicious, and out of all character for sincerity. – These ideas damp'd my Muse's fire.'[22] Nonetheless he succumbed to writing laments from time to time.[23]

Since he was familiar with both oral and written artistry, it is understandable that he should have drawn from the great corporate fund such themes and topics as the *chanson de malmarié*,[24] the romantic view of the rural population implicit in such works as 'The Cotter's Saturday Night',[25] praise of liberty,[26] and especially glorification of love and the lasses, found notably in such songs as the famous 'I love my Jean':

Tune—*Miss admiral Gordon's Strathspey*—

Of a' the airts the wind can blaw,
    I dearly like the West;
For there the bony Lassie lives,
    The Lassie I lo'e best:
There's wild-woods grow, and rivers row,
    And mony a hill between;
But day and night my fancy's flight
    Is ever wi' my Jean. –

I see her in the dewy flowers,
    I see her sweet and fair;
I hear her in the tunefu' birds,
    I hear her charm the air:

> There's not a bony flower, that springs
> By fountain, shaw, or green;
> There's not a bony bird that sings
> But minds me o' my Jean. –
>
>   (no. 227)

Sharing not only themes but also superficial content with both popular and oral literature and with his traditionally oriented world, Burns utilised stereotyped, pastoral names for his protagonists; see his many Elizas and Jockeys. And he referred almost as frequently to local events or persons, often women, as in his lines on Elizabeth Paton:

> 'Twas ae night lately, in my fun,
> I gaed a rovin wi' the gun,
> An' brought a *Paitrick* to the *grun'*,
>   A bonie *hen*,
> And, as the twilight was begun,
>   Thought nane wad ken.
>
> The poor, wee thing was *little hurt*;
> I *straiket* it a wee for sport,
> Ne'er thinkan they wad fash me for 't;
>   But, Deil-ma-care!
> Somebody tells the *Poacher-Court*,
>   The hale affair.
>   (ll. 37–48, no. 47, 'Epistle to J. R.
>   ******, Enclosing some Poems')

Local places too find specific inclusion – Stewart Kyle, Mauchline.[27] Additionally, Burns borrowed commonplaces, sometimes entire lines and phrases, from earlier oral and written literature as well as from life: 'An' she has twa sparkling, rogueish een';[28] 'An' durk an' pistol at her belt';[29] 'Now fare ye well, an' joy be wi you';[30] 'In *ploughman phrase* "GOD send you speed",/Still daily to grow wiser.';[31] 'saut tear blin't his e'e', reminiscent of 'Sir Patrick Spens' and other ballads;[32] and proverbs, such as 'Deil tak the hindmost'.[33] Burns also picked up the sexual slang of the vernacular and subtly incorporated it into his work, using, for example, the hunting metaphor with reference to Elizabeth Paton, printed above, and in 'The Hunting Song' (no. 190); he also used the term 'brose and butter' in his poem of that name (no. 78), referring, in the argot, to an abundance of semen. His references to traditional belief and custom are, of course, nowhere in greater concentration than in 'Halloween' (no. 73); but they are found in many works. The devil, so familiar a figure in Scots tradition that he is called 'auld cloven Clooty', 'Auld Nick',[34] appears from time to time,[35] as does death, personified, carrying a scythe over one shoulder and a three-pronged spear over the other.[36] Burns mentions belief in second-sight, that is the ability to foresee the future, a trait often attributed to poets.[37] And as part of his local, traditional orientation he alludes to legendary figures such as King Coil, said once to have been King of Kyle.[38]

Burns' most significant and pervasive use of traditional material as the basis for his works' content is, undoubtedly, in his songs.[39] He was deeply involved with song, that artistic complex of text and tune, throughout his life. His first known work, 'O once I lov'd' to the tune 'I am a man unmarried', written at fourteen, was a song; and his last work was a song. Thus songwriting framed his artistic life. Since, however, it became a very conscious process and his primary artistic mode after his Edinburgh stay, discussion of the songs will, for the most part, be left until Chapter 3.

The present, the local, Burns' own world is overwhelmingly obvious in the content of a group of poems often referred to as 'manners-painting'. Together these poems might well be called ethnographic or ethnoliterature, for they depict the environment from a variety of perspectives, exhibiting a multiplicity of aspects of life. Detailing various facets of life in eighteenth-century Ayrshire, these verbal pictures have served for subsequent generations as records of the life of the times: in fact, various works on eighteenth-century Scotland quote Burns as the source of their information and other publications provide corroborative parallel information.[40] I have enlarged the parameters of this group to include a number of works which contain, albeit sometimes briefly and incidentally, valuable detail about the life and times, which Burns incorporated into his works as important indicators of time and place.[41] Dealing with aspects of life which are traditional, long having been a part of the yearly round of existence, many of these poems focus on custom, those repeated practices which dominate life; on belief; and on various aspects of life found in rural Ayrshire. In most, the description of the traditional practices provides the broad canvas on which Burns paints his conception of life and against which he outlines various aspects for particular notice. His selection of detail is not random: elements were specifically chosen to make a point and, in the works judged the best, to enable implied social comment; the descriptions served well as valid backgrounds from which to work. As early as 1783,

Burns had articulated his own interest in the study of men, their manners and their ways 'and for this darling subject, I chearfully sacrifice every other consideration'.[42] 'Believe me . . . it is the only study in this world will yield solid satisfaction'.[43] This interest, widespread among the educated élite in the eighteenth century, no doubt stimulated Burns' selective descriptions of aspects of traditional life.

The bulk and most significant examples of Burns' focus on traditional life were probably written between 1784 and 1785. They include insignificant incidental detail of a man's wardrobe, refer to calendar customs such as Hogmanay and harvest home, to traditional food and drink as well as to hiring practices and welcoming gifts – to man and animal. Additionally, beliefs about witches and the devil find frequent articulation. Five extended examples should illustrate the centrality of his own traditional milieu, the way of life handed down from generation to generation, in his artistry. Here the description of ethnographic detail is not incidental, but integral.

Burns' ethnographic bent may well have reached its apogee in 'Halloween' (no. 73), his poem dealing with the sacred night when spirits overtly walk mortal territory and under proper ritual circumstances may foretell or enable prophecy of the future. The poem is explicitly descriptive of certain elements of the calendar celebration, is prefaced by an explanatory introduction, and is copiously footnoted by Burns to explain the rituals mentioned to the uninitiated. It is perhaps a universal human desire to know and, if possible, to control the future: in different times and places, the means of doing so will, of course, differ. In eighteenth-century Ayrshire, prognosticatory customs were practised on various days – Halloween being one – in an attempt to foretell future relationships between individuals of different sexes. In Burns' poem, the participants are young people looking forward to the next rite of passage, the next radical change in their own lives, and hoping to know something about what to expect. Burns vividly describes the various rituals – performed, at least to some extent, because of belief in their efficacy: pulling up stalks of kail, of oats; throwing yarn into a kiln; eating an apple in front of a mirror; pretending to winnow; and sewing hemp. Kinsley and others from the eighteenth to twentieth centuries have shown that all of these practices were both widespread and well-known. The practice of pulling up green kail stocks is a case in point: according to Eve Blantyre Simpson, a couple – eyes shut, hand in hand – should pull stocks from the garden of an unmarried man or woman. If the stock is stout, the future will be good; if the roots have no dirt attached to them, poverty will be their lot; furthermore, the taste of the stock's kernel will indicate the future spouse's temperament.[44] Similarly, William Grant Stewart discusses this 'customary art of divination'. A couple, blindfolded, pull up a stock of kail; its qualities enable prophesy of the future mate's size and shape. If dirt adheres to the root, they will have good fortune; the taste of the stem foretells the disposition of the future mate.[45] M. Macleod Banks, and others, also record the tradition.[46] Burns' own note touches on these same points, undoubtedly indicating his own observation of this practice:

> The first ceremony of Halloween, is, pulling each a *Stock*, or plant of kail. They must go out, hand in hand, with eyes shut, and pull the first they meet with: its being big or little, straight or crooked, is prophetic of the size and shape of the grand object of all their Spells – the husband or wife. If any *yird*, or earth, stick to the root, that is *tocher*, or fortune; the taste of the *custoc*, that is, the heart of the stem, is indicative of the natural temper and disposition.[47]

All of these rituals may give valuable hints about one's future – who one will marry, whether or not the girl will be a virgin, whether present courtship will be smooth, what status or occupation the future mate will have. But 'Halloween' would be rather a dry, anthropological account had not Burns particularised the general by peopling his celebration with willing, hopeful individuals – joined together in fun and anticipation in a calendar custom long known. Burns names spots they might visit – known in legend to be fairy rings – and he suggests the validity of the rituals when he has Grannie warn against certain practices – for, in the past, they have driven people mad, at least temporarily – and she describes one such account. A young lad, anxious to disprove her warning and simultaneously to prove himself to his assembled peers, takes it as a dare and goes out alone; but he succumbs to fear if not to madness. These are real people, come together, who interact – however disjointedly – before our eyes, making their beliefs and customs alive and functioning. The concluding stanza

> Wi' merry sangs, an' friendly cracks,
>   I wat they did na weary;
> An unco tales, an' funnie jokes,
>   Their sports were cheap an' cheary:
> Till *butter'd So'ns*, wi' fragrant lunt,
>   Set a' their gabs a steerin;

> Syne, wi' a social glass o' strunt,
>   They parted aff careerin
>   Fu' blythe that night.
>   (ll. 244–52, no. 73)

makes it clear that the rituals were performed in a social context which
included the telling of tales and jokes, the exchange of chatter, as well as
a traditional dish of sowens (a mixture of oatmeal and sour milk), with
butter, on this significant day of the year.

'Halloween' describes both belief and custom and the people who
hold them: thus the traditional milieu is, to all extents and purposes, the
subject of the poem. The preface and the epigraph from Goldsmith alert
one to Burns' distanced stance – these practices are of the uneducated
but worthy rural folk – and explain Burns' detached focus in the poem
proper. But the description and thus the poem itself are sympathetic and
there is no contrast with the ways of educated folk, essentially because
Burns describes his own physical – if not mental – milieu; and he has
given us a scene of multiple dimensions, having the force of reality. His
own world, however limited, was the basis of his artistry; such a work as
this shows his dependence on the people he knew – 'their manners and
their ways'. There would otherwise have been no poem.

In the song 'Tam Glen' (no. 236), we get a far less sustained
description of prognostication having to do with relationships of the
sexes both on Halloween and on St. Valentine's Day. Here the belief and
custom support the dominant idea of the song: that Tam Glen is the only
lad for her:

> Yestreen at the Valentines' dealing;
>   My heart to my mou gied a sten;
> For thrice I drew ane without failing,
>   And thrice it was written, Tam Glen. –
>
> The last Halloween I was waukin
>   My droukit sark-sleeve, as ye ken;
> His likeness cam up the house staukin,
>   And the very grey breeks o' Tam Glen!
>   (ll. 21–8, no. 236)

The traditional evidences used to support her choice are only part of her
argument, but they are valid within the poem's milieu. In this brief look

at the rationalising of a young girl, Burns has, in referring to shared traditional practices, made her dilemma far more interesting and lifelike, exemplifying yet again his debt to the milieu of his birth.

In 'The Holy Fair' (no. 70) Burns describes an annual event, an ingathering of Clergy and parishioners from an extended local area for worship and communion. Although the event was begun with the sacred in mind, the secular now reigns and Burns' deft flashes from scene to scene give us a look at this tradition. His selection of foci presents the events, contrasts them, and concludes that the effective reason for having such fairs is hardly the obvious religious one:

> How monie hearts this day converts,
>   O' Sinners and o' Lasses!
> Their hearts o' stane, gin night are gane
>   As saft as ony flesh is.
> There's some are fou o' *love divine*;
>   There's some are fou o' *brandy*;
> An' monie jobs that day begin,
> May end in *Houghmagandie*
>   Some ither day.
>
>   (ll. 235–43, no. 70)

This is not description for description's sake; it is a selective panoramic perspective, presenting a spectrum of viewpoints, which no doubt reflect reality. But in an age when the clergy and Kirk session had so much control over the lives of the people, such non-compliance appears startling. Burns was not deceived: it was not religion man loved and clung to; rather it was secular delight. Those who deny the truth, blind to what is in front of their eyes, proclaiming the sacred holiness of the day, they are wrong; they are hypocrites. We know what such 'holy fairs' were like because of Burns' description, but we must recognise that the description was but a vehicle and perhaps an essential one for Burns' comment about the people among whom he lived. Thus, the traditions of his day, generally known to his audience, provided the shared background, and through selective and judicious choice from a wide spectrum of behaviour, he forces the reader to question with him the Holy Fair's very being.

There are many remnants today of the visual acuity pre-eminent in days of old when oral, aural, and visual were the rule and reading and writing the possession of few. For goodness knows how long shops and taverns announced their function and name in signs hung prominently

to attract the cognoscenti – which in this case was virtually everyone –
with known and recognised symbols, rather than words. Such signs
were part of the known. In brief, hardly flattering verses, 'Versicles on
Sign-posts' (no. 244), Burns again plays against the known – a visual
traditional art/craft – to satirise qualities of various unnamed
individuals – such as the man too wont to smile:

> His face with smile eternal drest
> Just like the Landlord to his guest,
> High as they hang with creaking din
> To index out the country Inn –
>
> (ll. 6–9, no. 244)

But Burns' ethnography is perhaps most complete in the scene and
context described in 'The Cotter's Saturday Night' (no. 72). The
technique for such description may well have come from Robert
Fergusson's 'The Farmer's Ingle' and a model for comment from such
English authors as Gray, whose lines appear as epigraph to the poem,
but the basis of the poem is a description of the traditional and typical
life around him, illustrating all humanity's inherent dignity, nowhere
more obvious than among the poor of Scotland. Burns' depiction of a
man – weary from six day's toil – in domestic repose must be recognised
as filtered and skewed, an ideal rather than an actuality. But in the
description there is much detail about life: the gear of his work, his
ploughing, the indication of the coming Sabbath as a day of rest; the
visitation of his children fee'd out to plough, herd, or run errands; the
sharing of news while light sociable tasks like mending continue; the
modest supper of porridge and cheese followed by the family worship
around the fire, begun with the singing of a psalm, followed by the
reading of the scripture, and culminating with the prayer. There is
considerable evidence to support the accuracy of various portions of
Burns' account – concerning food, religious practices, and economic
circumstances. Henry Gray Graham describes the necessity earlier in the
eighteenth century of daily religious worship in the home, devolving
later to the Saturday-night observance of Burns' depiction.[48] Marjorie
Plant describes the centrality of 'meal' in the diet, supplemented in the
poem with cheese.[49] And R. H. Cromek describes the domicile of a
cotter and his house, including a description of family worship which he
suggests was never depicted more eloquently than by Burns.[50] Gilbert
Burns recorded that Burns was inspired by the invocation 'Let us
worship God' proclaiming the start of family worship. General accounts

of the eighteenth century confirm the veracity of Burns' presentation of
the life of the cotter, caught at the bottom of the economic heap in the
agricultural upheavals of the eighteenth century which did away with
much of the joint land tenure and communal work, thereby creating a
classed society with the 'have-nots', sending their children out to work
and yet still barely managing to survive, becoming more numerous. And
the testimony – early attributed to a servant of Burns' friend and
correspondent Mrs Dunlop but subsequently to others – that 'I've seen
the same thing in my ain faither's house mony a time, and he couldna hae
described it ony ither gate' suggests the reliability of his account.[51]
Another version recorded by John D. Ross tells of Burns' pleasure when
he asked a Mossgiel friend how she liked his poems – 'Weel, Rab, gin ye
canna write something we dinna ken, dinna put aff yer time writing sic
havers; I'm sure there's naething new in that; we see a' that ongauns
every day o' our lives.'[52] And biographical critics have suggested that
Burns was actually depicting here his own early environment – although
strictly speaking William Burnes was a class above, a tenant farmer,
although a poor one. Artistically Burns here combines his knowledge of
English and Scottish literary traditions; but far more importantly he
limns the traditional matrix, the way of life, choosing from it positive
and humanising elements for comment and reflection, as well as for
contrast. His own folkways provided him with the shared elements from
and through which to make his point. Unwittingly on the one hand, but
necessarily and predictably on the other, Burns was an ethnographer,
describing the life he knew best as an integral part of his own artistry.

The traditional milieu provided more than content for his poems and
songs; it also provided models for some of his verse forms and structures.
He used the ballad and folksong stanza pattern, to be described in
Chapter 3, throughout his life, both intuitively and consciously.
Additionally, he used the traditional form for his epigrams and epitaphs
which were usually topical and of questionable poetic value.

'To the Honble Mr R. M____, of P__nm__re, on his high Phaeton' (no.
464) illustrates Burns' epigrammatic bent, being a satiric thrust at a local
figure:[53]

> Thou fool, in thy Phaeton towering,
> Art proud when that Phaeton's prais'd?
> 'Tis the pride of a Thief's exhibition
> When higher his pillory's rais'd.

(no. 464)

Burns also used another traditional form, the epitaph,[54] sometimes seriously and sometimes mockingly, as well as blessings such as

> O, THOU, who kindly dost provide
> For every creature's want!
> We bless thee, God of nature wide,
> For all thy goodness lent:
> And, if it please thee heavenly guide,
> May never worse be sent;
> But whether granted or denied,
> Lord bless us with content!
> Amen!!!
> (no. 266)

While much of Burns' work utilised these traditional forms, most of his outstanding work used more literarily derived poetic forms. Occasional and extempore pieces, understandably, often relied on the traditional and time-honoured poetic patterns.

The very texture of much of his poetry – particularly in the pre-Edinburgh work – offers ample evidence of Burns' absorption in a local world, especially in his use of the Scots vernacular. His transference of the spoken dialect to the printed page shows an ear well-tuned to his milieu. Peter Giles suggests that Burns 'writes his best when he adheres most closely to his spoken dialect'[55] and Hans Hecht echoes this sentiment in stating:

> To reinforce his [Burns'] power of expression, his native dialect, with its wealth of vocabulary, its flexible phraseology, and at times its utterly fearless coarseness, came to his aid. Whenever Burns makes use of it, he reaches his zenith as an artist in words, and content and form are blended into an ideal unity.[56]

Although the bulk of the literature he read was in standard literary English, much has been made of his vernacular debt to the writings of Robert Fergusson. But Burns was using the vernacular before he read 'The Daft Days', 'Hallow-Fair', or 'The Farmer's Ingle'. Certainly his analysis of Fergusson's poetic success confirmed and strengthened his own preference for his native dialect, as well as providing him with a direct model for his own subsequent work. Many have commented on the alienation from readers and hearers that his use of dialect produced – then and now – though multiple and various translations have proven that something very substantial remains intact when translated into Russian, Japanese, even standard English, or copiously glossed. His use of the vernacular was probably a principal element in drawing him to the attention of the Edinburgh sages who saw Burns' Ayrshire dialect as *prima facie* evidence of his unlettered, rural, 'natural' voice. How they might have recognised him on the one hand because of this, seeing him in Herderian terms as a voice of the people, and on the other hand have encouraged him to write in standard English, which efforts momentarily produced such anglicised and essentially puerile effusions as 'Address to Edinburgh'

> EDINA! *Scotia*'s darling seat!
>   All hail thy places and tow'rs,
> Where once beneath a Monarch's feet,
>   Sat Legislation's sov'reign pow'rs!
> From marking wildly-scatt'red flow'rs,
>   As on the banks of *Ayr* I stray'd,
> And singing, lone, the ling' ring hours,
>   I shelter in thy honor'd shade.
>   (ll. 1–8, no. 135)

can only be explained with reference to the cultural confusion David Daiches describes in his extended essay on Scotland in the eighteenth century: a country at once romantically desirous of the independence, of the prestige of pre-Union days but realistic enough to see the necessity, within the political Union, of anglicisation.[57] Language was an implicit issue at this juncture. Restrospectively it seems hard to fathom a cultural movement which could lionise Burns, be enthusiastic over the traditional ballads and songs, and became agog with the still controversial Ossianic poems; but which could simultaneously, in denial, urge linquistic anglicisation, even hiring elocution teachers from England. Burns, for the most part an intuitive nationalist, opted for Scotland and the Scots vernacular.

Edward Eggleston's Hoosier poet, who used Burns as a model despite its attendant perils, said,

'I made varses in the country talk all the same, and sent 'em to editors, but they couldn' see nothin' in 'em. Writ back that I'd better larn to spell. When I could a-spelt down any one of 'em the best day they ever seed! . . . Now, you see, I could spell right ef I wanted to, but I noticed that Mr. Burns had writ his Scotch like it was spoke, and so I thought I'd write my country talk by the same rule.[58]

Burns' vernacular poetry had and still has far wider acceptance than the poetry of our hapless 'Posey Kyounty' rhymer, though they shared, as have many others, the preference for the familiar words and constructions of the spoken dialect each held in common with the local inhabitants; both preferred the traditional speech patterns.

Not all have denigrated Burns' vernacular pieces for their increasing linguistic unintelligibility. Robert Dewar and others laud this aspect of Burns: 'It is when he goes direct to the life of the folk whose "observation and remark" he courted, and copies the idiom of their daily speech, that [Burns] commands the applause he deserves.'[59] A look at one of his verse letters well exemplifies his superb vernacular ability. The second stanza of the justly acclaimed 'Epistle to Davie, a Brother Poet'

> It's hardly in a body's pow'r,
> To keep, at times, frae being sour,
> To see how things are shar'd,
> How *best o' chiels* are whyles in want,
> While *Coofs* on countless thousands rant,
> And ken na how to wair't:
> But DAVIE lad, ne'er fash your head,
> Tho' we hae little gear,
> We're fit to win our daily bread,
> As lang's we're hale and fier:
>   'Mair spier na, nor fear na,'
>   Auld age ne'er mind a feg;
>   The last o't, the warst o't,
>   Is only but to beg.
>
>   (no. 51)

shows Burns' deft use of his own dialect in poetic guise. And a variety of his early poems attest to this vernacular turn, often now by necessity glossed in order to communicate. The marvellous mock 'last will and testament' poem, 'The Death and Dying Words of Poor Mailie, the Author's only Pet Yowe, An Unco Mournfu' Tale' (no. 24) well illustrates Burns' linguistic talents:

> My poor *toop-lamb*, my son an' heir,
> O, bid him breed him up wi' care!
> An' if he live to be a beast,
> To pit some havins in his breast!
> An' warn him, what I winna name,

To stay content wi'. *yowes* at hame;
An' no to rin an' wear his cloots,
Like ither menseless, graceless brutes.

(ll. 43–50, no. 24)

The interior portions of Burns' poem 'The Brigs of Ayr, a Poem. Inscribed to J. B*********, Esq; Ayr' (no. 120), where the new and old bridges meet in an eighteenth-century version of the ancient and modern debate, also show the excellence and naturalness of Burns' use of the vernacular.

Auld Brig

I doubt na, frien', ye'll think ye're nae sheep-shank,
Ance ye were streekit owre frae bank to bank!
But gin ye be a Brig as auld as me,
Tho' faith, that day, I doubt, ye'll never see;
There'll be, if that date come, I'll wad a boddle,
Some fewer whigmeleeries in your noodle.

New Brig

Auld Vandal, ye but show your little mense,
Just much about it wi' your scanty sense;
Will your poor, narrow foot-path of a street,
Where twa wheel-barrows tremble when they meet,
Your ruin'd, formless bulk o' stane and lime,
Compare wi' bonie *Brigs* o' modern time?
There's men of taste wou'd tak the *Ducat-stream*,
Tho' they should cast the vera sark and swim,
Ere they would grate their feelings wi' the view
Of sic an ugly, Gothic hulk as you.

(ll. 91–106, no. 120)

Linguistic confusion, mirroring the cultural duality, is also evident in Burns' work as he switches from English to the Scots vernacular within the confines of an individual work. This alternation or code-switching undoubtedly reflected actual usage. Certain subjects such as philosophy and religion were discussed primarily in English, the vernacular being judged deficient for one reason or another. Since the Bible was not popularly translated into Scots, the 1611 English or King James Version was the accepted scriptural authority; thus by default, English became the language of religion. Dialogue and conversation, as in ordinary discourse, were apt uses for the vernacular. Burns replicates in several works this kind of linguistic shift, usually dependent on subject matter. Certainly this was an explicable means of communicating to his local audience for whom such shifts offered no confusion, though subsequent reading audiences, divorced from Scotland's eighteenth-century linguistic confusion, have seen them as artistic inconsistencies.

Again 'The Cotter's Saturday Night. Inscribed to R. A****, Esq.' (no. 72) provides an example. Describing the weekly family ingathering, the poem includes a depiction of family worship. Stanza 11, the meal, is described in Scots; as Christina Keith says, 'The vernacular comes in with the supper'.[60]

> But now the Supper crowns their simple board,
>   The healsome *Porritch*, chief of SCOTIA'S food:
> The soupe their *only Hawkie* does afford,
>   That 'yont the hallan snugly chows her cood:
> The *Dame* brings forth, in complimental mood,
>   To grace the lad, her weel-hain'd kebbuck, fell;
> And aft he's prest, and aft he ca's it guid;
>   The frugal *Wifie*, garrulous, will tell,
> How 'twas a towmond auld, sin' Lint was i' the bell.
>   (ll. 91–9, no. 72)

But by the conclusion of the next stanza, number 12, the shift to English is complete and stanza 13 initiates the description of the family worship, given largely in English:

> The chearfu' Supper done, wi' serious face,
>   They, round the ingle, form a circle wide;
> The Sire turns o'er, with patriarchal grace,
>   The big *ha'-Bible*, ance his *Father*'s pride:
> His bonnet rev'rently is laid aside,
>   His *lyart haffets* wearing thin and bare;
> Those strains that once did sweet in ZION glide,
>   He wales a portion with judicious care;
> '*And let us worship GOD!*' he says with solemn air.
>
> They chant their artless notes in simple guise;
>   They tune their hearts, by far the noblest aim:
> Perhaps *Dundee*'s wild-warbling measures rise,
>   Or plaintive *Martyrs*, worthy of the name;

Or noble *Elgin* beets the heaven-ward flame,
  The sweetest far of SCOTIA'S holy lays:
Compar'd with these, *Italian trills* are tame;
  The tickl'd ears no heart-felt raptures raise;
Nae unison hae they, with our CREATOR'S praise.
(ll. 100–17, no. 72)

Burns relied heavily on aspects of his traditional culture, on folklore, for the general content, the language and, to some extent, the structure of his poetry and songs. Additionally, he used the very situation and context of folklore by replicating actual traditional events in several of his works. This certainly lies at the heart of his work 'Love and Liberty – A Cantata' (no. 84) usually called 'The Jolly Beggars'. Here in fact there is a felicitous combination of ballad and song, form and content, Scots vernacular and English Scots diction, and context. Despite Thomas Crawford's statement that

> like everything else that Burns wrote, 'The Jolly Beggars, A Cantata', was influenced by literary tradition – by the burlesque cantatas so popular in the eighteenth century, where the trick consists in using recitatives to link songs set to popular tunes; by Gay's *Beggar's Opera*; and by innumerable stallballads and chapbooks celebrating the happy lives of beggars and tinkers and vagabonds of all sorts,[61]

which I believe overstates the sources of the work, one cannot deny the work's literary precedents – English and Scottish. However, I think it is just to look at the Cantata as a brilliant replication of traditional social interaction.

Traditional accounts and Burns suggest that the work grew out of an actual event in a local Mauchline tavern, witnessed by the poet, and artistically shaped. He is able to create order out of convivial chaos, out of a situation joining together a variety of vagabonds, sharing delight in their collective way of life if not genuinely joined as individuals. Burns presents us with both a general and a specific setting; the characters are at once types and particular individuals whose poetic recitative and song become the media for illustrating the social dynamics of this encounter of persons often judged to be at the bottom of the economic and moral heap. The event he depicts is no wooden, stilted account, for its description of exchange and participation creates vivid life before the reader's, and no doubt the hearer's, eyes/ears. In fact, Burns artistically gives a poetic account of individuals sharing their lives and pasts in poetry and song; in a way he conflates and makes one of two different traditional events – the telling of the past in personal experience stories, usually prose and repeated frequently enough to achieve a sense of artistic unity; and the sharing of songs by way of communication and entertainment. Such chance meetings of individuals found now in pubs, on trains and buses, offer the proper chemistry for the kind of event Burns depicts. He has altered perceived reality and – as always – transferred it to poetic medium. In other words, the witnessed actuality underwent a transformation into poetic and musical setting where it maintains the force of an actual interchange among persons congenial generally if not particularly. Burns thus raised actuality to artistry.

The linking of participants to appropriate poetic and song sentiments is deft and provides the internal consistency of the Cantata: the soldier is described by the narrator but his life finds expression in a song, which recounts his individual experience, fittingly accompanied by a well-known tune, appropriately titled 'Soldier's joy'. Likewise, his female companion, described by the narrator, sings a song to the tune 'Sodger Laddie' recounting her many 'loves'. After the narrator's distanced presentation of the next character, this 'raucle Carlin' laments the death of her John Highlandman to the tune 'O, an' ye were dead Gudeman' whose traditional text deals – in opposition to Burns' text – with a woman who would go away with a highland man if her husband were dead; nonetheless she slights him:

> *I wish that you were dead, goodman,*
> *And a green sod on your head, goodman,*
> *That I might ware my widowhead,*
> *Upon a ranting highlandman.*[62]

Certainly knowing the song as it existed in oral circulation enables one to see clearly what Burns is doing with an extant tradition. The Carlin's song is followed by another narrator introduction, this time of the fiddler who then gives his account of his profession of wandering about, playing and accepting life's good and bad. His girl is forcibly woo'd if not won by the tinker, who in turn addresses his new mate, singing to the appropriate tune 'Clout the Caudron', the traditional song text of which deals with a tinker 'willing' to mend pans and satisfy any woman's desires:

> Have you any pots or pans,
> Or any broken chandlers?

I am a tinker to my trade,
    And newly come frae Flanders,
As scant of siller as of grace,
    Disbanded, we've a bad run;
Gar tell the lady of the place,
    I'm come to clout her cauldron.[63]

Magnanimously wishing them well, the fiddler proceeds to seduce one of the bard's bevy of three. The bard is reminded of the traditional song 'Dainty Davy' which deals appropriately enough with seduction. Certainly Burns counted on the perspicuity of his readers and hearers to make the connection between his text and the traditional tune. Concluding his moment in the spotlight, the bard sings to the tune 'For a' that an' a' that', an affirmation of his rambling, carefree, live and let-live existence, and of women, sentiments shared by those present. The reaction of the crowd was loud and affirmative

    . . .−−−− and Nancie's waws
    Shook with a thunder of applause
    Re-echo'd from each mouth!
        (ll. 236−38, no. 84)

leading to the final scene of the Cantata − where all unite in drink while the poet sings to the tune 'Jolly Mortals, fill your glasses', a moving reaffirmation of their collective way of life,

    Here's to BUDGETS, BAGS and WALLETS!
        Here's to all the wandering train!
    Here's our ragged BRATS and CALLETS!
    One and all cry out, AMEN!
    A fig for those by LAW protected,
        LIBERTY'S a glorious feast!
    COURTS for Cowards were erected,
        CHURCHES built to please the Priest.
        (ll. 274−81, no. 84)

reinforcing the present scene and all of their lives in general. Burns' ability, based on book and traditional knowledge, to use a tune and the text associated with it, which was appropriate to the context described − or ironically pertinent − is subtle and artistic, a wedding of known and unknown to create a new piece. In poetry and song Burns depicts the social and convivial interaction so often duplicated as near strangers are joined for a moment in unity and friendship, telling of their pasts and agreeing, however momentarily, in the chemistry of the exchange. Such momentary unity expressed by the assembled company mirrors such brief and intense chance encounters in reality. And the actual traditional interaction, seen by Burns and transformed by his creativity and vision, becomes the foundation for the poem.

Burns' debts to his own milieu are many and varied – content and form, language and context or situation. Identifying these various levels presents a fuller picture of the cultural tools Burns had at his disposal in producing his poetry and songs – tools heretofore largely minimised in assessing his work. But it is well to mention that these traditional manifestations of culture were but one major ingredient in shaping his work; for, as a very literate poet, Burns was extensively aware also of both the Scottish and English literary traditions. The principal focus here has been in surveying Burns' intuitive use of his own oral and traditional milieu because it has been so frequently neglected, as background and basic to his creativity. Perhaps his communicative power derived ultimately from his ability to forge something quite different by using aspects of both oral and written precedents. Invariably, both are a part of his work.

2 Edinburgh and After: Burns' Conscious Collecting of Folksongs

I am engaged in assisting an honest Scots Enthusiast, a friend of mine, who is an Engraver, and has taken it into his head to publish a collection of all our songs set to music, of which the words and music are done by Scotsmen. – This, you will easily guess, is an undertaking exactly to my taste. – I have collected, begg'd, borrow'd and stolen all the songs I could meet with.

Ferguson, *Letters*, 1:179, no. 193

Burns went to Edinburgh late in 1786 to arrange for a new edition of his poems and songs. The traditional base of much of his work had caught the attention of a group of implicit nationalists interested in persisting evidences of a distinctly Scottish cultural tradition, which they saw not only in the works of Burns but also in the Ossianic poems and in traditional balladry and song. The inspiration for this nationalism was largely backward-looking and antiquarian and was the result of Scotland's eighteenth-century identity crisis: in 1603 James VI of Scotland had become James I of England, uniting the crowns of the two nations; that union had been further cemented in 1707 with the union of the parliaments, conclusively marking the end of Scotland as an independent nation. The Jacobite Risings, Highland-inspired, of the first half of the eighteenth century failed to restore Scotland to separate status. Thus a return to political independence seemed impossible and, in fact, was not favoured by everyone. However, a movement did develop to preserve Scottish cultural identity. The cultural nationalists looked to the past and to the countryside; their interest was antiquarian and pastoral. They greeted Burns as a rustic voice of Scotland and happily supported his Edinburgh edition.

27

Burns immediately recognised this enthusiasm for what it was and took advantage of it; one might almost say he flaunted his humble origins, dressing the part. But more importantly, he was influenced by cultural nationalism and its antiquarian thrust. Being in Edinburgh, away from his immediate traditionally based milieu, enabled him to see the cultural value of his own environment. In Edinburgh he achieved the proper perspective to discern consciously the breadth and depth of the oral artistry of his milieu, as traditional artistry which flowed from the people and was transmitted from generation to generation by word of mouth. He saw this material as an important part of Scotland's past which should be saved as one way perhaps of reaffirming Scotland. Nationalism, then, contributed both to his fame in Edinburgh and to his own subsequent artistic and creative endeavours.

Burns' newly acquired perspective and nationalism were almost immediately channelled into a productive endeavour: in 1787 Burns met the Edinburgh engraver, James Johnson, who was already involved in a project – one volume of what eventually became six was almost ready for press – to print all the traditional music of Scotland. Burns was immediately drawn to this project; he had experienced traditional song firsthand in the milieu of his birth; he had been writing similar songs. Johnson's work, in fact, focused Burns' songwriting, gave it purpose, influenced the direction of his future artistic work, and inspired his wish to be the anonymous bard of Scotland (all to be discussed in Chapter 3). It also inspired Burns to collect, edit, and annotate folksongs as a way of preserving Scotland's cultural heritage. Johnson's *The Scots Musical Museum* provided Burns with the means to 'study men, their manners, and their ways' which as early as 1783 he had said was 'the joy of my heart'.[1]

In many ways Burns was so excited by the engraver's plan that he all but took over; he began to make contributions, and by the second volume he was virtual editor, certainly prime director of the project. He wrote prefaces and contributed items, texts and tunes, giving directions on how they should be arranged and presented.[2] He solicited items from others; he made lists of contents; he prodded Johnson, in some of the twenty-one letters directed to him, to get the work into print;[3] he read proofs.[4] For the remainder of his life, the *Museum* occupied all the time he could give it, for he was thoroughly in sympathy with its aims.

Burns and Johnson agreed that their collaboration should focus on the traditional vocal music of Scotland. What was meant by *traditional* is debatable: perhaps simply music which bore some intuitive mark of Scotland, either being sung by her people or composed – tune or text –

by a native.[5] Neither Johnson nor Burns clearly discriminated between folksongs, usually anonymous and passed on orally, and songs by known authors, often learned from chapbooks or song collections. Both kinds formed the basis of popular music in eighteenth-century Scotland and such collections as Allan Ramsay's *Tea-Table Miscellany* and Joseph Ritson's *Scottish Songs*, as well as the *Museum*, show a juxtaposition of old and new, traditional and non-traditional; in fact they reflect popular taste. The *Museum* was not the first Scottish collection to be printed; earlier in the eighteenth century W. Thomson's *Orpheus Caledonius: A Collection of Scots Songs* (1725–33, second edition in two volumes), Allan Ramsay's various publications, David Herd's *Ancient and Modern Scottish Songs, Heroic Ballads* (1769–76, second edition in two volumes), to mention but a few miscellanies, had led the way. All were stimulated in part by the antiquarian and nationalistic urge to preserve what was Scottish before it was forgotten.[6] Unlike many eighteenth-century collections, the *Museum* printed for each tune a text, for each text a tune – outwardly not reflecting the persistent bias of printing only one or the other in totality. But it becomes clear, primarily through Burns' correspondence, that the purpose of the *Museum* was essentially to preserve the tunes of Scotland; and to make them more memorable – perhaps more singable – words were provided because tune and text, in the view of Johnson and Burns, were inseparable. That the tunes took precedence is amply illustrated by various statements of Burns such as: 'Here, once for all, let me apologise for many silly compositions of mine in this work. Many beautiful airs wanted words'[7]; and 'I, often gave Johnson verses, trifling enough perhaps, but they served as a vehicle to the music' (Dick, 120). The tunes were foremost, but they had to have a text to make them whole, a concept not universally accepted in ballad and folksong scholarship until the mid-twentieth century and still only given lip-service in some quarters.[8]

Burns personally contributed the bulk of the material ultimately published in *The Scots Musical Museum*. Much of this material he procured by active, conscious collecting, though we know little about his technique except for the glimpses he left in written appeals to correspondents for songs – texts or tunes or both – that he had heard them perform before or had reason to believe they knew.[9] Such appeals are usually prefaced by a brief, enthusiastic report of the *Museum* and its purpose, followed by a request for an item. While a contemporary of Burns, Professor Thomas Gillespie of St Andrews, 'related how Burns was in the habit of tying his horse outside her (Kirsty or Betty Flint's) cottage door and sitting by her fireside while she sang "with a pipe of the most overpowering pitch"',[10] we seldom know exactly how he collected or from whom, one notable exception being the tunes he specifically stated were collected from his wife, Jean Armour Burns, whose rural background was and continued to be traditionally oriented;[11] Burns describes her voice as being 'the finest "wood-note wild" I ever heard'.[12] Mostly, he simply records that an item was collected. Tradition makes much of Burns' personality, of his instant capacity for rapport; he undoubtedly found collecting natural, easy, and congenial.

Direct, stated evidence of his conscious collecting is derived from three sources: his letters; the annotations of *The Scots Musical Museum* in the Interleaved Copy which he prepared for his neighbour at Ellisland, Robert Riddell of Glenriddell; and the Excise Manuscript, Edinburgh University Library, Laing II. 210[9].[13] In general Burns tells his friend and correspondent John Richmond that considerable amounts of his time on his Highland tour, made during his stay in Edinburgh, were taken up with learning Highland tunes and picking up 'Scotch songs' (Ferguson, 146); and to Rev. John Skinner, author of the popular 'Tullochgorum', he says, 'I have been absolutely crazed about it [Johnson's *Museum*], collecting old stanzas, and every information remaining respecting their origin, authors, &c, &c' (Ferguson, 147). But more specifically he relates that he has collected 'O'er the moor amang the heather' from Jean Glover, to whom he attributes it. In this instance, almost the only one, he also gives a brief look at her and her background when he says that she was 'a girl who was not only a whore, but also a thief; and in one or other character has visited most of the Correction Houses in the West. She was born, I believe, in Kilmarnock. I took down the song from her singing as she was strolling through the country, with a slight-of-hand blackguard' (Dick, 328). Of the song beginning 'My Harry was a gallant gay' sung to the 'Highlander's Lament' he says, 'The chorus I pickt up from an old woman in Dunblane . . .' (Dick, 209) and the song text of 'Auld lang syne' 'from an old man's singing' (Ferguson, 586). The 'Bob o' Dumblane' he learned 'on the spot, from my old Hostess in the principal Inn there', and he quotes several verses as a sample (Excise, p. 2). But he collected tunes as well. He indicates that he 'first heard the air ("Bhannerach dhon na chri") from a lady in Inverness, and got the notes taken down for this work' (Dick, 157). He tells George Thomson, with whom he also collaborated on a collection of songs, in one of fifty-six letters which contain a variety of cogent statements about songs, that he still has 'several M.S.S. Scots airs by me, which I have pickt up, mostly from the singing of country lasses'

(Ferguson, 554; see also p. 34). He collected a tune, never before collected or printed, from 'a country girl's singing' – 'Craigie-burnwood' (Ferguson, 557). And in another letter to Thomson he asks; 'Do you know a droll Scots song, more famous for its humor than delicacy, called, The grey goose & the gled? – Mr. Clarke took down the notes, such as they are, at my request.'[14] These are concrete statements in Burns' own words.

Other evidence of Burns' collecting comes from the annotations of the *Museum* prepared by William Stenhouse, with later additions by David Laing and Charles Kirkpatrick Sharpe, in *Illustrations of the Lyric Poetry and Music in Scotland*. Stenhouse annotated the items in the *Museum* by referring to a vast body of historical material as well as to considerable amounts of holograph material, some of which appears to be no longer extant. Stenhouse's work is generally held in good repute and his evidence must be considered. On the basis of his research, a number of items – excluding those items definitely written by Burns – he says were transmitted to James Johnson by Burns and a quantity of these he says were collected by him as well.[15]

In addition to Stenhouse's direct statements about Burns' own collecting and Burns' own indications, there are indirect evidences in the letters, the Interleaved Museum, and the Excise Manuscript. In these far more numerous instances, one surmises that the items were collected.[16] For example, of 'Waukin o' the fauld' Burns says: 'There are two stanzas still sung to this tune, which I take to be the original song when Ramsay composed his beautiful song of that name in the Gentle Shepherd. – It begins

> I will ye speak at our town,
> As ye come frae the fauld, &c–'
>   (Excise, p. 1)

He does not say he collected this, but he probably did or alternately he recalled it from his youth, as was often the case.[17] In the Excise Manuscript Burns, in annotating 'Saw ye nae my Peggy', indicates that: 'The original words, for they can scarcely be called Verses, seem to be as follows; a song familiar from the cradle to every Scotish ear. –

> Saw ye my Maggie,
> Saw ye my Maggie,
> Saw ye my Maggie,
>   Linkin o'er the lea?

High kilted was she,
High kilted was she,
High kilted was she,
    Her (coa)ts aboon her knee. —

What mark has your Maggie,
What mark has your Maggie,
What mark has your Maggie,
    That ane may ken her be?'
                    (Excise, pp. 7–8)

Of 'Hughie Graham' Burns says: 'There are several editions of this ballad. This, here inserted, is from oral tradition in Ayrshire, where, when I was a boy, it was a popular song' (Dick, 303); or of 'The beds of sweet Roses' — 'This song, as far as I know, for the first time appears here in print. When I was a boy it was a very popular song in Ayrshire. I remember to have heard those fanatics, the Buchanites, sing some of their nonsensical rhymes, which they dignify with the name of hymns, to this air' (Dick, 7). And he most emphatically says, 'Dainty Davie – I have heard sung, nineteen thousand, nine hundred, & ninety-nine times' (Ferguson, 586). This kind of recollection or self-collection is most common in Burns' comments on the songs in the *Museum*. Burns did collect, but it is impossible to know for sure how he went about it – whether he collected by 'learning' the songs himself or whether he noted them down in writing – probably a combination of the two. It is also possible that some of his collecting was even more haphazard – that he actually wrote down only bits and pieces which perforce had to be highly edited later to make a whole.

Burns' knowledge of the popular song repertoire of his time was not limited to oral experience and collecting; he knew of the wider repertoire through the collections of tunes and texts which so abundantly flooded the market in eighteenth-century Scotland on broadsheets, in chapbooks, and in books. Burns' firsthand and derived knowledge of Scotland's song formed the basis of his editorial work for the *Museum* and later for his commentaries on individual items. By his own admission, he was an expert, having 'paid more attention to every description of Scots songs than perhaps any body living' (Dick, 13). As a boy he possessed a collection of songs, probably *The Lark*, and he 'pored over them, driving my cart or walking to labor, song by song, verse by verse' (Ferguson, 125). He was familiar with the list of songs in Wedderburn's *The Complaynt of Scotland*, with Ramsay's work –

especially *The Tea-Table Miscellany*, with Bishop Percy's *Reliques of Ancient English Poetry* and David Herd's *Ancient and Modern Scottish Songs, Heroic Ballads*,[18] with Ritson's collections of English and Scottish songs, with John Pinkerton's work. In a letter to George Thomson, which further supports his claim to thorough book knowledge of the subject, he asked Thomson to send him the tunes for which he wanted words, together with the first line of the usual text: 'I say, the first line of the verses, because if they are verses that have appeared in any of our Collections of songs, I know them'.[19] Books primarily on tunes he referred to even more frequently; he often mentioned Oswald's *Caledonian Pocket Companion* and additionally the collections by Aird, McGibbon, Gow, Cummin, Anderson, Dow, McDonald, and Corri. In fact Burns can say in a letter to Johnson, 'I want much Anderson's Collection of strathspeys &c., and then I think I will have all the music of the country'.[20] His examination of books was not limited to the texts and tunes; he was familiar with the historical material in introductions such as Ritson's famous essay on Scottish songs, with theoretical and historical treatises like Dr Beattie's *Essays on Poetry and Music*, William Tytler's *Dissertation on the Scottish Music* and with such relevant periodical publications as *The Bee*. He was aware of various controversies such as those revolving around editorial principles: he knew the criticism levelled against Pinkerton (Ferguson, 569). Burns, in fact, must have known virtually all the important collections of his day and they, together with his collecting, influenced his editing work for the *Museum*.

In a letter to William Tytler of Woodhouselee, Burns writes:

Inclosed I have sent you a sample of the old pieces that are still to be found among our Peasantry in the West. I had once a great many of these fragments; and some of these here entire; but as I had no idea then that any body cared for them, I have forgot them. – I invariably hold it sacriledge to add any thing of my own to help out with the shatter'd wrecks of these venerable old compositions; but they have many various readings.[21]

This letter, written in 1787 approximately four months after his first meeting with James Johnson, augured well for Burns' work in collaboration with him. And surely some material, especially ballad texts, was sent to Johnson exactly as he remembered or had collected it. But as so often has been the case with previous and subsequent editors, the actions of Burns did not always live up to his bold and praiseworthy sentiment.

Burns sent many texts to Johnson in altered form, having amended or corrected them because they were judged to be indelicate ('Let me in this ae night'); he expanded some fragments – a chorus, a stanza, or several lines – to make a complete text ('I'm o'er young to marry yet'); he was inspired by a tune or tune title to write a song ('The Gardner wi' his paidle – or, The Gardner's March–'); he used a traditional idea or imitated the form and diction of traditional songs to make a new one; he submitted material written completely by himself or by known authors; and he took some texts directly from broadsheets. As a poet, he probably could not help touching up here and there, much as he did with his own poems and songs, many of which went through successive editions, multiple recreations, having some relationship with the oral recreative process. As a product of his time, Burns followed the existing editorial practices and recognised that certain subjects were taboo in polite society (Ferguson, 554). He often felt the urge to conflate, to create a perfect version. But he collected, edited, altered, and amended so that the songs could be preserved. In his editorial work he was also influenced and governed by an aesthetic ideal moulded in part by the traditional milieu from which he came; and his aesthetic ideal at times so reflected the traditional aesthetic sensibilities that some of his own compositions and editions were picked up and transmitted orally, in chapbooks, and in published editions, re-entering the popular musical repertoire from which their inspiration had sprung.[22]

The tunes which Burns as virtual editor of the *Museum* communicated to Johnson had three sources: those collected from oral tradition, those written by contemporaries and friends like Allan Masterton and Robert Riddell of Glenriddell, and those abstracted from one of the many books of tunes available to Burns. Dick has suggested that Burns did Scottish music a very good turn indeed in this latter endeavour, for he abstracted only the basic melody, leaving the florid embellishments behind, thus restoring them to something approximating their original state in oral tradition. Burns, not being a professional musician, was much less likely to touch up the tunes. In fact there has been much discussion of Burns' ability to deal with music at all. Early biographers, taking their cue from Burns' childhood teacher John Murdoch, claimed him a musical illiterate. Murdoch's estimate was based on a limited exposure to Burns; and Burns' own subsequent performance suggests that he was extremely well-informed musically. He must certainly have read music easily, for he chose tunes for some of his own texts out of the available songbooks; in the Hastie Manuscript, he gives a few bars of item 52, 'Ca' the ewes' but completely wrote out the melody for a verse of item 122, 'Here's his health in water'; he played the fiddle and used it to help acquaint himself with tunes before writing for them.[23] His editorial practices sometimes led him to choose only a portion of a tune – especially of the dance and instrumental ones found in books – to accompany a text or to alter the tune slightly to fit the text well: in the Hastie Manuscript, for example, he gives the following note to item 39 to the tune 'Braes o' Balquhidder', beginning 'When in my arms, wi' a' thy charms': 'Note. The Chorus is the first, or lowest part of this tune – Each verse must be repeated twice to go through the high, or 2nd part –.'[24] The fact that he saw the tunes as foremost may have been responsible for his general reluctance to alter them.

Before discussing Burns' annotations of his material, I should mention in passing that Burns' collecting and study of tradition were not limited to the *Museum*. He also contributed material to George Thomson's *A Select Collection of Scotish Airs*.[25] Thomson asked Burns to write or provide twenty-five texts in English to accompany tunes selected by Thomson. Burns, however, sent Thomson many more texts written or chosen by him to fit a particular Scottish tune. Thomson, like Johnson, was interested in including all Scottish tunes. However, Burns and Thomson were in basic disagreement about what constituted a good song: Thomson sought 'improved' texts in English, suitable for gentle ears, and tunes arranged by the noted composers of the day; Burns, on the other hand, wanted to preserve their Scottish qualities. Burns' sometimes lengthy justifications for his views can be found in his correspondence with Thomson. There is a third book of songs associated with Burns' name, *The Merry Muses of Caledonia*, which was first published four or five years after Burns' death. This collection of bawdy songs has caused considerable embarrassment over the years to certain Burns' enthusiasts because an admitted interest in bawdry is antipathetic to middle-class morals. It is interesting to note that enthusiasts have long recognised Burns as a collector with reference to the *Merry Muses* – better to have collected than written! And probably the first recorded instance of Burns' collecting is a version of a bawdy song 'Brose an' Butter' which exists in a holograph of 1785 on the back of the draft of a letter to Margaret Kennedy of Daljarrock. Burns enjoyed such songs, collected them for his and his friends' edification, and worked over many of them in ways similar to his editorial practices vis-à-vis the texts for the *Museum*.[26] It is much more difficult, however, in this case to discover the originals on which he worked as their circulation was oral rather than written, save for such manuscript collections as those made by Burns. Burns circulated his manuscript among friends and fellow enthusiasts (Ferguson, 604) and had Peter Hill make a copy of it for Andrew Erskine. Gershon Legman and James Kinsley conjecture that Peter Hill, using the copy made of Burns' manuscript, holograph material such as letters containing bawdy songs sent to his friends, and existing oral material shared by members of the Crochallan Fencibles — an Edinburgh male convivial society to which Burns belonged — pieced together the edition titled *The Merry Muses of Caledonia; A Collection of Favourite Scots Songs, Ancient and Modern; Selected for use of the Crochallan Fencibles.*[27] After his Edinburgh experience Burns was, in fact, far more conscious of the whole spectrum of traditional life than he had been before; and on an informal level he collected and recorded narratives, practices and customs, beliefs and sayings as well as the songs and music of primary importance in this chapter. On his travels he collected historical traditions,[28] proverbs, and sayings; and he confessed to Mrs M'Lehose, the Clarinda of his correspondence, that 'I like to have quotations ready for every occasion. — They give one's ideas so pat, and save one the trouble of finding expression adequate to one's feelings' (Ferguson, 178). And on the same subject, he said to Mrs Dunlop, 'Do you know, I pick up favorite quotations, & store them in my mind as ready armour, offensive or defensive, amid the struggle of this turbulent existence' (Ferguson, 524). The antiquarian and nationalistic spirit of the times encouraged Burns' conscious observation and collection of traditional material.

Not only did Burns collect and subsequently edit songs, but he also annotated this material, using his wide knowledge of oral tradition gained both from firsthand experience and from book study. Often these annotations were comparative and involved pointing out differences in various versions; sometimes they were historical and conjectural. They are not always correct, nor is proof always provided; seldom does Burns support an assertion or tell the basis of his conclusion. This is understandable when one realises what a limited amount of time was actually at Burns' disposal for this kind of work. Many of the annotations, however, are exceedingly valuable and show the depth of his knowledge on the subject of folksong.

Over and over again Burns pinpoints the unique qualities of Scots music, qualities which make him love it and qualities which distinguish it from other national musics: 'There is a certain something in the old Scotch songs, a wild happiness of thought and expression, which peculiarly marks them, not only from English songs, but also from the modern efforts of song-wrights, in our native manner and language'

(Ferguson, 147). But he also developed a more exact notion of a Scottish Prosody as containing:

> a certain irregularity . . ., a redundancy of syllables with respect to that exactness of accent & measure that the English Poetry requires, but which glides in, most melodiously with the respective tunes to which they are set. . . . There is a degree of wild irregularity in many of the compositions & Fragments which are daily sung to them by my compeers, the common people—a certain happy arrangement of old Scotch syllables, & yet, very frequently, nothing, not even *like* rhyme, or sameness of jingle at the ends of the lines. ——[29]

He tells Thomson, who often criticised some of the Scottish songs for just those reasons Burns praised them and who wanted to anglicise them, 'let our National Music preserve its native features. – They are, I own, frequently wild, & unreduceable to the modern rules; but on that very eccentricity, perhaps, depends a great part of their effect' (Ferguson, 559).

Not only was Burns at pains to define Scotland's national, traditional music, but he was also aware of differences between ballads, stories told in song, and the more lyric folksongs he personally favoured. Although he frequently uses the word *ballad* interchangeably with *song*, he specifically advises Thomson in a way which indicates his knowledge of their inherent differences when he says: 'You must, after all is over, have a Number of Ballads, properly so called. – Gil Morice – Tranent Muir – Mcpherson's Farewell – Battle of Sheriffmuir, or, We ran & they ran . . . Hardiknute – Barbara Allan' (Ferguson, 586).

Burns also hoped to provide histories and backgrounds to the songs he collected and edited. He sought to identify the author: as a poet himself, he knew an extraordinary pride in authorship and imputed such to others. And he felt sorry for those whose names were lost: always he saw an individual author behind a song. He was quick to attribute where possible and since a number of pieces in the *Museum* had known authors, this was not difficult.[30] But he was aware of the inherent problems involved in discovering who an author was, recognising the unpredictable nature of oral and popular channels of transmission. With some amusement he told Thomson, 'I myself, have lately seen a couple of Ballads sung through the streets of Dumfries, with my name at the head of them as the Author, though it was the first time ever I had seen them –' (Ferguson, 646). Here he is referring to a broadsheet or chapbook attribution capitalising on his name and fame to sell a product, an advertising gimmick with much precedent. Actually, Burns planned to publish an edition of all the songs he had written for George Thomson and for the *Museum* 'lest I should be blamed for trash I never saw, or be defrauded by other claimants of what is justly my own' (Ferguson, 695); but his early death prevented this. To Rev. Skinner he wrote, 'I have heard your "Tullochgorum." particularly among our west-country folks, given to many different names, and most commonly to the immortal author of "The Minstrel", who indeed never wrote anything superior to "Gie's a sang, Montgomery cried"' (Ferguson, 203). Of many songs, he can say only that they are old;[31] their authors' names are lost. Often he indicates what portion of the text is his or Ramsay's or some other known author's, giving a sample of the old verses.[32] He could make such statements because of his wide oral and book knowledge which prepared him for his comparative comments. And Burns recognised other results, too, of sometimes long oral tradition, a term which he used (Dick, 303), such as the variation in texts (Ferguson, 557) and tunes and titles[33] though he does not speculate on their causes. Of 'Waly, waly' he says, 'In the west country I have heard a different edition of the 2nd Stanza. Instead of the four lines beginning with "When cockle shells" &c; the other way run thus:–

> O, wherefore need I busk my head,
> Or wherefore need I kame my hair
> Sin my fause luve has me forsook,
>   And says he'll never luve me mair.'
>   (Dick, 158)

In the song 'For lake of gold she's left me, O!': 'The country girls in Ayr Shire instead of the line: – "She me forsook for a great Duke"; say "For Athol's Duke she's me forsook", which I take to be the original reading' (Dick, 163). Burns recognised that in oral transmission words may be changed or altered when not understood and gives the interesting example of the alteration of the Gaelic title and words 'Leiger m'choss' to 'Liggeram Coss' (Ferguson, 593). He was cognisant of regional variation as well:

> The people in Ayrshire begin this song ('Johnny Faa, or the Gypsie Laddie') –

> The gypsies cam to my Lord Cassili's yet.

They have a great many more stanzas in this song than I ever yet saw in any printed copy. The Castle is still remaining at Maybole where his lordship shut up his wayward spouse and kept her for life.

(Dick, 181)

Elsewhere he says that this is one of the few songs he thinks definitely originated in Ayrshire (Dick, 161). But he also knew that songs with wide distribution could be and were often localised (Dick, 191). Burns wanted, then, to know the place of origin if possible: 'This tune ("The tither morn") is originally from the Highlands. I have heard a Gaelic song to it, which I was told was very clever, but not by any means a lady's song' (Dick, 345). Of 'Go to the Ew-bughts, Marion' he said:

I am not sure if this old and charming air be of the South, as is commonly said, or of the North of Scotland. There is a song apparently as ancient as *Ewe-bughts Marion*, which sings to the same tune, and is evidently of the North. It begins thus:—

> The lord o' Gordon had three dochters,
>   May, Marget, and Jean,
> They wad na stay at bonie Castle Gordon
> But awa to Aberdeen.[34]

He also conjectured on the subject of date of origin: 'Bess the gawkie' 'shews that the Scotish Muses did not all leave us when we lost Ramsay and Oswald, as I have good reason to believe that the verses and music are both posterior to the days of these two gentleman' (Dick, 4). And of 'There's nae luck about the house', in his words 'one of the most beautiful songs in the Scots, or any other language', he postulates that 'it is long posterior to Ramsay's days. About the year 1771 or '72, it came first on the streets as a ballad; and I suppose the composition of the song was not much anterior to that period' (Dick, 44). In a more complex vein, he writes about 'Highland laddie':

As this was a favorite theme for our later Scotish Muses, there are several airs & songs of that name. – What I take to be the oldest, is to be found in the Musical Museum, beginning, 'I hae been at Crookie-den' – one reason for my thinking so is, that Oswald has it in his coll[n]. by the name of, 'the auld Highland laddie'. – It is also known by the name of 'Jinglan Johnie', which is a well-known song of four or five stanzas, & seems to be an earlier song than Jacobite times. –As a

proof of this, it is little known to the peasantry by the name of
'Highland laddie', while every body knows Jinglan Johnie. – the song
begins

> Jinglan John, the meikle man
> He met wi' a lass was blythe & bonie.
> (Excise, p. 10)

Burns also attempted to discover possible routes of dissemination. On
this subject he several times noted the similarity between certain Irish
and Scottish tunes (Ferguson, 576) and suggested how difficult it was to
know where they were really begun or how they spread. On the latter
point he suggested that a body of material, especially tunes, was
common to both because 'the wandering Minstrels, Harpers, or Pipers,
used to go frequently errant through the wilds both of Scotland &
Ireland, & so some favorite airs might be common to both' (Ferguson,
576). And further he added: 'In the neighbourhood & intercourse of the
Scots & Irish, & both musical nations too, it is highly probable that
composers of one nation would sometimes imitate, or emulate, the
manner of the other –' (Ferguson, 647). Of 'Jockie's Gray breeks' he
said, 'though this has certainly every evidence of being a Scotish air, yet
there is a well known tune & song in the north of Ireland, called, "The
Weaver & his shuttle O'', which though sung much quicker is, every
note, the very tune –' (Excise, p. 6).

Although he tended to lump all the popular songs – oral and written –
together, he recognised their differences, that the oral songs had a
certain quality which made them memorable and transmittable: 'The
two songs in Ramsay, one of them evidently his own, are never to be met
with in the fireside circle of our Peasantry; while, what I take to be the
old song is in every shepherd's mouth –' (Excise, p. 8). Ramsay he
imitated but also judged: the old words had something Ramsay did not;
Burns recognised this and so did his 'compeers'.

In addition to these notes which touch on matters of authorship, on
oral tradition and its characteristics like variation and localisation, on
routes of dissemination and place of origin – all of which show an
amazing amount of sophistication for a tenant farmer/exciseman beset
with financial, family, and health difficulties – there are a variety of
interesting historical notes which add to the history of the songs
annotated. In the Excise Manuscript, especially, Burns includes a
number of anecdotes and traditions which are related to songs:

I insert this song ('Bob o' Dumblane') to introduce the following anecdote which I have heard well authenticated. In the evening of the day of the battle of Dumblane (Sheriffmoor), after the action was over, a Scots officer in Argyle's army observed to his grace, that he was afraid the Rebels would give out to the world that *they* had gotten the victory – 'Weel, weel,' returned his Grace alluding to the forego-ing ballad; 'if they think it be na weel bobbit, we'll bob it again.' –
(Excise, p. 2)

Burns provides an anecdote about how the song 'Kirk wad let me be' helped a Covenanting clergyman escape a band of soldiers by acting in a very unministerial way, singing loudly and possibly composing the song on the spot (Excise, p. 3); and he describes a 'dramatic interlude at country weddings' which uses the first stanza of the same item (Excise, p. 3). The second Bishop Chisholm of Dunblane, he has heard, would like to hear 'Clout the Caldron', if he were going to be hanged, because of its soothing qualities (Excise, p. 11). He gives the tradition, commonly known, about 'Dainty Davie':

This song, tradition says, & the composition itself confirms, was composed on the rev. David Williamson's begetting the daughter of Lady Cherry trees with child, while a party of dragoons were searching her house for him to apprehend him for being an adherent to the Solemn League & Covenant. – The pious woman had put a lady's night-cap on him & had laid him abed with her own daughter, & passed him to the soldiery as a lady, her daughter's bedfellow.
(Excise, p. 11)

Elsewhere he quotes Stephen Clarke's opinion that the tune 'Cumnock Psalms' was based on a Catholic chant (Ferguson, 637). And of the much used tune 'Hey tutti taitie', Burns says: 'There is a tradition, which I have met with in many places of Scotland, that it was Robert Bruce's March at the battle of Bannock-burn' (Ferguson, 582). He occasionally provides information, often anecdotal, about the authors of various songs as he did with Cunningham the player, author of 'Kate of Aberdeen'.[35] He identifies and discusses topographical places such as the birch trees in 'The bush aboon Traquair' (Dick, 80). He quotes Dr Blacklock as a source of various historical notes (Dick, 89, 160). And he explains elements in songs out of his vast knowledge: 'The title of this air (14th of October) shews that it alludes to the famous King Crispian, the patron of the honorable Corporation of Shoemakers. Saint Crispian's

day falls on the fourteenth of October, old style, as the old proverb
tells:—

> "On the fourteenth of October
> Was ne'er a sutor sober!" '[36]

He often implies that a song is based on fact (Dick, 174).

Above all, Burns repeatedly confirms his theoretical position that a
song is a unity of text and tune.[37] When he writes to Johnson or
Thomson or various casual correspondents about songs, he almost
invariably gives the names of both text and tune, or a few lines of the text
and then a name for the tune. So that for 'This is no mine ain house'
which appears in the *Museum*, he says that only the first half-stanza is
old; Ramsay wrote the rest; then he writes four verses of old words,
following them with the important, completing information: 'The tune
is an old Highland air, called *Shuan truish willighan*' (Dick, 216).
Additionally he suggested that the tune itself often conveyed the spirit of
its title (Dick, 18) which he believed alluded to the first text used to the
tune. Texts, he felt, because they were so often localised, were replaced
with new words in a new locale or at a later time, but tunes persisted,
being in his words 'the language of nature' and thus more universally
applicable and persistent (Dick, 16). It almost goes without saying that
he recognised that more than one text might be sung to a given tune;
conversely a text might itself be sung to different tunes. It takes,
however, a text and a tune to make a song. Burns knew this and his
annotations and letters amply show that he did more than pay lip-
service to this position.

The evidence that Burns knew something beyond the texts and tunes
of the songs is not overt at all. To find these valuable statements about
sources, his own and those of others, and his historical notes and
theoretical views, one must go behind the printed material which he
published, or which he knew was published, and consult his letters, his
annotations of song in the Interleaved Museum, and the Excise
Manuscript as well as the valuable historical work done by such persons
as Stenhouse, Laing, Sharpe, and Dick. It is only then that Burns as
collector, historical student, annotator (and songwriter for that matter)
can be seen. His annotations are most valuable for as Henry G. Farmer
has said: 'The history of the "auld sangs" of Scotland would not have
been so well documented had it not been for the poet's discreet and
lengthy annotations'.[38]

No doubt there are a variety of reasons why the annotations were not published: certainly additional cost was one, purpose and audience were another. Burns began his work for the *Museum* in the guise of National Bard and he sought to become, through his editorial and poetic work, the collective voice of the people. He was not eager to admit how many songs were his own because he tried to pass them off, in the *Museum* particularly, as Scotland's voice; some of the prefaces he wrote for the *Museum* illustrate this: 'Ignorance and Prejudice may perhaps affect to sneer at the simplicity of the poetry or music of some of these pieces; but their having been for ages the favorites of Nature's Judges – the Common People, was to the Editor a sufficient test of their merit'.[39] And 'Consciousness of the well-known merit of our Scotish Music, and the national fondness of a Scotch-man for the productions of his own country, are at once the Editor's motive and apology for this undertaking'.[40] He could hardly then admit himself to be the author or amender of half the items.[41] Some of the songs he edited, as well as his own original ones, however, did have all the earmarks of traditional pieces, circulating orally themselves. Burns did not admit his role and thus his texts alone are of limited utility in determining what was actually circulating before and during his time; they are inaccurate records of collecting unless one looks behind them to his own annotations and to those of subsequent scholars.

There is evidence, however, that Burns, unlike many collectors/editors of his time and afterwards, began to realise as he delved more and more deeply into the subject through collecting, active participation, and study that the annotations he was capable of making were of equal importance with the texts and tunes he had recovered. In a letter to George Thomson, referring to Thomson's plan to republish Dr Beattie's *Essays On Poetry and Music*, Burns says: 'On my part, I mean to draw up an appendix to D^{r}s essay, containing my stock of anecdotes, &c, of our Scots Airs & Songs' (Ferguson, 535). But, even more important, he wrote to James Johnson, probably in 1792, asking for another interleaved copy of the *Museum* so 'that I may insert every anecdote I can learn, together with my own criticisms and remarks on the songs. A copy of this kind I shall leave with you, the Editor, to publish at some after period, by way of making the Museum a book famous to the end of time, and you renowned for ever'.[42] Such a publication would certainly have placed Burns in the very vanguard of folksong scholarship if not as its leader. However, the book, if begun, was never completed. Earlier he had annotated some items for Robert Riddell of Glenriddell in the Interleaved Museum. No doubt the hypothetical interleaved book would have followed that plan but have been more extensive. Although Farmer has suggested that the Excise Manuscript contains missing pages from the Riddell Interleaved Museum, this is highly improbable; however, it is possible that the Excise Manuscript, written after November 1791 when Burns became an exciseman and thus had access to the paper on which it is written, was a first stage of the fuller annotations Burns projected, for the notes and comparative comments are generally more expansive in the Excise Manuscript than in the Interleaved Museum. It is a great loss that the hypothetical Interleaved Museum was not completed, but it adds to Burns' stature as a student of folksong that it was projected as a completing aspect of the *Museum*.

In view of modern standards of collection and transcription it is impossible to condone Robert Burns' editorial work except by saying that he at least provided information in his annotations, and probably planned more, that give some indication of the original from which he worked. While this is not an acceptable excuse by today's standards, it is historically accurate to say that Burns was following the editorial principles of his time – those of Ramsay and especially of Percy. His editorial work differed in quality and kind from most of theirs because he was both a poet *and* a product of the songs' traditional milieu so that what he did to the texts was more likely to fit the folk aesthetic ideal, to be similar to the oral recreative process, and to be returned to the folk, than what they did. It is interesting to note here that the most rigid and vitriolic editor of Burns' time, Joseph Ritson, is amazingly easy on Burns whom he calls 'a natural poet of the first eminence' when he notes in a footnote only that 'Mr. Burns, as good a poet as Ramsay, is, it must be regretted, an equally licentious and unfaithful publisher of the performances of others. Many of the original, old, ancient, genuine songs inserted in Johnsons *Scots Musical Museum* derive not a little of their merit from passing through the hands of this very ingenious critic'.[43] Walter Scott, a poet too, followed Burns, not Ritson, in his own editing, and said of the songs Burns edited that he 'restored its original spirit, or gave it more than it had ever possessed'.[44] Gershon Legman, who has thoroughly studied Burns' editing of bawdy songs, says

> that Burns was wrong in attempting to 'purify' the bawdy Scottish folksongs he collected, and in part wrote, in the polite versions he later produced specifically to accompany and to preserve the musical heritage of their folkloristic tunes. To the modern folklorist, Burns did almost equally wrong in attempting to improve these folk-collected texts, even when his improvement consisted not of expurgat-

ing them but of making them, in some cases, a good deal bawdier and always more personal. This is, however, the right of every folk-poet and singer.[45]

At least in the case of the *Museum* he gives information which makes it possible to discover some of what he did.

Robert Burns undoubtedly deserves a place in the history of folksong study. Most of the people enumerated as folksong scholars in eighteenth- and early nineteenth-century Scotland such as Walter Scott, Allan Cunningham, R. H. Cromek, William Motherwell, C. K. Sharpe, James Hogg, John Pinkerton, and Robert Jamieson were ballad enthusiasts: Burns did not ignore narrative folksong; he was actually interested in all divisions of folksong but he favoured the lyric. He was not alone in preferring or publishing lyrics: a number of collections such as those by Allan Ramsay had appeared, and lyric folksongs were regularly included in the predominantly ballad collections; but Burns is alone as a lyric enthusiast in collecting, annotating, and developing a theoretical position about the material. As such he should be seen as a central figure in the history of folksong study. Because his focus was different from the dominant ballad interest and because his contact with this interest was indirect and limited to print, he has been overlooked. It is easy to understand why – beyond the difference in focus, lyric rather than narrative – Burns has been ignored, for he differs in a number of ways from this group of ballad men. Many of these men were primarily editors: he was additionally a conscious collector as well as a knowledgeable scholar who realised the necessity for considerable annotation. And Burns, unlike many of these men, came from the very background where traditional songs were culturally functional. Unlike these men, however, Burns' work was done primarily in isolation. He did meet and/or correspond with a variety of antiquaries and cognoscenti of his day: his neighbour at Ellisland, Robert Riddell of Glenriddell, who has some claims to being an amateur folklorist and antiquarian himself; William Tytler (*Dissertation on the Scottish Music*), Dr Beattie (*Essays on Poetry and Music*), and Dr Blacklock – all said to be textual collaborators in the *Museum* (Ferguson, 145); Rev. Hugh Blair, David Stewart Erskine – 11th Earl of Buchan, James Sibbald, William Smellie. But he wrote to or knew these men as Scotland's poet, a rustic bard, rather than as a genuine antiquary and scholar. His contact with activities and interests similar to his own was through the written printed word and there is every reason to believe he knew just about everything available. In this isolation he differs from the ballad men who had a

complex network of communication, often epistolary. They shared a
limited number of manuscript and human resources: a number of
editors, for example, drew upon the traditions of Mrs Brown of
Falkland. Burns' sources were different and multiple; they were his and
his alone. In a sense, Burns occupies a *cul de sac* in the history of
folksong study: he took from tradition and the books available but he
had no direct contact with persons involved in similar endeavours. But
he did influence: he and his works, by their example, were among the
stimulating forces in the rise and development of German Romanticism,
which later restimulated the earlier interest and study of Scottish
traditional material which had inspired Burns when he went to
Edinburgh in 1786. Certainly he posthumously influenced the persons
who came after him, especially on the subject of editing. Allan
Cunningham was most probably led to his forgeries, that is, imitations
of traditional songs passed off as traditional, because of Burns' success in
doing that himself. Scott, too, followed him. It is interesting to note the
number of known ballad scholars and editors who also worked on
Burns, mostly as editors, thus in a way similar to their ballad work. They
were doubtless influenced by him: Allan Cunningham published an
edition of *The Complete Works of Robert Burns*; R. H. Cromek, the
influential and important *Reliques of Robert Burns* and editions of his
works; James Hogg and William Motherwell, *The Works of Robert
Burns*, whose commentary was enriched by communications from Peter
Buchan. Incidentially, Motherwell served at various times as secretary
and president of the Paisley Burns Club. Robert Chambers edited *The
Life and Works of Robert Burns* as well as other more limited
publications; C. K. Sharpe annotated the annotations of Stenhouse's
Illustrations of the Lyric Poetry and Music in Scotland, intended to
accompany the *Museum*. Walter Scott admired Burns' work and
reviewed books on him as in the *Quarterly Review* for 1809; and his son-
in-law John Gibson Lockhart published a *Life of Robert Burns*. And at
the end of the nineteenth century, Andrew Lang, a more broadly-based
folklore scholar than the ballad editors above, edited both *Selected
Poems of Robert Burns* and *The Poems and Songs of Robert Burns*.
  Burns might be called a saviour of folksongs because in the words of
many commentators, he 'rescued' old wrecks of Scottish culture and
saved them, often by editing and making hitherto unprintable songs,
printable; in this sense he might he called a populariser, preparing the
songs for that collection of popular taste, *The Scots Muscial Museum*.
Burns can also be called a revivalist – a person who witnessed a decline
in interest, a waning of influence of song and who collected to preserve,

sometimes working over the songs until they had renewed vitality.[46] He was exceedingly influenced by the antiquarian and nationalistic concerns of his day – concerns which became focused after his stay in Edinburgh and which encouraged him consciously to collect, edit, study, and annotate a body of songs – especially lyrics. Certainly one could say of Robert Burns, both in his practice and intent, as he said of the antiquary Francis Grose –

> A chield's amang you, taking notes,
> And, faith, he'll prent it.[47]

3 The Antiquarian and Nationalistic Impulse: The Later Songs and Poems

> Ev'n then a wish (I mind its power)
> A wish, that to my latest hour
>   Shall strongly heave my breast;
> That I for poor auld Scotland's sake
> Some useful plan, or book could make,
>   Or sing a sang at least.
>   'The Answer' to the Guidwife of Wauchope-House

Burns' Edinburgh experience, especially his introduction to antiquarian and nationalistic concerns circulating there, definitely had artistic repercussions. This is particularly obvious in his song output, for after Edinburgh song – no doubt inspired by his collaborations with Johnson and Thomson – became his primary artistic mode.

He had of course written songs before. His first known work had been the song, 'O once I lov'd', written when he was seventeen to praise his female harvest companion, Nelly Kilpatrick; it was composed to be sung to the traditional tune she often sang, 'I am a man unmarried'. But he turned to song with a vengeance after Edinburgh because he saw songs and especially the tunes which accompanied them as being distinctly Scottish. Not only did he collect songs – both texts and tunes – which were circulating orally, but he also edited partial song texts to make them whole, and he created completely new works as well. Before he went to Edinburgh, he had also made wholes of parts and written totally new song texts, but he had done so more or less intuitively because the composition of songs, the wedding of text to tune, was an accepted form for a local poet; old and new songs were frequently performed in gatherings of friends. Burns' experiences in Edinburgh made him aware of song as Scottish material endangered by the movement towards anglicisation. He aspired to be Scotland's anonymous bard, a national rather than a local poet, by joining words – all or partially of his own making – to Scottish tunes. This conscious endeavour occupied the remainder of his life and led him to produce hundreds of songs. Unfortunately, it is almost impossible to determine the exact number because he composed so much in the form and spirit of traditional song and allowed many of his works to be published without his name attached.[1]

In working with song, Burns was representing and reinforcing an old tradition, for singing of songs – often passed on orally – had long been an aspect of social life, though few studies have dealt with their social function. Instead most scholars have abstracted texts and less frequently tunes from their possessors, whom they have often dismissed as uncreative members of the lower or rural classes. Thus both the songs' possessors and the songs' functions have been deemed beneath interest;[2] the texts alone were worthy of interest for the light they might shed on the development of written literature, especially prose narrative. Only one type of folksong has been singled out for extensive study – the ballads, stories told in stanzaic song. Fewer lyrics have been systematically collected and published, perhaps because they have been perceived to be less stable and more ephemeral than ballads; thus lyrics have been largely ignored – except with reference to Burns[3] – though some texts had been included along with ballad texts in various early publications, such as those of David Herd. Burns knew ballads, but he preferred lyrics. The paucity of both material and study of the lyric makes it difficult to determine definitively what Burns in fact wrote or his debts to the traditional material on which he surely built. Comparative texts, so abundant for the ballad, are often lacking. The fact that he both wrote and rewrote and edited *and* collected makes the issue of identifying his works problematic: one cannot claim a song as his just because it exists in holograph. Many of Burns' own songs have themselves circulated orally along with anonymous traditional material and with the songs he edited and rewrote and collected. All have been treated equally in oral transmission: all are subject to change, to variation, to the dynamic process which makes a song a folksong. The singers often do not know the author; conversely they may both accurately or inaccurately attribute. This adds further to the difficulty of determining what Burns really wrote. At this late date any study of Scotland's traditional lyrics

will be incomplete because the available data itself is incomplete and
historical material irrecoverable, but such a study, built by comparative
examination of extant printed and manuscript collections, might
provide both a more realistic estimate of the lyric's existence than the
preponderance of ballad studies would suggest and offer – particularly
relevant here – a basis for determining the extent of Burns' lyric song
production as well as his specific debts to the traditional lyric.[4]

In his songwriting, he certainly drew heavily on traditional models for
content, form, and style. His use of content is both obvious and
pervasive: at times he took a tune title or a few lines and built a new song
around it; at other times he utilised whole stanzas and fragments; he
adapted bawdy songs – sometimes bowdlerising them, sometimes
making them bawdier; he also used the themes and commonplaces
native to the oral material. Where sources of Burns' songs have been
sought in the past – J. C. Dick was an early master of this and the notes
in Henley and Henderson's Centenary edition contain ample
examples – the tendency has been to find parallel lines and stanzas in
books or in manuscripts – the assumption being that Burns, who did in
fact know most relevant published material and perhaps some manu-
script collections, drew his lines, titles, and fragments from such sources.
It would be much more accurate, in view of his conscious collecting
activities and his lifelong association with song, to suggest that Burns
got much of the material orally and that both he and the editors of the
books and the writers of manuscripts – if they collected from oral
tradition – were tapping and recording an oral tradition, which – like
the ballad repertoire of Scotland – probably existed all over the Scots-
speaking area of Scotland. It is literary bias that makes many assume
that Burns derived most of his material from books.

Perhaps Burns' inspiration for 'A Fragment. When *Guilford* good our
Pilot stood' (no. 38) was the tune named after the battle of
Killiecrankie,[5] one episode in a long history of conflict between
Highlanders and English: the text refers to the American Revolutionary
War and subsequent British elections. One line 'Up, Willie, Waur them
a', man!' echoes an oft-repeated cry of Jacobite songs; and that line itself
is given as the tune for 'The Laddies by the Banks o' Nith' (no. 270) and
is repeated in the chorus – the whole being a political piece in favour of
Johnstone and belittling his opponent – and is thus an example of
possible inspiration derived from a tune title. The clause is also used
essentially as a repeated line and as the title of Burns' redaction of a song
(no. 212), included in Kinsley as Burns' work. Since it has been widely
reported in various versions,[6] all dealing with another Highland/English

conflict, and since Burns said he got the version from Tom Niel,[7] this song should certainly be put in a separate category of songs, not written, but collected by Burns.[8] A comparison of Burns' first stanza with that of David Herd's version is illustrative:

> *Burns*: When we gaed to the braes o' Mar,
> > And to the wapon-shaw, Willie,
> > Wi' true design to serve the king
> > And banish whigs awa, Willie. –
> > Up and warn a', Willie,
> > Warn, warn a';
> > For Lords and lairds came there bedeen
> > And wow but they were braw, Willie. –

> *Herd*: When we went to the field of war,
> > And to the Weaponshaw, WILLIE,
> > With true design to stand our ground,
> > And chace our faes awa', WILLIE;
> > Lairds and Lords came there bedeen,
> > And vow gin they were pra', WILLIE
> > *Up and war'em a'*, WILLIE,
> > *War 'em, war 'em a'*, WILLIE.[9]

'Up and warn a' Willie –' is not an isolated instance of attribution to Burns of traditional material. Often James Kinsley, editor of the most recent, complete, and scholarly edition of Burns' work, *The Poems and Songs of Robert Burns*, includes such material in the Burns' corpus but contradicts, to an extent, his own attribution by placement, in the commentary. Of 'Gude Wallace' (no. 584) he says, 'It is clear at least that Burns collected the ballad from oral tradition; but there is no evidence that he revised it'.[10] Further, Kinsley says of 'The rantin laddie –', (no. 575) 'There is, then, no evidence that Burns made much change in what he collected; and he did not attempt to complete the poem, or to make good the break after l. 30'.[11] Additionally, he attributes various versions of Child ballads to Burns, such as 'Tam Lin' (no. 558, Child, 39); 'Lord Ronald my Son' (no. 352, Child, 12); 'Hughie Graham' (no. 342, Child, 191); 'Geordie – An old Ballad' (no. 358, Child, 209); 'Leezie Lindsay' (no. 565, Child, 226), and 'Johnie Blunt' (no. 368, Child, 275). Various songs which Burns said he collected, for example 'Auld lang syne' (no. 240) and 'A waukrife Minnie' (no. 311), are also included as Burns' own work. The difficulties of accurately determining what Burns did write, particularly in the area of song, are evident and are hampered at every turn, both by scholarly bias and by the paucity of organised comparative material, so much needed when studying a figure like Burns whose roots in oral tradition were very deep.

Fortunately, Burns has left some information which indicates his creative process. 'Then Guidwife count the lawin' (no. 346) belongs to that category of songs which were built from fragments or stanzas – if one accepts Burns' statement that 'the chorus of this is part of an old song, one stanza of which I recollect:—

> Every day my wife tells me
> That ale and brandy will ruin me;
> But if gude liquor be my dead,
> This shall be written on my head,
> O gude wife count, &c.'[12]

Burns takes this sentiment and uses traditional phrases and words as well as the chorus to produce a song about the conviviality of all, of low and high estate, in drink:

Lively

> Gane is the day and mirk's the night,
> But we'll ne'er stray for faute o' light,
> For ale and brandy's stars and moon,
> And blude-red wine's the rysin Sun.

Chorus
Then guidwife count the lawin, the lawin, the lawin,
Then guidwife count the lawin, and bring a coggie mair.

There's wealth and ease for gentlemen,
And semple-folk maun fecht and fen;
But here we're a' in ae accord,
For ilka man that's drunk's a lord.
    Cho⁵. Then goodwife count &c.

My coggie is a haly pool,
That heals the wounds o' care and dool;
And pleasure is a wanton trout,
An' ye drink it a', ye'll find him out.
    Cho⁵. Then goodwife count &c.

                                        (no. 346)

A less substantiated borrowing of a stanza from oral tradition may
occur in 'Duncan Davison':

    A man may drink and no be drunk,
        A man may fight and no be slain:
    A man may kiss a bony lass,
        And ay be welcome back again.
                    (ll. 21–4, no. 202)

Henley and Henderson conclude that Burns got the stanza from Herd's
manuscript which he might have seen in Edinburgh:[13]

        I can drink and no be drunk,
        I can fight and no be slain,
        I can kiss a bony lass,
        And ay be welcome back again.[14]

The well-known bothy ballad, 'The Barnyards o' Delgaty', includes a
variant stanza:

        I can drink and nae be drunk,
            I can fight and nae be slain,
        I can court anither's lass,
            And aye be welcome to my ain.[15]

One might speculate that Burns and John Ord and David Herd before
them had each collected this floating verse. It is impossible to determine
whether or not Burns wrote this stanza or any number of texts.

The bawdy songs present an even greater problem, for few were published because they were considered to be offensive. Gershon Legman, Sydney Goodsir Smith, James Barke, and James Kinsley have worked extensively with this material; and they conclude that Burns often added verses to the end of bawdy songs and presented the content from a female perspective;[16] that he often bowdlerised the songs for the *Museum*; and that he collected many of the items rather than writing them. Smith suggests that bawdry has been and continues to be widespread: 'The composition of obscene verse in Scotland is of such a quality and has so extensive a tradition as almost to merit a chapter to itself in the discussion of any given period of Scottish literature'.[17] Kinsley's statement concerning 'Had I the wyte she bad me' exemplifies the problem of attributing a song to an individual who was at times a reflection of an oral tradition: 'The *Muses* song may be traditional. The second and third stanzas are admittedly in the enthusiastic and violent manner of Burns's acknowledged bawdry, but that manner is itself in the folk tradition'.[18] Because this oral world was his heritage, he understandably worked within it to communicate. Perhaps he wrote these songs guided by the traditional models; maybe he collected them;[19] possibly he edited them. Again holograph material can mislead, sometimes being only a record of his collection. But it is safe to say that traditional song played a very important part in providing Burns with inspiration, even if one is not able to point definitively to all of the songs he used as sources.

One of the most blatant ways in which Burns used the material he knew as model was through parody and imitation. Parody, of course, by poking fun, reinforces the subject at hand. His parody of a ballad in 'Grim Grizzle' (no. 530) is a perfect example: the text describes a woman in authority who wanted her herdsman 'John o' Clods' to train the cattle to defecate at a specific time and place. And in such songs as 'Lord Gregory' (no. 399) Burns imitates traditional subject matter: exiled, a young woman seeks admittance to her lover's hall. In both parody and imitation, something more than content, however, is involved: dominant is the use of traditional form – the poetic structures of the oral artistic world.

Burns repeatedly used the ballad and folksong structure – the four-line stanza which both accompanies and complements the four standard musical phrases. This stanza form, rhyming abcb, having a 4343 stress pattern – frequently called common metre – was widely known, from sacred as well as secular traditions: used in the Metrical Psalms, it dominated the folksong tradition as well. When Burns wrote songs, when he wedded text to tune, when he accepted the general contours of the traditional stanza form, when he included a chorus, he built on oral forms which he knew well as a member of a group where such structures were familiar.

One kind of folksong is narrative – the ballad; and Burns consciously used the stanza form and narrative thrust in several items. 'The Five Carlins – A Ballad – Tune, Chevy chase' (no. 269) is a good example: the title signals his use of ballad form, content, and tune. Beginning

> There was five Carlins in the South,
>   They fell upon a scheme,
> To send a lad to London town
>   To bring them tidings hame. –
>   (ll. 1–4, no. 269)

the text describes a disagreement over who should represent the song's characters in London, and was inspired by a local election. While narrative and couched in traditional stanza form, the content comes close to parody as Burns virtually paraphrases the final stanza of the traditional ballad Ben Jonson would have written himself, 'The Hunting of the Cheviot' or 'Chevy Chase':

> God save our *king*, and blesse this land
>   with plentye, ioy, and peace,
> And grant hencforth *that* foule debate
>   twixt noble men may ceaze!
>   (Child, 162)

Burns writes, in inconclusively concluding his ballad,

> So how this weighty plea may end,
>   Nae mortal wight can tell:
> God grant the King, and ilka man,
>   May look weel to themsel. –
>   (ll. 89–92, no. 269)

He uses, of course, the tune, wedded to the traditional ballad text 'Chevy Chase' in this imitation, parody, statement, which is undeniably couched in general folksong and specific ballad form.

While Burns employed traditional dialect in his poems, excelling in dialogue and conversational use, his songs for the most part are merely sprinkled with the vernacular. But in addition to traditional subject matter and form, he incorporated aspects of oral style into his songs. Repetition has long been recognised as an oral stylistic device and in his songs Burns repeated both words, lines, and stanzas.[20] In 'I hae a wife o' my ain' (no. 361) the word *naebody* concludes the second and fourth lines of each of the four stanzas, building almost incrementally – incremental repetition being another frequently named characteristic of traditional song, particularly ballads.

> I hae a wife o' my ain,
>   I'll partake wi' naebody;
> I'll tak Cuckold frae nane,
>   I'll gie Cuckold to naebody. –
>
> I hae a penny to spend,
>   There, thanks to naebody;
> I hae naething to lend,
>   I'll borrow frae naebody. –
>
> I am naebody's lord,
>   I'll be slave to naebody;
> I hae a gude braid sword,
>   I'll tak dunts frae naebody. –
>
> I'll be merry and free,
>   I'll be sad for naebody;
> Naebody cares for me,
>   I care for naebody. –

(no. 361)

Linking incremental repetition with line repetition, Burns' song 'The rantin dog the Daddie o't' (no. 80) concludes each stanza with the title phrase as in the initial stanza:

> O Wha my babie-clouts will buy,
> O Wha will tent me when I cry;
> Wha will kiss me where I lie,
> The rantin dog the daddie o't.
>   (ll. 1–4, no. 80)

And quite a number of his songs[21] repeat the vocable *O*, largely as in traditional song, to fill out the metre and fit the melodic line, as exemplified by the final stanza of 'Green Grow the Rashes. A Fragment.' (no. 45):

> Auld Nature swears, the lovely Dears
> Her noblest work she classes, O:
> Her prentice han' she try'd on man,
> An' then she made the lasses, O.
>   (ll. 17–20, no. 45)

Here he also uses a refrain, another oral song device, often – as in this instance – probably taken wholesale from a traditional model:

> *Green grow the rashes, O;*
> *Green grow the rashes, O;*
> *The sweetest hours that e'er I spend,*
> *Are spent among the lasses, O.*
>   (no. 45)

His songs thus owe much to the traditional songs he had grown up with. After his stay in Edinburgh he turned increasingly to this medium for his artistry by editing, patching, and creating texts which could accompany Scottish tunes; the shift to songwriting as his principal endeavour was inspired by the Scottish nationalistic and antiquarian sentiments he acquired during his brief stay in the capital. He built on the content, form, and style of traditional song as a way of expressing his sense of unity with all of Scottish artistry; he sought, through song, to be the anonymous voice of Scotland, to speak for and to his fellow Scots, to give them texts to accompany the tunes; his motivation was nationalistic.

The same influences also affected Burns' poetic work after the
Edinburgh stay and are particularly obvious in his most celebrated work
of this period, 'Tam o' Shanter'. Here the primary stimulus was
antiquarian and was inspired by his contact with Francis Grose's project
to record the physical antiquities of Britain – the material remnants of
the past.

'Tam o' Shanter' was in a way written to order. While Burns was
living at Ellisland Farm near Dumfries, his neighbour and friend, a local
man of considerable substance, sometime antiquary Robert Riddell of
Glenriddel, enjoyed Burns' company – no doubt both because he was an
oddity, 'a ploughman poet' in his eyes, but also because Burns shared
with Riddell an interest in antiquities, both physical and oral. And
Riddell shared his friend Burns with various visitors to his estate for one
or both of these reasons. It was the latter, no doubt, that led Riddell to
introduce Burns to Francis Grose, author of *Antiquities of England and
Wales* (1772–87), who was visiting Scotland in 1789 preparatory to
publishing *Antiquities of Scotland* (1789–91). With the enthusiasm of a
native in exile (he was living in Dumfriesshire, the county just southeast
of his native Ayrshire at the time), Burns recalled buildings and ruins in
Ayrshire which, with patriotic and antiquarian fervour, he insisted
should be included: one such spot was the ruin of Alloway Kirk, near the
Brig o' Doon, in whose churchyard his own father was buried. Grose's
technique in preparing his books – amusingly detailed in a descriptive
poem by Burns called 'On the Late Captain Grose's peregrinations thro'
Scotland, collecting the Antiquities of that Kingdom' – was to visit
various physical antiquities, carefully sketching them, and to write an
historical description. Grose agreed to include a sketch of Alloway Kirk
if Burns would write a poem about it. Burns did, basing his poem upon
legendary traditions: 'Tam o' Shanter' was published in the second
volume of Grose's *Antiquities of Scotland* in 1791.[22] (See Plate 1.)
Grose's introduction pays tribute to Burns' participation: 'To my
ingenious friend Mr. Robert Burns I have been variously obligated; he
not only was at pains of marking out what was most worthy of notice in
Ayrshire, the country honored by his birth, but he also wrote, expressly
for this work, the pretty tale annexed to Aloway Church.'[23]

The poem itself relies heavily on traditional content, so often the
source of Burns' works. Here Burns consciously utilised legendary
traditions he had heard as a member of a traditional group. Such
material undoubtedly was shared at the same kinds of gatherings where
songs were transmitted: both were part of the oral artistry of his early
environment. Just as with song, however, he was probably not

consciously aware of this material's significance until his Edinburgh experience which introduced him to the nationalistic and antiquarian movement and provided him with the necessary perspective to see the value of this material to Scotland.

Burns then was certainly in sympathy with Grose's work; and to assure Alloway Kirk's inclusion in the *Antiquities of Scotland*, he wrote a poem which was based on traditional legends. In preparing to fulfil his part of the bargain, Burns recalled several legends about Alloway Kirk in a letter to Grose:

Sir,
Among the many Witch Stories I have heard relating to Aloway Kirk, I distinctly remember only two or three.

Upon a stormy night, amid whirling squalls of wind and bitter blasts of hail, in short, on such a night as the devil would chuse to take the air in, a farmer or a farmer's servant was plodding and plashing homeward with his plough-irons on his shoulder, having been getting some repairs on them at a neighbouring smithy. His way lay by the Kirk of Aloway, and being rather on the anxious look-out in approaching a place so well known to be a favorite haunt of the devil and the devil's friends and emissaries, he was struck aghast by discovering, through the horrors of the storm and stormy night, a light, which, on his nearer approach, plainly shewed itself to proceed from the haunted edifice. Whether he had been fortified from above on his devout supplication, as is customary with people when they suspect the immediate presence of Satan; or whether, according to another custom, he had got courageously drunk at the smithy, I will not pretend to determine; but so it was that he ventured to go up to, nay into the very Kirk. – As good luck would have it, his temerity came off unpunished. The members of the infernal junto were all out on some midnight business or other, and he saw nothing but a kind of kettle or caldron, depending from the roof, over the fire, simmering some heads of unchristened children, limbs of executed malefactors, &c. for the business of the night. It was, in for a penny, in for a pound, with the honest ploughman; so without ceremony he unhooked the caldron from off the fire, and pouring out the damnable ingredients, inverted it on his head, and carried it fairly home, where it remained long in the family a living evidence of the truth of the story.

Another story, which I can prove to be equally authentic, was as follows.

On a market day in the town of Ayr, a farmer from Carrick, and

consequently whose way lay by the very gate of Aloway kirk-yard, in
order to cross the river Doon at the old bridge, which is about two or
three hundred yards farther on than the said gate, had been detained
by his business till by the time he reached Aloway it was a wizard hour,
between night and morning.

Though he was terrified with a blaze streaming from the kirk, yet as
it is a well known fact, that to turn back on these occasions is running
by far the greatest risk of mischief, he prudently advanced on his road.
When he had reached the gate of the kirk-yard, he was surprised and
entertained, through the ribs and arches of the old gothic window
which still faces the highway, to see a dance of witches merrily footing
it round their old sooty blackguard master, who was keeping them
all alive with the power of his bagpipe. The farmer stopping his horse
to observe them a little, could plainly descry the faces of many old
women of his acquaintance and neighbourhood. How the gentleman
was dressed, tradition does not say; but the ladies were all in their
smocks; and one of them happening unluckily to have a smock which
was considerably too short to answer all the purpose of that piece of
dress, our farmer was so tickled that he involuntarily burst out, with a
loud laugh, 'Weel luppen, Maggy wi' the short sark!' and recollecting
himself, instantly spurred his horse to the top of his speed. I need not
mention the universally known fact, that no diabolical power can
pursue you beyond the middle of a running stream. Lucky it was for
the poor farmer that the river Doon was so near, for notwithstanding
the speed of his horse, which was a good one, against he reached the
middle of the arch of the bridge, and consequently the middle of the
stream, the pursuing, vengeful hags were so close at his heels, that one
of them actually sprung to seize him: but it was too late; nothing was
on her side of the stream but the horse's tail, which immediately gave
way to her infernal grip, as if blasted by a stroke of lightning; but the
farmer was beyond her reach. – However, the unsightly, tailless
condition of the vigorous steed was to the last hours of the noble
creature's life, an awful warning to the Carrick farmers, not to stay
too late in Ayr markets. –

The last relation I shall give, though equally true, is not so well
identified as the two former, with regard to the scene: but as the best
authorities give it for Aloway, I shall relate it. –

On a summer's evening, about the time that Nature puts on her
sables to mourn the expiry of the chearful day, a shepherd boy
belonging to a farmer in the immediate neighbourhood of Aloway
Kirk, had just folded his charge, and was returning home. As he

passed the Kirk, in the adjoining field, he fell in with a crew of men and women, who were busy pulling stems of the plant ragwort. He observed that as each person pulled a ragwort, he or she got astride of it, and called out, 'Up horsie!' on which the ragwort flew off, like Pegasus, through the air with its rider. The foolish boy likewise pulled his ragwort, and cried, with the rest, 'Up horsie!' and, strange to tell, away he flew with the company. The first stage at which the cavalcade stopt, was a merchant's wine cellar in Bourdeaux, where, without saying, by your leave, they quaffed away at the best the cellar could afford, untill the morning, foe to the imps and works of darkness, threatened to throw light on the matter, and frightened them from their carousals. –

The poor shepherd lad, being equally a stranger to the scene and the liquor, heedlessly got himself drunk; and when the rest took horse, he fell asleep and was found so next day by some of the people belonging to the merchant. Somebody that understood Scotch, asking him what he was, he said he was such-a-one's herd in Aloway, and by some means or other getting home again, he lived long to tell the world the wondrous tale. –

> I am, Dr Sir,
> Robt Burns[24]

Just as Burns often collected and edited folksongs, sometimes changing them to fit his own traditionally formed aesthetic sensibility, in 'Tam o' Shanter' he built a poem upon a legend he had heard in his contemporary Ayrshire.

It was the second legend included in Burns' letter to Grose which was most significant in the writing of 'Tam o' Shanter'. While Burns' version is localised in Ayrshire, it should be pointed out that this legend is found elsewhere: it has certain affinities with a legend, recorded and classified by Reidar Th. Christiansen in *The Migratory Legends* as no. 4015 'The Midnight Mass of the Dead':

At a certain place (A1), on a certain occasion (A2), some person (A3) for some reason or other entered a church at night (A4). Inside he found a congregation totally unknown to him (B1), as was also the officiating clergyman (B2), and as he was sitting down, someone (B3) warned him, telling him to leave and in what manner to do so (B4). As he rose to leave, those present tried to detain him (C1), even pursued him to the door (C2). He made good his escape (C3), but lost his coat or shawl (C4) which people found next morning on the doorsteps of the church all torn to pieces (C5).[25]

Burns' prose account may well be a version of this number, although Katharine M. Briggs in *A Dictionary of British Folk-Tales* lists 'Tam o' Shanter' in her Tale Type Index as no. 3051, fitting it into Christiansen's scheme.[26] Additionally, she lists one version, 'The Witch of Biggerdale', not printed in her volume but found in H. L. Gee, *Folk Tales of Yorkshire*.

At Biggersdale in Mulgrave Woods, not far from Whitby, lived a wicked witch called Jeanie. She terrorised the countryside by her spells and incantations. Her home was in Hob's Cave, and she became so troublesome to the farmers in the neighbourhood that one of them, a young man who thought himself no end of a bold fellow, determined to put an end to her.

Mounting his horse, he ventured to ride through the woods till he arrived at her den. He dared to call her name, but before he could dismount the witch rushed upon him with such fury that, for all his brave promises to his friends, he turned his horse about and galloped off as quickly as he could.

The enraged witch followed like the wind, and the farmer's only hope was that he might cross running water before she caught up with him. Downhill he rode, faster than he had ever ridden before, the witch – a creature as ugly as sin – shouting to him to stop and threatening him with horrible punishments if she caught up with him. She seemed likely to do so, for she was gaining on the terrified rider. Under trees and over briars he raced, lashing his panting horse as he went, and every now and then glancing fearfully over his shoulder, only to see Jeanie rushing after him, her wand raised above her head.

But luck was with the young farmer. Spurring his horse in one last frantic effort he leapt from the bank into the stream. Even so, Jeanie was so close behind him that as the horse splashed into the water she struck its flanks with her wand, cutting the poor beast in two. For all that, the forepart of his steed carried the farmer safely to the other side before it fell dead under him.[27]

While Burns' primary debt is to the second legend in the letter to Grose quoted above, he incorporated both general and specific details from the first: a stormy night on which the devil is abroad; the man, possibly drunk, returning home late by Alloway Kirk, a known haunt of the devil and his followers; the lighted ruins of the church; and the chance view of such ritual materials as unchristened children and portions of executed malefactors. But the second account provides the narrative structure and outline which controls the tale of Tam, as a contemporary critic and friend of Burns suggested in objecting to the conclusion, which he admitted – and Burns agreed – was no doubt dictated by the content of the 'popular tale'.[28] From the market day in Ayr to the closing moral – that the tailless horse will provide a warning – Burns borrows from his prose version: a Carrick farmer's way home takes him by Alloway and across the Doon. Having stayed late, returning home around midnight, he sees the church filled with light, observes the witches dancing in their smocks; one witch, more attractive than the rest, is attired in a very short slip which makes her dancing all the more appealing. He cries out to encourage her and quickly retreats across the bridge, leaving only his horse's tail behind. Fortunately for Tam, devils and witches cannot cross running water.[29]

The legends which Burns utilised as the principal structure and content of his poem can be divided into individual beliefs; these can in turn be corroborated, confirming their existence as a part of the traditional culture, by referring to repositories of traditional motifs and beliefs such as Ernest W. Baughman's *Type and Motif-Index of the Folktales of England and North America*, Margaret Alice Murray's *The Witch-Cult in Western Europe*, Thomas Davidson's *Rowan Tree and Red Thread*, Stith Thompson's *Motif-Index of Folk-Literature*.

The central portion of the poem, Tam's encounter with the Witches' Sabbath (Baughman, G243), takes place around midnight (Baughman, G303.6.1.1). Murray suggests that: 'The actual hour at which the Sabbath was held is specified in very few cases; it appears to have been a nocturnal assembly, beginning about midnight and lasting till early dawn or cockcrow';[30] Davidson adds that 'the meetings were usually held at night and in secret. Sometimes in an open but secluded place, sometimes in a churchyard, occasionally in a house'.[31] The setting here is a churchyard ('in nearly all the witch confessions we are told the initiation ceremonies were conducted in churchyards or other con-secrated ground'[32]) in the midst of stormy weather which Reginald Scot said witches could control: 'They may at their pleasure send raine, haile, tempests, thunder, lightening'.[33] Both male and female witches (Baughman, G220.0.2) are present as is the devil (Baughman, G303.6.2.2) who appears in the form of a dog (Baughman, G303.3.3.1.1 (a)), paralleling Murray's description that 'the Highland witches in the eighteenth century saw the devil as a dog; he was "a large black ugly tyke" '.[34] The dog was only one form the devil might take: 'The animal forms in which the Devil most commonly appeared were bull, cat, dog, goat, horse, and sheep'.[35] Murray suggests that the typical Sabbath began with homage to the devil, continued with the reports on work and ritual sacrifice, and concluded with dancing and feasting.[36] The witches dance (Baughman, G247) and the devil attends (Baughman, G303.6.2.1), providing the music (Baughman, G303.25.23) by playing the bagpipes. Murray quotes a corroborative report from 1655: 'One Night going to a dancing upon Pentland-hills, he [the devil] went before us in the likeness of a rough tanny-Dog, playing on a pair of Pipes, and his tail played ey wig wag wig wag'.[37] It is this scene which Tam comes upon and which his horse balks at approaching, sensing the unnaturalness of the event (Baughman, B521) and eventually saving Tam (Baughman, B523). Lines 131–41 describe the remnants of ingredients from the witches' rituals and sacrifices: flesh of children was often boiled, the thicker part used for ointment to help one fly, the thinner portions drunk for magical power.[38] Unbaptised babies belonged to the devil.[39] Since witches and fairies are often conflated, motifs relating to fairies may provide some corroboration: the witches chase Tam after he watches them dance (Baughman, F261.4) and yells at them; they attempt revenge, perhaps for being identified (Baughman, F361.3) and pursue him (Thompson, G267), flying through the air (Baughman, G242); but they are powerless to cross the Doon (Baughman, G273.4) in pursuit. However, they have some revenge in removing Tam's horse's tail which remained a moment too long on their side of the water (Baughman, R265; Thompson, G273.4.1). The legends as a whole as well as the individual parts were firmly rooted in known traditional beliefs.

Both the legend and parts of the legend can be established as aspects of the shared traditional culture through the discovery of parallels. These traditional materials can then be compared with the finished poem to discover, at least in part, those elements which Burns himself created and introduced. As I suggested earlier, this kind of comparative data is unavailable for lyric folksongs and makes determining Burns' debt to the traditional lyric, especially in terms of content, virtually impossible. For 'Tam o' Shanter', however, there is considerable comparative material which makes tentative identification of Burns' contributions possible.

The general frame and introduction are largely Burns'. The general setting (after a long market day, when it is tempting to stop for a drink even though it is late and a long way home to a wife who may be angry) narrows to a specific setting, Ayr, which Burns praises (he wanted to preserve the names and locales of his area), and an individual, Tam. This is followed by the first moral comment, a foreshadowing of events to come, which confirms the fact that Tam should have taken his wife's advice or minded her prophecies. Burns adds the tavern scene (friends drinking, telling stories, talking, oblivious to storm) as well as the psychological effect of this on Tam: he is happy and content but must go. Tam's good mount, Meg or Maggie; his attempt to remain calm by singing, all the while riding fast and holding on to his blue bonnet even when approaching spots where evil has occurred (no doubt lines 89–97 allude to local legendary material, to memorates perhaps he had heard) are details added to the prose redaction. Maggie sensed strangeness, a detail Burns probably included from his traditional knowledge (Baughman, B521); and the Scottish dances, rather than imported ones, reflect Burns' nationalism. He adds the open coffins and deft candle-holding corpses, many details of ritual apparatus, and the comment on Tam's view of the dancers. The allusion to Nannie's subsequent deeds may have been prompted by his own traditional knowledge as no doubt was the suggestion that the devil too was entranced; for witch and devil rituals were often sexual in nature. Further Burns builds suspense before the chase, interpolates comments that Tam will be punished, and alters the final moral – do not drink too much or think about short smocks. Burns has done more than stick to his prose outline; he has added other traditional material; and he has probably created detail as well.

The analysis above has dealt primarily with discrete content and has largely ignored the whole – the complete poem – which was essentially based and structured on the second prose account to Grose. That account records a legend, and knowledge of the legend as a form of oral communication may add further to the recognition of Burns' debt to his oral milieu. For Burns not only used legend content, he also recreated in the poem aspects of the legend context, the situation of legend exchange. He had done something similar in his earlier work, 'The Jolly Beggars', discussed in Chapter 1. In 'Tam o' Shanter' his use of content and context is both more subtle and more accurate and may well reflect a heightened awareness of traditional material and its context.

The legend has been one of the most elusive oral genres to define. Linda Dégh and Andrew Vazsonyi have suggested that a belief about which there is a certain ambiguity and ambivalence is the essential core of the folk legend.[40] The core belief provokes alternate reactions from the hearers – belief, indifference, scepticism, disbelief, opposition – which are often voiced as interrupters in the narrative account. The

belief, included in the narrative, together with the reactions make up the
folk legend. Thus the folk legend is defined both by its content and by its
context.

In terms of content, 'Tam o' Shanter' contains the pivotal belief
factor. In fact Burns so subtly introduces beliefs throughout the poem
that the reader or hearer is led in crescendo fashion to the final belief and
is forced to respond from his or her own matrix, external to the poem, to
the final action. The poem adheres as well to other accepted ideas of
what a legend is: Burns establishes a setting for the poem, localised to
create verisimilitude, a stock-in-trade of the legend teller: Carrick, Ayr,
the nearby village of Alloway and its ruined kirk, the adjacent river
Doon and its old bridge, and the local pub hostess Kirkton Jean. It is a
cold market day; work is done; weary men are resting and recouping
themselves by drinking while their wives sit at home, alone, getting
angrier by the minute. From the general we move to the specific, aided
by the good story-teller's ability to enable us to see both setting and
situation through vivid images:

> This truth fand honest *Tam o' Shanter*,
> As he frae Ayr ae night did canter,
> (Auld Ayr, wham ne'er a town surpasses,
> For honest men and bonny lasses.)
>
> (ll. 13–16)

Tam has often stopped for such a drink, and his wife as often has
predicted dire results – that he would drown in Doon, or be caught by
warlocks who regularly gather at Alloway Kirk:

> She prophesied that late or soon,
> Thou would be found deep drown'd in Doon;
> Or catch'd wi' warlocks in the mirk,
> By *Alloway's* auld haunted kirk.
>
> (ll. 29–32)

Here Burns introduces elements of belief and on the face of it, such a
possibility as witches and warlocks at Alloway Kirk is accepted as given.
(However, when the poem moves full circle to witches and warlocks at
Alloway in the concluding scene, this belief is, for some, not so readily
accepted.) But, ignoring his wife's prophecies, Tam once again has a
rollicking good time after market day – singing, hearing and telling
stories, talking, flirting, and all the while drinking as time passes quickly.

And it is midnight – 'night's black arch the keystane'. It is stormy, the kind of night the devil would like; this is another belief accepted in passing. Tam finally leaves in this awful weather, singing to ward off fears, keeping a look-out for hobgoblins, whose existence one again accepts. On his ride he passes first a spot where a man was drowned in snow, then the place where a drunkard broke his neck, the place where a murdered child was found, and a well where a woman hanged herself (more accepted beliefs). As if this is not enough – these spots so identified with human malevolence – Tam approaches Alloway Kirk where a full-fledged Witches Sabbath is in progress, described in detail:

> And, vow! *Tam* saw an unco sight!
> Warlocks and witches in a dance;
> Nae cotillion brent new frae *France*,
> But hornpipes, jigs, strathspeys, and reels,
> Put life and mettle in their heels.
> A winnock-bunker in the east,
> There sat auld Nick, in shape o' beast;
> A towzie tyke, black, grim, and large,
> To gie them music was his charge:
> He screw'd the pipes and gart them skirl,
> Till roof and rafters a' did dirl—
>
> (ll. 114–24)

Though they are usually ugly and old, one witch is young and extraordinarily appealing, both to Tam and to the Devil; forgetting himself, Tam yells out a compliment, breaking either the spell or his non-participation, and the witches and warlocks roar after him, managing to get revenge on him for seeing them only by catching the horse's tail as it was crossing water into safety.

The central action in the poem is initiated by two violations, initially by Tam's ignoring his wife's request that he should come home rather than socialising and secondly by his violation of the accepted principle – for believers – that one should not interrupt supernatural beings: one should avoid at all costs letting it be known they are being observed. The one violation, understood by all, prepares for the second about which there can be alternate views: to the believer, Tam actually saw; to the sceptic, he was so drunk, he thought he saw or dreamt he did; to the non-believer, he saw nothing: this tale could not be true. And did his horse really lose her tail or is there a more rational explanation such as the local tradition that the man identified as the real Tam, Douglas Graham,

'explained the loss of his market money and bonnet – and the depilation
of his mare's tail by some wags in Ayr'?[41] Although belief has been
introduced subtly before the arrival at Alloway Kirk – that witches do
congregate, that hobgoblins exist – the finale offers the first real
confrontation, for the reader or hearer must here make a decision, must
believe or not; and this decision or choice of participation will affect the
final reactions of the reader/hearer of the poem. In the real legend such
reactions would become part of the complex; here the complex is frozen
in print, but the reactions nonetheless come to the reader.

The outline and essential elements of 'Tam o' Shanter' are found in
Burns' letter to Francis Grose; and the prose versions there are
compelling. But the poetic retelling goes beyond the prose source and in
writing approximates some of the devices of the oral context. Burns does
this largely through his additions to the legends in the Grose letter. No
doubt, he intuitively realised the bareness of the text without the hints at
reaction, the comments, the cumulative response he knew existed in
legend-telling from firsthand experience; and he sought to replicate a
typical context. The very frame he adds presents a situation in which
such legends – texts and responses – might surely be told. His tale of
Tam follows the initial action, though it might have been a part of the
communication of narratives he suggests took place in the introductory
setting.

> The night drave on wi' sangs and clatter;
> And ay the ale was growing better:
> The landlady and *Tam* grew gracious,
> Wi' favours, secret, sweet, and precious:
> The Souter tauld his queerest stories;
> The landlord's laugh was ready chorus:
> The storm without might rair and rustle,
> *Tam* did na mind the storm a whistle.
>
> (ll. 45–52)

And the narratives told then (perhaps those referred to in lines 89–96)
may actually have prepared or predisposed Tam for the subsequent
events. The inclusion of moral comment (see lines 17–18, 33–6, 105–10,
201–4) and narrative interrupters (lines 53–66, 151–62, 179–80)
parallels aspects of the legend in context. Additionally, Burns' use of
imagery, his building of suspense by interrupting the flow of the
narrative as well as the moral asides and comments given above become
written substitutes for gestures, dramatic pauses, and for the comments

of hearers usually found in oral legend exchanges. David Daiches suggests, for example, that Burns' interruption at line 105, 'Inspiring bold John Barleycorn!' 'effectively keeps the reader in suspense and gives him an excuse to dismiss, if he so wishes, all that Tam saw as the product of the man's drunken imagination'.[42] These guides to the legend, or breaks in the narrative, parallel aspects of oral legend exchanges and allow the reader or hearer to consider the events described. The stance of the narrator is one of belief, though slight hints at alternative reaction are planted – maybe he is drunk and hallucinating, an 'out' provided for the sceptic. No matter how one reads the poem, the conclusion – the loss of Maggie's tail – demands a response:

> Now, wha this tale o' truth shall read,
> Ilk man and mother's son, take heed:
> Whene'er to drink you are inclin'd,
> Or cutty-sarks run in your mind,
> Think, ye may buy the joys o'er dear,
> Remember Tam o' Shanter's mare.
>
> (ll. 219–24)

All in all, Burns uses more than the content; he replicates the situation in which legends are told, and by the way he builds the story, he brings each reader/hearer into the situation so that the conclusion always demands response.

Students of the legend have also pointed out that narrators of legends always take a stance towards the legend and its belief core, usually one of acceptance. It has generally been assumed that Burns could not have believed this tale and that his poem presents a satiric view of such a belief. This assessment may not be completely accurate: in eighteenth-century Scotland, there was considerable belief in witchcraft, in such gatherings as Tam witnessed, and in its attendant experiences; even if belief in witches was not complete, even if an individual wavered, in the context of a legend-telling, due to circumstances of time, place, state of mind, and other factors belief might momentarily exist; Burns, in his letter to Grose, suggests the veracity of the legends in the transitional or metanarrational[43] passages: 'The last relation I shall give, though equally true, is not so well identified as the two former, with regard to scene'.[44] Burns, and his immediate audience, could and did believe in witches. And Burns, like a legend-teller, takes a stance and his stance and the evidence later given in the poem continue to assert this belief.

Why else would Meg, Tam's horse, preternaturally feel the otherness of the situation at Alloway Kirk?

Although Burns' letter is a composite, his poetic retelling of the legend comes close to duplicating the genuine legend context; for there is comment from outside the narrative, interrupting and commenting as the poem proceeds. What really happens is that Burns as narrator/author recreates the context of legend-telling and adds comments similar to those which might be made if the legend were being told in its natural context. Burns, in poetic form, duplicates this responsive quality in such a way that hearers and readers also find themselves responding, especially to the unresolved and uncommented upon final action, belief – the loss of Meg's tail. Thus, the way in which Burns has used legend content and context also provokes response from readers and hearers of the poem.

In some ways, 'Tam o' Shanter' represents Burns' most mature and vital integration of traditional material, for the poem incorporates far more than legend and other traditional content: it recreates aspects of the context of legend-telling – including localisation, the belief stance of the narrator, and the various responses to the beliefs imbedded in the narrative. His heightened awareness of traditional material after his Edinburgh experience no doubt accounts for the sophisticated way he handled this material. He was able in 'Tam o' Shanter' to preserve aspects of a legend which might otherwise have died. His collecting, editing, patching, and writing of songs also served the same purpose. Both are results of the conscious antiquarian and nationalistic enthusiasm he acquired in Edinburgh.

4 Tradition's Use of Burns: The Songs and Poems

> ... wherein is he great, except that his own songs at once found receptive ears amongst the people; they were re-echoed by the binders and reapers in the field, and he was greeted with them by his boon-companions in the alehouse.
>
> Goethe

Burns' own traditional environment provided the inspiration for much of his artistry. At first this had been reflexive; but finally it was reflective. His closeness to his own milieu on a variety of levels made his work appeal: his sensitivity to the world he shared with his audience enabled him to create well-turned phrases, characters, memorable lines, and songs which became a part of the very traditional culture which had initially inspired his work – both poems and songs. He borrowed from tradition but amply repaid that loan by creating works of art which in and through time have replenished that traditional fund.

Material enters oral tradition because it reflects the shared values and perceptions of a group of persons. Once adopted, it often loses signs of original authorship – particularly as it is removed in time and place from its creator. The hallmarks of this traditional material are stability and change: aspects of the tradition continue to exhibit qualities of the original but each performance may show variation. Oral circulation supports this dynamic process, which does not insist on textual fixity in the written literary sense.

Lines, phrases, songs, and poems by Burns have achieved oral currency; nearly anonymous, agreeable to change, these tangible memories of his creativity underline Burns' ability to speak for and to his fellow Scots. In his own day this was true and poor farm servants are said to have saved for months to buy a chapbook edition of his work: 'I can well remember, how that even ploughboys and maid-servants would have gladly bestowed the wages which they earned the most hardly, and which they wanted to purchase necessary clothing, if they might procure the works of BURNS'.[1] Every home has traditionally – if no other books – the Bible and Burns, copies of which often sustained soldiers on the battle field.[2] And I have been told that Scottish schoolchildren, evacuated during the war, were given a copy of Burns as they left their homeland. While the books, the editions of his poems, have received in some quarters almost amulet status, the songs and poems have achieved an almost independent oral existence, though the availability of correcting texts may have acted as constraining factors to radical variation.

Various lines and phrases have been taken from their literary context and elevated to traditional proverbial status. One informant suggested that people 'unknowingly quote [Burns] more than any other poet', for his words can be appropriately applied to many situations.[3] One need not long frequent pubs before hearing various persons, deep in 'spirits', described as 'bousing at the nappy' and maybe 'getting fou and unco happy' – memorable lines from 'Tam o' Shanter'.[4] In a similar context, referring to topics and opinions, I have listened to the admonition that 'Some books are lies frae end to end, / And some great lies were never penn'd' from 'Death and Doctor Hornbook'.[5] Often the exact words are slightly altered, though the specific sense is maintained. Burns' lines and songs are dealt with as traditional material; the concept of absolute fixity of text does not exist. As humanism both nationally and internationally continues to be an ideal, Burns' already popular and frequently reiterated lines from the 'Song – For a' that and a' that' have become almost slogan: 'Than Man to Man the warld o'er, / Shall brothers be for a' that. – '[6] Lines expressing truisms become supportive and explanatory of current occurrences: 'Man was Made to Mourn';[7] 'O wad some Pow'r the giftie gie us / *To see oursels as others see us*!' from 'To a Louse, On Seeing one on a Lady's Bonnet at Church'.[8] But undoubtedly the most frequently cited of all Burns' lines concludes the account of Cumnock boxes: during the time when Cumnock boxes of sentimental wood were in vogue, Adam Armour, Jean's brother, proposed to make some from the repenting stool on which Burns sat; but he found that 'The best laid schemes of men and mice gang aft agee [sic]' for it was worm eaten.[9] And the primary character in one poem has become a generic name for the sanctimonious – Holy Willie.[10]

While poems have provided a majority of Burns' lines raised to oral proverbial status, some songs as well as poems, frequently complete, have entered oral tradition. Undoubtedly, this was possible because Burns had heard traditional songs all through his life and this repetition had reinforced in him the traditional aesthetic. As was suggested in Chapter 3, Burns' close relationship with oral tradition adds to the difficulty of determining his authorship; and authorship must be established before his works circulating in oral tradition can be identified. Because of the complexity of his involvement with tradition, this is a virtually impossible task. His own songs have often been anonymously juxtaposed with traditional material as well as with songs by discernible authors. Gershon Legman suggests that this was the case with *The Merry Muses of Caledonia*, that the editor of the material for the Crochallan Fencibles joined holograph material, songs by other club members, and bawdry orally current to form the book.[11] And it is dangerous with Burns to assume, as many editors have, that a song text in Burns' hand is tantamount to authorship: Burns actively collected material, recording it naturally in writing. Knowing extant collections of eighteenth-century Scottish folksongs and ballads, studying in detail Burns' attitude toward song found extensively in the Interleaved Museum and in his letters, especially those to George Thomson, enables one to suggest with considerable assurance that certain items in Burns' hand were not written, but collected by him, sometimes from his own memory – thus excluding them from his own corpus. 'O my Luve's like a red, red rose' may provide an example: it has long been acclaimed as one of Burns' most exquisite songs, but Burns described it as 'a simple old Scots song which I had pickt up in this country'.[12] And in a letter to William Tytler of Woodhouselee in August of 1787, he refers to six items – a song beginning 'In Edinburgh braes there is a well', sung to an air similar to one called 'For lake o' gold', usually titled 'The rowin't in her Apron'; a stanza beginning 'Ye're like to the timmer o' yon rotten wood', sung to the tune 'Bonie Dundee'; 'Young Hynhorn' (Child, 17); a song titled 'Willie's rare &c' (see Child, 212, 214, 215); two stanzas of a song called 'The lass o' Livistone'; and 'Rob Roy' (Child, 225). Only the first two items are definitely attributed to Burns by Kinsley; the remaining four appear in an appendix of items 'admitted at various times to the canon of Burns's work, either wrongly or on inadequate evidence'.[13] Burns' letter, below, should settle the matter: all six belong to oral tradition:

Sir,

    Inclosed I have sent you a sample of the old pieces that are still to be found among our Peasantry in the West. I had once a great many of these fragments; and some of these here entire; but as I had no idea then that any body cared for them, I have forgot them. – I invariably hold it sacriledge to add any thing of my own to help out with the

shatter'd wrecks of these venerable old compositions; but they have
many various readings. – If you have not seen these before, I know
they will flatter your true old-style Caledonian feelings; at any rate, I
am truly happy to have an opportunity of assuring you how sincerely I
am,

Revered Sir,
your gratefully indebted, humble serv!
Robert Burns

Lawnmarket
Monday noon[14]

The difficulties of attribution are many.

The situation is further muddied by Burns' own wish, particularly in
his work for Johnson's *The Scots Musical Museum*, to be Scotland's
anonymous poet, speaking for her, and by the simultaneous existence in
oral tradition of an old song and the newer one Burns based on it. In
some way, certainly Burns agreed with Andrew Fletcher of Saltoun's
quote from 'a very wise man': 'If a man were permitted to make all the
ballads [used loosely to refer to all folksongs] he need not care who
should make the laws of a nation.'[15] In his role 'as the embodied spirit of
Scottish song',[16] Burns discouraged attributions in the *Museum*,
developing a code to indicate items he had written: 'R', 'B', and 'X'
identified his own, 'Z' old songs on which he worked. But he did not use
the code with any consistency or with complete accuracy. Working to
preserve Scotland's songs – texts and tunes – as a monument to
Scotland, he often, as discussed earlier, worked up fragments or altered
extant texts he did not like into wholes. An interesting example of his
editing and the subsequent existence of his and the traditional versions
side by side is an item, called by Burns 'My bonie laddie's young but he's
growin yet –':

Slowish

O Lady Mary Ann looks o'er the castle-wa',
She saw three bonie boys playin at the ba',
The youngest he was the flower amang them a',
My bonie laddie's young but he's growin yet.—

O Father, O Father, an ye think it fit,
We'll send him a year to the College yet,
We'll sew a green ribban round about his hat,
And that will let them ken he's to marry yet. –

Lady Mary Ann was a flower in the dew,
Sweet was its smell and bonie was its hue,
And the langer it blossom'd, the sweeter it grew,
For the lily in the bud will be bonier yet. –

Young Charlie Cochran was the sprout of an aik,
Bonie, and bloomin and straught was its make,
The sun took delight to shine for its sake,
And it will be the brag o' the forest yet. –

The Simmer is gane when the leaves they were green,
And the days are awa that we hae seen,
But far better days I trust will come again,
For my bonie laddie's young but he's growin yet. –[17]

A parallel tradition, though more narrative in content, exists in many versions typically titled 'The Trees They Do Grow High'. An early version, probably called 'Craigston's Growin', provides parallels from oral tradition to three of Burns' five stanzas: the first, fifth, and sixth:

The Trees they are high and the leaves they are Green
The days are awa that I hae seen
But better days I thought wou'd come again
An' my bonny bonny boy was growin.

I've been climbing a Tree that's too high for me
I've been seeking fruit thats nae growin
I've been seeking hot water beneath the cold Ice
An' against the stream I've been Rowin.

Father she said, you've done me much wrang
You've wedded to a young, young man
I'd have wedded ane wi a staff in his han
'Afore I had wedded a Boy.

O Daughter I did you no wrang
For the wedding you to o'er young a man
You've your Tocher in you ain han
An' your bonny love daily growin.

O Father if ye think it fit
We'll send him a year to the College yet
We'll tie a green Ribbon around his hat
To let them ken that he's married
Four & Twenty cambric braids she had plait
An' sent to College wi him.

She lookit o'er her Father's castle wa'
Saw four & Twenty bonny boys playin at the Ba
But her ain love was foremost amang them a'
Young Craigston's daily growin.

In's fourteenth year he was a married man
In's Fifteenth year he had a young son.
In's Sixteenth year his grave grew green
Alas! for Craigston's Growing.

The Trees are high & the leaves are green
The days are awa that I hae seen
An' anither may be welcome where I hae happy been
Take up young Craigston's Growin.[18]

Burns may well have collected from himself or another the very stanzas he printed in the *Museum*, writing stanzas three and four himself. Or he may have found stanzas in Herd's manuscript as Henley and Henderson suggest.[19] We will never know. Attribution with Burns is a complicated matter and is, of course, a prior consideration before identifying which of his songs achieved oral circulation.

It is not only scholars who have had difficulty with attribution; the people have and do as well, sometimes recognisably over-, and sometimes underattributing. Often this is sheer guesswork; at other times it is based on a keen literary sense – identifying on the basis of subject matter, particularly impersonal lyrics about women or lovely rivers. And no doubt some attributions are made to make an item approved or acceptable, for association with Burns' name gets it a hearing. The chap books were capable of both: a chapbook in the Lauriston Castle Collection, National Library of Scotland, no. 2786–29, 'Burns' Celebrated Songs', Edinburgh, printed by J. Robertson, Horse-Wynd,

1805, is guilty of overattribution. The contents include 'Of a' the airts the Win' can blaw'; 'Gude forgie me for Liein' ('Ae day a braw wooer cam' down the lang glen'); 'The Soger's Return' ('When wild war's deadly blast was blown'); 'Tom Tough or Yo Heave Ho'; 'The Wounded Hussar'; 'Jenny's Bawbee'; 'Gin a Body meet a Body'; 'Come under my Plaidy'; 'Crazy Jane'; 'God Save the King'. Burns did not write the last seven. Chapbook no. 2788–7 from the same collection provides no attributions at all. Titled 'Songs of Bonnie Scotland by her Sweetest Singers', it includes 'Wandering Willie'; 'Afton Water'; 'The lass of Ballochmyle'; 'O' a' the Airts'; 'Ae Fond Kiss'; 'My Nannie's Awa'; 'Down the Burn, Davie'; 'Gae bring to me a pint o' wine'. So it is well nigh impossible to determine with any exactitude what Burns really wrote or edited or collected; however, assuredly some of each category had and still have oral circulation.

Many of Burns' own songs have circulated orally because they adhere to the people's expectations of what a lyric folksong should be. In oral transmission, they receive variation, abhorred by many Burns enthusiasts who themselves often unwittingly contribute to the alteration of the printed version. Many individuals know only the chorus; it is few who carry in memory the whole. So it is with other traditional folksongs: not everyone is a great bearer of tradition. It should be reiterated that Burns' attitude to some of his songs approaches a preference for traditional fluidity as he changed – sometimes because of audience, sometimes because of memory – texts and tunes from one publication or holograph copy to another.

The great ballad singer of the twentieth century in Scotland, Jeannie Robertson, had numerous Burns' songs in her repertoire and her daughter Lizzie Higgins suggests she was 'daft' over Burns before her ballad repertoire was discovered and acclaimed.[20] She learned Burns' songs much as she acquired the rest of her repertoire. But there are some who would deny Burns' songs traditional status because they are by him, even though they are partially transmitted orally and are characterised by contraction, localisation, and other kinds of variation. The Border shepherd, Willie Scott, is said to have spoken out against this attitude, saying Burns' songs are as traditional as one can get.[21] A brief look at Jeannie Robertson's version of 'Flow Gently Sweet Afton' or 'Afton Water' should indicate this, exhibiting the traditional stability resulting from a desire for continuity as well the change which necessarily exists when an item circulates more in oral than in written transmission.

Jeannie's text shows at once the marks of probable book origin or reinforcement, and variation resulting from memory and oral circulation. The first two stanzas show the greatest amount of stability, the middle portion the most change, with the conclusion hitting a middle ground, exhibiting more variation than the beginning but less than the middle section: this textual pattern of stability and change conforms to generalisations about musical stability in oral tradition.[22]

Burns' text

Flow gently, sweet Afton, among thy green braes,
Flow gently, I'll sing thee a song in thy praise;
My Mary's asleep by thy murmuring stream,
Flow gently, sweet Afton, disturb not her dream.

Thou stock dove whose echo resounds thro' the glen,
Ye wild whistling blackbirds in yon thorny den,
Thou green crested lapwing thy screaming forbear,
I charge you disturb not my slumbering Fair.

How lofty, sweet Afton, thy neighbouring hills,
Far mark'd with the courses of clear, winding rills;
There daily I wander as noon rises high,
My flocks and my Mary's sweet Cot in my eye.

How pleasant thy banks and green vallies below,
Where wild in the woodlands the primroses blow;
There oft as mild ev'ning weeps over the lea,
The sweet scented birk shades my Mary and me.

Thy crystal stream, Afton, how lovely it glides,
And winds by the cot where my Mary resides;
How wanton thy waters her snowy feet lave,
As gathering sweet flowerets she stems thy clear wave.

Flow gently, sweet Afton, among thy green braes,
Flow gently, sweet River, the theme of my lays;
My Mary's asleep by thy murmuring stream,
Flow gently, sweet Afton, disturb not her dream.[23]

Jeannie's text

Flow gently sweet Afton, among thy green braes,
Flow gently I'll sing thee a song in thy praise.
My Mary's asleep by the murmuring stream,
Flow gently sweet Afton, disturb not her dream.

Thy stock dove whose echo resounds through the glen,

Ye wild, whistling blackbird in yon thorny den,
Thy green crested lapwing, thy screaming forbear,
I charge you disturb not my slumbering fair.

How wanton thy hills and green vallies below
Where wild in the woodlands the primroses grow
For oft as mild evening sweeps over the lea
The green scented birk shades my Mary and me.

Thy crystal stream Afton, how lovely it glides,
And winds by the cot where my Mary resides.
How wanton thy waters, her snowy feet lay
As fathering sweet floweries, she stands by clear waves.

Flow gently sweet Afton, amongst thy green braes,
Flow gently sweet river, my theme of my lay.
My Mary's asleep by the murmuring stream,
Flow gently sweet Afton, disturb not her dream.[24]

The majority of changes show word substitutions, involving both similar initial sounds and the same syllable count: the for thy; thy for thou; lay for lave; floweries for flowerets; stands for stems; amongst for among. The most noticeable change is the deletion of the third stanza. The first textual phrase of stanza four substitutes 'how wanton thy hills' for 'how pleasant thy banks' and may reflect memory of the omitted third stanza which focuses on hills. Other substitutions in the fourth stanza are sweeps for weeps and green for sweet. The tune printed with the song in the *Museum*, 'not otherwise known',[25]

Slow and tender

is not the tune used by Jeannie. Rather her tune is based on a two-strain setting of the text made by Alexander Hume (1811–59), sung by Jeannie with the characteristic ornamentation and emphases which made her renditions of the 'big' ballads so memorable.

Slow, with much liberty

26

Many of Burns' songs are no longer sung to the melody originally intended. Some of the substitutions are the result of published melodies; others are derived from an individual's dissatisfaction with the tune designated and a conscious adoption of an alternative. Jeannie Robertson, in talking of tunes, indicated that she must like both the tune and the text in order to learn a song: if she did not like the tune, she often set the text to a tune she liked.[27] Whatever the ultimate source of Jeannie's version, it is clear that her rendering, both in text and tune, exhibits variation as well as stability, those hallmarks of traditional song.

Poems too have entered tradition in a variety of ways. In Burns' own day, he often read his poems or recited them to a circle of friends in a context where traditional material was performed; in this way – from multiple hearing – others probably learned and in turn transmitted them. In 1972 I heard a Burns enthusiast say that alterations were acceptable within reason – especially to aid communication. Just as Burns changed his poems and songs to accommodate them to different audiences, so would my informant change material today to make it more relevant. And Burns' peoms, notably 'Tam o' Shanter', have been used in recitation, in dramatic performance, as artistic communication.

In yet another way Burns' songs and poems have influenced subsequent tradition. Many have been the imitators, often anonymous; and some of their products have become a part of tradition. But parody too, which must know a genre to use it, abounds. By poking fun, it reinforces the original as well as making a statement. Though there is

Plate 1   The ruins of Alloway Kirk from Francis Grose, *Antiquities of Scotland* (London: Hooper & Wigstead, 1797), with permission of the Pierpont Morgan Library

Plate 2   From James Gould, *Burnsiana: A Memento of the "Burns Centenary Collection", January 25th 1859, Now in the Poets' Corner Mitchell Library, Glasgow.* One copy, bound in Edinburgh, 1883. Volume 6, page 62. By permission of The Mitchell Library

Plate 3 Found in *Lucas's Etchings*, privately printed, 1847. By permission of The Mitchell Library

Plate 4 From James Gould, *Burnsiana: A Memento of the "Burns Centenary Collection", January 25th 1859, Now in the Poets' Corner Mitchell Library, Glasgow.* One copy, bound in Edinburgh, 1883. Volume 7, page 29. By permission of the Mitchell Library

Plate 6 The Alexander Nasmyth Full-length Portrait, Scottish National Portrait Gallery, No 1062. By permission of the Scottish National Portrait Gallery

Plate 5 From James Gould, *Burnsiana: A Memento of the "Burns Centenary Collection", January 25th 1859, Now in the Poets' Corner Mitchell Library, Glasgow*. One copy bound in Edinburgh, 1883. Volume 3, page 6. By permission of The Mitchell Library

Plate 7 The Archibald Skirving Portrait, Scottish National Portrait Gallery, No 745. By permission of the Scottish National Portrait Gallery

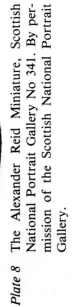

Plate 8 The Alexander Reid Miniature, Scottish National Portrait Gallery No 341. By permission of the Scottish National Portrait Gallery.

Plate 9 The John Beugo Engraving: published in Burns' *Poems, Chiefly in the Scottish Dialect* (Edinburgh: William Creech, 1787). Print provided by the Scottish National Portrait Gallery

Plate 10 'Burns and Highland Mary Pledging Troth' from James Gould, *Burnsiana: A Memento of the* "*Burns Centenary Collection*", *January 25th 1859, Now in the Poets' Corner Library, Glasgow*. One copy, bound in Edinburgh, 1883. Volume 8, page 77. By permission of The Mitchell Library

Plate 11 Burns Supper, by permission of The Scotsman Publications Limited

Plate 12 Burns Supper, by permission of The Scotsman Publications Limited

some question about his authorship of 'Auld Lang Syne',[28] scholars to date have not quibbled much about the attribution.[29] And as a song, the parodies and potential parodies may be limitless. The chorus of 'Auld Lang Syne' said to be 'Done up in tartan' is as follows:

> Shall Gaelic speech be e'er forgot
> An' never brocht to min'.
> For she'll be spokit in Paradise
> In the days o' Auld Lang Syne.[30]

And the anecdote told to Hamish Henderson of the School of Scottish Studies by Lucy Stewart provides another example of this song's use in tradition:

'The Twa Fools'
   There was aince two men oot in a big liner, and there were twa feels [fools] one was a cook; the ither een was one of the crew. So they had been on deck ae day and there was een aafie bothered wi a stutter – he'd an aafie bad stutter. An the cook he fell overboard.
   So he ran to the captain to tell the captain that the cook had fell overboard. He tried to tell the captain but he couldnae get oot the words for stutterin. He stuttert and stuttert and stuttert. The captain he got fed-up and he, he says, 'Good Gracious, man,' he says. 'if ye cannae say yer words,' he says, 'sing them.' So he startit to sing,

> 'Should auld acquentance be forgot,
> An niver brocht til min'
> The bloomin cook's fell overboard
> And he's fifty miles behind.'[31]

Burns not only took and derived inspiration from tradition; he gave to it as well. The acceptance of some of his work into oral traditional circulation underscores his closeness to the traditional milieu of his time and suggests the importance of that world to an examination of his art. The aesthetic sensibility which guided much of his work was a shared sensibility – thus enabling some of his own productions to enter the shared, oral expressive culture of eighteenth-century Scotland. Through this process, he became a national figure, implicitly the anonymous voice of Scotland, explicitly the national poet.

5 Tradition's Use of Burns: The Legendary Tradition

> You may ha'e another Nelson
> Sailing o'er the waves;
> You may ha'e another Wellington
> Commanding so'dgers brave;
> You may ha'e another Shakespere [*sic*]
> Or a Byron in their turns;
> But you, or me will never see,
> Another Rabbie Burns.

'These verses were sung in our club (Detroit Burns Club) by one of our members. It was learned from his uncle who probably composed the words to the tune from some old melody, author unknown.'

Burns' own milieu was a traditional one: on the very personal level, he unconsciously accepted many of its practices and concerns; as an artist in words he drew from it in a multiplicity of ways; and as a collector of folksongs he recorded one aspect of that on-going oral tradition, folksongs, for posterity. As inheritor of a cultural tradition, he lived in large measure by it, taking from it, and giving back to it. Unwittingly, he also provided the ever-developing tradition with an immense body of additional material, for he became the central figure in a legendary tradition, which at different times has largely included three narrative genres – personal experience stories, legends, jokes and anecdotes – which reflect changing attitudes and perspectives towards Burns.

It is not difficult to understand why Burns the man was chosen to be a figure in tradition. Undoubtedly he stood out: though of poor stock, he achieved a measure of fame and success. In fact, he was the tangible embodiment of a success story as poet and as man. However, he was also a man of the people, whom one could and can call familiarly Rab or Rabbie. Rooted in the rural agricultural class, he remained true to his environment, wrote about the ordinary and everyday things of life understood by all, and proclaimed as man and poet his sympathy for the earth's creatures – man and beast. A man with such empathy for nature that he would take the extra time needed to release his horse from the cart at the limekilns,[1] a man whose experience was the familiar experience,[2] whose feelings are identical with those today[3] could be both friend and compatriot and ideal.

Burns became an ideal because he was at one and the same time like everyone else and different. He was a recognised poet; he was not afraid to speak out against injustices felt by himself and those who shared his background; in articulating the self-limiting moral and religious precepts of his day, he voiced the people's concerns and unstated rebellion. For a time, he was both implicitly spokesman for many Scots and the representative of the ideal Scotsman. The legendary tradition that grew up about Burns is firmly based in the historical reality of his documentable life, but the traditions about Burns have been shaped, directed, and moulded to endow him with the qualities and traits of the ideal Scot, paving the way for him to become virtually the symbol of Scotland during the late nineteenth century.

Since their beginnings, the legendary traditions concerning Burns have been both written and oral – befitting a country which early recognised and sporadically implemented universal literacy as prerequisite for religion and, thus, for the 'compleat' life. With the act of 1543, the Roman Catholic Church had proclaimed the right of all to read the Scriptures and with the Provincial Council of 1549 allowed – if not provided – for instruction concerning sacred writings. But it was the New Kirk, the Prebyterianism of John Knox, which hastened Scotland's literacy. Expressing it eloquently in his *Brief Declaration to England* in 1556, Knox articulated an ideal position which became if not the specific model, at least a recognisable goal: 'For the preservation of religion it is most expedient That scholes be universally erected in all cities and chief townes, the oversight whereof to be committed to the magistrates and godly learned men of the said cities and townes'.[4] Conceived of in four layers, beginning with parish schools for learning to read via the Catechism and relevant religious writings, progressing from thence to the grammar schools stressing Latin instruction, the educational plan of Knox reached its apogee in high schools for the study of classical languages, logic, and rhetoric and in the Universities, largely established to train the clergy. In theory exemplary, the implementation was less than universal; however, schools were widely instituted as a cornerstone of the Calvinisation of Scotland.[5] Intended to

create a country of Bible readers and Biblical scholars, literacy could not
be limited to the acquisition of religion alone; and somewhat like the
results of eating from the Biblical tree of knowledge of good and evil, the
achievement of literacy was both positive and negative, for it at once
made sacred as well as profane writing accessible.

By the late eighteenth and early nineteenth century, the rudiments of
literacy were available to most and reading was a recognised medium for
communication. Beside it, however, the oral tradition continued as it
does today to carry much of the vital communication. Thus, the
legendary traditions about Burns were circulated both through oral and
written (and more recently electronic) means. In many instances the oral
account came first, was preserved in print, and often re-entered oral
tradition from a reading and fortuitous retelling, the process continuing
potentially to infinity. Alternately, in other instances, the written might
have initially fed the oral. Perhaps the most accurate way of illustrating
the complexity of the interaction and possible simultaneity of oral and
written modes of communication is to provide a concrete example. An
informant told me, in 1973, that it was a tradition to stick a pitch fork
into the top of a haystack, covering it then with a sheet, to let all the
neighbours know that Burns was visiting and that they were welcome to
come. A more recent account, communicated to me in writing, localises
and particularises this tradition: it is set at Covington Mains and was
identified as a family tradition. Was this originally oral or written? A
similar narrative appears in the Chambers–Wallace edition of Burns[6]
and in the somewhat fictionalised biographical series by James Barke.[7]
Do these latter capitalise on and report oral tradition or do they initiate?
What is important is that the tradition, widely accepted, has circulated
in all available media. It fits the collective notion of what would be right
vis-à-vis Burns. Records of traditions about Burns from the last century
are today totally written – some in books which are definitely records of
oral exchanges, others in accounts drawn from earlier written treat-
ments. The important factors are that the ultimate source or origin is
ignored; that similar narratives appear in many books; that the accounts
are varied: thus, the printed records exhibit both the anonymity and the
variation which characterise oral tradition, folklore. They are definitely
a part of the tradition, as are accounts transmitted more recently
through the electronic orality.

The legendary tradition which has grown up about Burns is neither
believed nor accepted by all Scots. There is a wide spectrum of
response – positive, negative, ambivalent, neutral – recalling the mul-
tiple responses possible to the single legend complex imbedded in Burns'

poem 'Tam o' Shanter'. But the positive belief in or acceptance of the validity of the traditions dominates, at least sentimentally, and cuts across class lines. It is well to remember that Scots, long rightly proud of their tradition of personal independence and individualism, do not on this or any other issue necessarily agree.

Burns has been and continues to be the subject of much speculation and the central figure in many narratives. Significantly, he – as writer – probably played an important part, initially, in establishing certain attitudes towards himself, attitudes which continue to be found in the legendary tradition today. Overstating his humble origins, he signed himself 'A Peasant' when he wrote to John Sinclair, compiler of the *Statistical Account of Scotland*, about the Dumfriesshire lending library he and Robert Riddell instituted;[8] and he played much on his limited education and rude origins in the Preface to the Kilmarnock edition.[9] Underlining the latter and implying a light-hearted flippancy about his art, he told his correspondent and brother poet John Lapraik,

> I am nae *Poet*, in a sense,
> But just a *Rhymer* like by chance,
> An' hae to Learning nae pretence,
>   Yet, what the matter?
> Whene'er my Muse does on me glance,
>   I jingle at her.[10]

And his seemingly autobiographical song, beginning 'There was a lad was born in Kyle', appropriately wedded to the tune 'Dainty Davie' whose traditional text describes another man's successful dalliance with the 'fair sex', provides impetus for at least some subsequent (or simultaneous?) traditions – that the weather was inhospitable on the day of his birth, that a satisfactory prophecy about his future had been madè then, and that he recognised his reputation as a man very attracted to the lasses.

Tune, Daintie Davie

Brisk

There was a lad was born in Kyle,
But what na day o' what na style,
I doubt it's hardly worth the while
   To be sae nice wi' Robin.

   Robin was a rovin' Boy,
     Rantin' rovin', rantin' rovin';
   Robin was a rovin' Boy,
     Rantin' rovin' Robin.

Our monarch's hindmost year but ane
Was five-and-twenty days begun,
'Twas then a blast o' Janwar' Win'
   Blew hansel in on Robin.

The Gossip keekit in his loof,
Quo' scho wha lives will see the proof,
This waly boy will be nae coof,
   I think we'll ca' him Robin.

He'll hae misfortunes great and sma',
But ay a heart aboon them a';
He'll be a credit till us a',
   We'll a' be proud o' Robin.

But sure as three times three mak nine,
I see by ilka score and line,
This chap will dearly like our kin',
   So leeze me on thee, Robin.

Guid faith quo scho I doubt you Stir,
Ye'll gar the lasses lie aspar;

> But twenty fauts ye may hae waur –
> So blessins on thee, Robin.[11]

Thus Burns' own writings probably influenced subsequent attitudes and opinions about himself and his origins or alternately fostered already extant family traditions, facts, or rumours.

The appetite for the 'inside scoop' on Burns increased with his death and almost immediately memoirs of him such as those by Robert Heron and Maria Riddell[12] appeared in print, the former probably being the first published account insinuating that Burns was a drunkard and died as a result. Formal editions as well as the burgeoning chapbook editions of his work kept his life – its vagaries and varieties – in the public eye. Newspapers and magazines both fed and capitalised on the widespread public interest. Antiquaries and acquaintances were led to interview friends who had had any sort of connection with Burns.[13] The written reiteration, restimulation, and recirculation of traditions about Burns began shortly after his death and continues to this day, typically in such works as the somewhat fictionalised biographical series of five novels by James Barke, *Immortal Memory*, and in plays, such as Robert Kemp's 'The Other Dear Charmer', which focuses on Burns' relationship with Clarinda.

But the written is certainly not the only – or perhaps even the dominant – medium for the dissemination of the 'kerygma' of Burns; the oral, whether initiator or inheritor, played and plays its role. Television and radio, the electronic orality, speed up the process today. Focusing on the man, all media intermesh, firmly supporting the fabric of tradition so richly woven about Robert Burns.

Families have assumed an important role in transmitting accounts of Burns, to some a near sacred figure, a divinity in Scotland. Friends, too, pass on time-tested and honoured accounts. The Burns Federation Clubs, now almost worldwide, share information about Burns in their meetings and through their publication, the *Burns Chronicle*, and do their part in keeping the memory of Burns alive. The Burns Suppers, to be discussed in Chapter 6, have loosely formalised the fostering and transmission of aspects of Burns' life.

As an institution, the schools, however, have not done much to disseminate information and traditions about Burns, whether from printed or oral sources. Partly this reflects the low status long given to 'native' literature and arts in the once consistent trend towards anglicisation. Today, however, most children learn a smattering of Burns' poetry in school and can rattle off a few lines from 'To a Mouse';

and some schools hold competitions for recitations of Burns' poetry often sponsored by Burns Clubs, but the children learn little about the man himself. This may reflect the multiplicity of traditions about his life and the difficulty of determining *the* truth. And, of course, some of the traditions present unsavoury actions and attitudes – judged from the perspective of generalised middle-class morality. So what one learns by and about Burns at school is often severely limited. It is not the children or young people for the most part who take an interest in the Burns' traditions. The younger the person, the less is known of and about Burns; but adults, almost to a person, know about specific aspects of his life, can quote at least a line or two, and more importantly, have an opinion about this man and his relevance or lack of significance to themselves and to Scotland. Interest in and knowledge of Burns is perhaps predominantly an adult concern, grown into and developed as human beings simultaneously achieve mature identity as individuals and as Scots. Burns plays a role in this process.

Burns is a part of Scotland's traditional culture, both as a man and as a poet. In his own day as well as in ours his humanity and his personality have intrigued: narratives and songs as well as illustrations represent facets of his being. Seen as a whole the traditions form an extensive legendary cycle dealing with the life and loves of Robert Burns. In actuality, various segments of the legend have a largely fragmentary and isolated existence. But viewed collectively, one can identify the various facets of his existence which have been chosen for memory and stress as part of the legendary tradition. And the people respond variously to the traditions.

This legendary cycle might be called the unofficial biography of Robert Burns because the details and narratives are for the most part not included in or integral to the standard biographical treatments; nor, of course, are the details and narratives necessarily true. In many cases concrete supporting documentation is not available, but the specific material may be analogous to provable material. For example, there is considerable evidence to document Burns' encounters with women: his own poem to his first illegitimate child by Elizabeth Paton – 'A Poet's Welcome to his love-begotten Daughter; the first instance that entitled him to the venerable appellation of Father' – and the ample correspondence between himself and Agnes Maclehose, the Sylvander and Clarinda letters. These exploits have not become a part of the traditional cycle while countless other narratives pay tribute, in almost infinite variety, to the same theme and impulse. Many aspects of the Burns tradition have been anthologised in popular books which pander to the public's desire for little-known facts. Before the rise of contemporary academic scholarship with its concern for research, facts, and subsequent documentation, books quite naturally mixed known with possible or even impossible accounts to make a whole. Thus, nineteenth-century editions and biographies contain a mixture – the documentable evidence as well as the narratives and accounts passed on as true by tradition, their oral and written persistence attesting to their value to the people. It would be inaccurate to suggest that all these accounts have appeared in oral tradition, though I would suggest that their repetition, variation, anonymity, and persistence combine to present a legendary view of Burns – a man born to poor parents, raised to work the land, trained later for the excise, who achieved lasting immortality physically through his 'way with women' and spiritually through his poems and songs; a distinctive character, his art and 'view of the world' coincided in numerous improvised works. The particular accounts, whether circulating in oral or written tradition, support the general and overriding legend. Through time, this general tradition has moved towards fewer foci, understandably, as specific memory of or contact with Burns has become historically impossible.

The order used here to illustrate the major components of the legendary tradition is interpretative in the sense that it brings together material not usually, if ever, told or transmitted as a cycle. I have used a loose biographical approach to present, as descriptively as possible, a full range of traditional material about Burns. The individual traditions given are in no way exhaustive but are rather suggestive of the range of traditions which have existed and do still exist. The sources are both written and oral: some of the more detailed and highly patterned narratives date from the nineteenth century; the current oral tradition is more elliptical. It should be noted too that, as a figure of prominence for nearly two hundred years, Burns has magnetically pulled in some recognised floating episodes.[14] In most instances, a representative text will be printed in presenting the legendary biography. Multiple accounts on a particular topic such as Burns' way with women or the circumstances of composition indicate the relative significance of the topic within the tradition.

Robert Burns was born in a small cottage in Alloway, a suburb of Ayr, on 25 January 1759, a date still celebrated by many Scots. Accounts of the raging weather on or near the day of his birth appear in many biographical narratives:

Robert Burns was born in a clay-built cottage on the 'banks of bonnie Doon', and tradition relates that such a tempest raged that the gable of the lowly dwelling was blown down, and the mother, with her infant, had to seek shelter in an adjoining hut still more humble.[15]

'Tis now one hundred years ago, on a fearful stormy night, on the eve of the Poet's birth, that his father was hastening for assistance to Ayr, and in dashing through the ford which the rain had so greatly swollen as to check foot passers crossing, when old Burns, with his characteristic kindness to a woman wistfully sitting by the torrent, turned his steed and carried her across, and then proceeded on his important errand. Judge of his astonishment when again reaching home he saw the same woman sitting in his ain ingle corner, most anxiously waiting the expected event. She was a spaewife, and when the baby was placed in her lap, uttered the famous prediction which in after years Burns made into song.[16]

His own song 'There was a lad', quoted earlier, may have provided the seed for subsequent traditions, particularly concerning the prophecy.

Burns' childhood, while filling his head with traditional culture, especially song, later used in his mature works, has been largely ignored by tradition. It was probably typical in most aspects. His father was uncommonly concerned with education, that is book learning, and did all that he could to provide his children with various kinds of knowledge which might hopefully enable them to escape the uncertainties of tenant farming. He initiated Burns' desire for knowledge:

Burns, even when a child, read everything he could and whenever he could. 'A country woman in Dunscore once remarked, who had seen Burns riding slowly among the hills reading, "That's surely no a good man, for he has aye a book in his hand!"'[17]

Burns' achievements later owe, of course, considerably to this learning, desultory and self-acquired as it was.

One might say that the adult Burns had three occupations: he was a farmer, excise collector, and author; each of the three has stimulated distinctive traditions. While the term *farmer* is quite accurate, tradition has largely opted to refer to Burns as a ploughman. Essentially, ploughmen were farm workers fee'd by a farmer, that is, paid to work and often accommodated on the farm during the period of employment. In his father's household, Burns was actually a kind of substitute ploughman because the family financial circumstances precluded hiring many outsiders; but his status, as son of a tenant farmer and later as joint tenant with his brother Gilbert at Mossgiel and independently at Ellisland, was considerably above that of hired man. He himself fostered the rural, unlettered stance in the introduction to the first, the Kilmarnock, edition of his works, published in 1786, but first alludes to his occupation at plough in the second, or Edinburgh, edition in 1787, perhaps consciously adopting the idea from Henry Mackenzie's 1786 review of his work in *The Lounger:* 'The Poetic Genius of my Country found me as the prophetic bard Elijah did Elisha – at the *plough*; and threw her inspiring *mantle* over me . . . I was bred to the Plough, and am independent'.[18] Being a ploughman, theoretically one close to the soil and thereby close to the 'soul', the 'roots' of a nation, was an ideal occupation for Burns, and appealed to the Edinburgh literati as similarly placed individuals appealed in Germany, especially following Herder's ideas about romantic nationalism. A. M. Kinghorn suggests that 'Burns's poetic personality is grounded in the prejudices of the literary critics who first welcomed him as a "*rusticus abnormis sapiens*" and daffed their hats to "a native genius" fit to rank with the great ones of European literature'.[19] Of course, Burns had purposely played up to this idea; and the pose was readily capitalised on and continues to have marked oral currency. This idea led naturally to a variety of pictorial representations, reflecting tradition's occupational preference for Burns. (See Plates 2, 3, 4, 5.) Tradition simultaneously suggests a widespread ignorance of the ploughman's work – his dress and accoutrements: for example, a farmer once conversed with another farmer about a German print of Burns at the plough:

'This is the poet Burns?'
'Weel, I suppose it's meant for him,' replied the farmer; 'but did ye ever see a man at the pleugh wi' his kirk coat on? Whaever pentit that picture kent little about Burns and far less about the harness o' a pleugh horse. Man, the hale thing is ridiculous!'[20]

Burns took on the additional job of tax or excise collector in 1789, continuing in a half-hearted fashion to farm until 1791. The excise job may well have cramped his style for, being government employment, it curtailed by necessity of survival the vitriolic and satiric responses he had earlier levelled against the Church, forcing him to veil his ideas which were opposed to government policy and the suppression of liberty. The job also necessitated contact with ordinary individuals like himself, trying to save money and eke out an existence by avoiding taxation where possible. Traditional accounts pay tribute to Burns' understanding and empathy,[21] also suggested in a letter of report to his superior in the excise, Robert Graham of Fintray: 'I recorded every Defaulter; but at the Court, I myself begged off every poor body that was unable to pay'.[22]

From Professor Gillespie we learn that on a fair day in August, 1793, in the village of Thornhill, a poor woman, Kate Watson by name, had, for that day only, and doubtless by the particular desire of a thirsty population, converted without license her cottage into a public-house. 'I saw the poet,' says the Professor, 'enter the door, and anticipated nothing short of an immediate seizure of a certain grey-beard and barrel, which, to my personal knowledge, contained the contraband commodities our bard was in quest of. A nod, accompanied by a significant movement of the forefinger, brought Kate to the doorway or trance, and I was near enough to hear the following words distinctly uttered: — "Kate, are you mad? Don't you know that the supervisor and I will be in upon you in the course of forty minutes? Good-bye t'ye at present." Burns was in the street in the midst of the crowd in an instant, and I had access to know that the friendly hint was not neglected. It saved a poor widow from a fine of several pounds for committing a quarterly offence by which the revenue was probably subject to an annual loss of five shillings.'[23]

Jean Dunn, a suspected trader in Kirkpatrick-Durham, observed Burns and Robertson — another exciseman — approaching her house on the morning of a fair, slipped out of the back door, apparently to evade their scrutiny, leaving in her house only her attendant for the day and her daughter, a little girl. 'Has there been any bewing for fair here to-day?' demanded the poet as he entered the cabin. 'O no, Sir,' was the reply of the servant, 'we hae nae licence for that.' 'That's no true,' exclaimed the child, 'the muckle black kist is fu' o' the bottles o' yill that my mother sat up a' night brewing for the fair.' 'Does that bird speak?' said Robertson, pointing to one hanging in a cage. 'There is no use for another speaking-bird in this house,' said Burns, 'while that lassie is to the fore. We are in a hurry just now; but as we return from the fair we'll examine the muckle black kist.'[24]

The poet and a brother exciseman one day suddenly entered a widow woman's shop in Dunscore, and made an extensive seizure of smuggled tobacco.

'Jenny,' said the poet, 'I expected this would be the upshot; here Lewars, take note of the number of rolls as I count them. Now, Jock, did ye ever hear an auld wife numbering her threads before check reels were invented? "Thou's ane, and thou's no ane, and thou's ane a' out – listen."' As he handed out the rolls, he went on with his humorous enumeration, but dropping every other roll into Jenny's lap. Lewars took the note with as much gravity as he could muster, and saw the merciful conduct of his companion as 'if he saw it not'.[25]

Tradition has tended to view writing as a casual pursuit, only vaguely cerebral, demanding little sustained thought. And in Burns' day, many were the local poets or village rhymers – always writers by avocation; because jotting down or thinking up rhymes could thus take little time, the process appeared effortless and spontaneous. Burns fell heir to this opinion: a number of narratives describe the casual, everyday circumstances which led to certain compositions.

Burns was an excellt Plow & workman but when under the Influence of the Poëtic fever, not steady – then he was silent with his lips frequently in motion. So good natured that his boys directed him rather than he the boys.[26]

While Burns was thrashing, etc. his companions had often much difficulty to keep pace with him, for he was often either slow or very quick, according to the state of his mind [whether or not he was composing mentally], his violence soon exhausted him, when he threw himself on the straw quite worn out.[27]

Next day while he was composing the Poem on the mouse, he was driving & unloading two carts, earth & lime, which his brother & and another man filled from a heap at a distance – so absorbed was he Burns that one time he forgot to unload one of the Carts and returned it with its load to the heap, not much to the pleasure of his Brother.[28]

J. B. sat beside Burns in Church on the day when the Incident occured wh gave occasion to the Poem of the Louse, & was surprized when Burns awakened him, the middle of the same night, & repeated to him all the stanzas, requesting his opinion of them, – this was the most surprizing Proofs of the facility with which Burns composed, that Came within J. B.'s Knowledge –[29]

It is said that Burns was seen one day pacing too and fro along his favourite walk beside the river 'Nith'. Some hours afterwards his Bonnie Jean with her two children Robert and Francis Wallace, join him, but perceiving he is deeply absorbed 'crooning to himself' she, guided by true womanly tact retires with her little prattlers and from behind some 'lang yellow broom' growing upon the bank keeps a loving look out, unseen by the poet. He becomes increasingly excited, and this continued till he finished the poem ['Tam o' Shanter'], and with a sod dyke for desk, committed it to paper.[30]

Why should we speak of *Scots wha hae wi' Wallace bled*, since all know of it, from the King to the meanest of his subjects? This dithyrambic was composed on horseback, in riding in the middle of tempests, over the wildest Galloway moor, in company with a Mr. Syme, who, observing the poet's looks, forbore to speak, – judiciously enough, for a man composing *Bruce's Address* might be unsafe to trifle with. Doubtless this stern hymn was singing itself, as he formed it, through the soul of Burns; but to the external ear, it should be sung with the throat of the whirlwind. So long as there is warm blood in the heart of Scotchman or man, it will move in fierce thrills under this war-ode; the best, we believe, that was ever written by any pen.[31]

On Sunday 26th August 1787, Burns and Nichol visited Carron Iron Works, 3 miles south of Falkirk, and could not gain admittance because it was Sunday. On returning to Carron Inn, Burns wrote an impromptu verse on the window of the Inn, using a diamond with which he had written on other windows of inns, which leads me to believe he knew he would be known to posterity.[32]

At the end of the bridge which crosses the Ayr below Barskimming mill, there is a cottage in which an old man named Kemp lived with his daughter Kate. Kate was a trim lass, whose charms brought Burns from Mossgiel to see her one evening. It happened that Kemp's cow had strayed, and Kate had gone to look for it. The poet set off to search for both. As he crossed the bridge he met the miller of Barskimming on his way to visit Kate. 'Well, miller, what are you doing here?' said he. ' Deed,' said the miller, 'I was gaun to spier that question at you.' 'Why,' said the poet, 'I cam' down to see Kate Kemp.' 'I was just gaun the same gate,' said the miller. 'Then, ye need gang nae farther,' said Burns, 'for baith her and the coo's lost, and the auld man is perfectly wild at the want o' them.' The rivals strolled together by the river side, chatting in friendly fashion. Soon, however, Burns became silent, and strode along in a pensive mood. Suddenly he turned, bade the miller good-night, and hurried off towards Mauchline. Next time he met the miller, he apologised for his rudeness, and explained that he had been composing a poem. To make amends, he read his composition to the miller. It was 'Man was made to Mourn'.[33]

At Loudoun Manse after dinner they danced. Here is a description of the aftermath: 'Dr. Lawrie's son, who succeeded him in the Manse of Loudoun, used to tell of Burns's visit. Though the dance was not so long as the poet indicates, the family were waiting breakfast next morning and Burns had not appeared. Young Mr. Lawrie was sent upstairs to see what detailed him. He met him coming down. "Well, Mr. Burns, how did you sleep last night?" "Sleep, my young friend! I scarcely slept at all – I have been praying all night. If you go up to the room, you will find my prayers on the table." ' The prayer was that well-known petition:

> O thou dread Pow'r who reign'st above,
>   I know thou wilt me hear;
> When for this scene of peace and love,
>   I make my pray'r sincere.
>
> 'When, soon or late, they reach that coast,
>   O'er life's rough ocean driven,
> May they rejoice, no wand'rer lost,
>   A family in Heaven!'[34]

Burns himself suggested·that women often inspired his poetic creations:

There is certainly some connection between Love, and Music & Poetry, and therefore, I have always thought it a fine touch of Nature, that pass-age in a modern love composition

'As towards her cot he joggd along'
'Her name was frequent in his song –'

For my own part I never had the least thought or inclination of turning Poet till I got once heartily in Love, and then Rhyme & Song were, in a manner, the spontaneous language of my heart.[35]

The account below affirms such emotional inspiration:

He was fond of the ladies . . . Now, aye, my – daughter, when she
was a – a nurse, and she had –, there had been a lot of English girls
training with her, you see and used to annoy her you see: 'Oh, Burns
he was a dirty dog.' And just got her back up one day and she said, 'He
wasn't a dirty dog at all. He's no worse than what we have today. But
he – none of the chaps are clever enough to go home and write a poem
about girls.'[36]

Initially a representative of the village poet or bardic tradition where a
rhymer frequently expressed thoughts or emotions widely shared, Burns
acted in a way as a kind of voice of the people. He, like official poet
laureates to this day, often wrote frankly occasional poems, spur of the
moment effusions like the lines 'On Dining with Lord Daer', which
he sent to Dr Mackenzie, saying, 'The foregoing verses were really
extempore, but a little corrected since'.[37] He frequently alluded to the
extempore quality of various poems and songs; and even today, his
ability to compose spontaneously is often cited: 'It [his poems] came
through naturally; I mean he didn't have to set down – he just sat down,
as far as we are led to believe, and just wrote it right off'.[38] Such a talent,
perhaps better called penchant, Burns shared, of course, with many
poets: Donald the Hammerer – Donul nan Ord – son of Alexander, the
first Invernahyle, improvised the following lines after making peace with
Argyll who had ridiculed him because of his laugh:

Ugly Laugh is the name of the rock;
An ugly mocker 'twill ever be,
But if you will look on your own wife's face,
As ugly a sight you at home may see.[39]

Some of the impromptu verses featured in the accounts (frequently
stressing circumstances of composition, thus related to the previous
examples) are included in editions of his works. The majority are not.
Many show Burns as outspoken, blatantly ridiculing another (especially
the many epitaphs and epigrams attributed to him); others focus on
specific contests to create poems; some show his unique responses
to various situations. Taken as a whole, the accounts of Burns'
improvisatory productions reflect the public's view of poetic
creativity.

... and when I [Young] found him [Nicol] & Burns over their Whiskey-punch bandying *extempore* translations and imitations of English, Scotch & Latin Epigrams, I could not help considering them as good exemplifications of the Italian *Improvisatori*.

One remarkable instance still occurs to me. When Burns gave Nicol the following strange epitaph to translate into Latin, –

> 'Here lies old John Hildibrode
> Have mercy on him, gude God,
> As he would hae on thee, if he were God
> And thou wert old John Hildibrode.'

After a little consideration, Nicol gave furth a Latin edition of this nonsense, which I thought greatly superior to the original.[40]

But when Mr. Cunningham was making such a general *exposé* of the Works of Burns in this line, he might have included the following, written by him upon a relation of mine, Mrs. Young, formerly Mrs. Grizzel Craik, the widow of Thomas Young Esq. of Lincluden College, founded by Archibald the *Grim* Earl of Douglas –

> Here lies with Death, aul Grizzel *Grim*
> Lincluden's ugly witch,
> O Death! thou surely art not nice
> To lie with sic a b – – –ch. –[41]

I saw on a pane of Glass [at the George Inn] the following lines on a noted character in Dumfries, a little hump-backed, irascible, litigious lawyer of the name of *Glen* –

> David Glen, the best of little men
> Of the lawyer Kind *when drunk*

which on a former occasion pointed out to Mr. Syme & Burns then present, the latter took out his diamond pen & added the words *Sober* or *drunk* – – – –[42]

In 1786–7 when Burns was on his border tour, he wrote the following verses; he was a natural versifier. Burns always strung a verse or wrote on a window or something. He went into Cockleferry to get his dinner – so they say – I'm not saying its true. And he said when he came out he wrote this down:

If ere I come this road
This buggers house I'll mind be God
Three and six an for the dinner
Oh the damned infernal sinner.[43]

Burns whiled away the time waiting for an elegant gentleman reading a gilt bound copy of Shakespeare which was wormy; he wrote these lines:

'Through and through the inspired leaves,
    Ye maggots, make your windings;
But, oh! respect his lordships's taste,
    And spare his golden bindings.'[44]

One another occasion he visited a painter who was depicting Jacob's Dream. He put his criticism on the back:

'Dear____, I'll gie ye some advice,
    You'll tak' it no uncivil;
You shouldna paint at angels mair,
    But try and paint the devil.
To paint an angel's kittle wark,
    Wi' Auld Nick there's less danger;
You'll easy draw a weel-kent face,
    But no sae weel a stranger.'[45]

Burns once silenced a boring snob who boasted that he knew persons in high places:

'No more of your titled acquaintances boast,
    And in what lordly circles you've been;
An insect is only an insect at most,
    Though it crawl on the curls of a queen.'[46]

Once he went to church at Lamington, Clydesdale; the church was cold and uncomfortable and the sermon was boring. He left the following as tribute.

'As cauld a wind as ever blew,
    A caulder kirk, and in't but few;
As cauld a preacher's ever spak' —
    Ye'll a' be het ere I come back.'[47]

When Burns was given a servant's seat in the dining hall, he responded with the following rhyme:

> I was not appointed piper here
> To blow up his back side.

This is also told of a Highland piper, similarly placed.[48]

In the year 1789, before Burns's reputation as a poet had become generally acknowledged, he and some of his companions were enjoying themselves in a road-side public house, whither, by accident, a person named Andrew Horner, who fancied himself a great poet, having written a great deal, happened to stop on his way to Edinburgh to find a publisher for his verses.

In the course of conversation, being rather overcome by the fumes of the toddy, he explained the reason of his journey 'to the great city', when one of the company made a wager with him, that he would find a man in the room who would compose a better verse in a given time than he could. Andrew being rather confident in his muse, took the wager, the time allowed being ten minutes, and commenced: —

> 'In seventeen hunner eighty-nine,'

but was not able to get any further when the time expired.

Burns was then called to try his rhyming skill, and with the polite remark that if Mr. Horner was willing, he would borrow the line written. Andrew consented, and Burns, in his rapid round hand, put down the following: —

> 'In seventeen hunner eighty-nine,
> The deil got stuff to mak some swine,
>   An' put it in a corner;
> But afterwards he changed his plan,
> An' made it something like a man,
>   An' ca'd it Andrew Horner.'

Horner was so much dispirited at his own defeat and the wit and ready genius of Burns, that he threw all his verses into the fire, swearing he would never write another verse, but be content to attend to his farm and let poetry alone for the future.[49]

A poet of some pretensions wrote Burns for an opinion of two of his poems; Burns' reply:

'DEAR CIMON GRAY, –
       The other day
    When you sent me some rhyme,
I could not then just ascertain
    Its worth, for want of time;

But now, to-day, good Mr. Gray,
    I've read it o'er and o'er,
Tried all my skill, yet find I'm still
    Just where I was before.

Wi' auld wives minions, give our opinions,
    Solicited or no,
Then of its faults, my honest thoughts
    I'll give, and here they go:

Such damned bombast, no time that's past
    Will show, or time to come;
So Cimon, dear, your song I'll tear
    And fling it doon the lum.'[50]

Well, again amongst auld folk I heard this one. I heard that Burns
went across with a boat to Ireland. When he landed at the other side
into Ireland – from Ayrshire – the boat hauled up along the quay, you
see, and there was crowd of people waitin' for some of their people
comin' off. So the great Irish poet was there. (Now this may be just a
story, I don't know.) But they called him McGee and he was a poet. So
he was standin' on the quay and he looks into the boat and he sees this
people standin'. So he lookit at this man specially which had tooken
his attention. There's nae doubts about it, Burns had aboot him
somethin' that wad have taken people's attention. That's true. And he
said:

        By the cut of your hair
        And the clothes that you wear
        I ken you are Burns
        Frae the auld toon o' Ayr.

And Burns lookit up at him and he said:

        You're on the land
        And I'm on the sea:
        By the cut o' your gob
        I think you're McGee.[51]

Robbie Burns was a Scotch poet and Tom Moore was an Irish poet, and Bobbie Burns was painting the front of his house, and Tom Moore walked down the street. He says:

> 'You Scottish fool
> Leave down your tool
> And let Tom Moore pass by.'
> 'Oh,' he says,
> 'You Irish ass
> You have room to pass
> Between the wall and I.'[52]

Well, it was in Dr. Ferguson's house in Edinburgh here that-a-Tannahill, of course Dr. Ferguson invited Burns and Tannahill and Lady Nairne to his house to have a nice enjoyment and drinks all round of course. And of course a they was tryin' to compete with one anothers poems and sayins' and Lady Nairne she went to the door and she cried Cock a doodle do and came back into Dr. Ferguson's house and Dr. Ferguson says well Robbie says could you, could you end up beating that sayin'? So Burns – an, ah-stood up and he says

> And to the door the lady flew
> To imitate the cock that crew
> She crewed so loud the little sinner
> You doubtly thought the cock was in her.

And of course they all dropped their jugs and laughter and Dr. Ferguson he fell near into the fire in laughing. And Tannahill went to the door and he said, There's no a star in all the carrey (sky) and Burns went to the door and Burns come back and says oh no Tanny, he says, that's no use, he says the carreys full of stars he says. That's no use he says. So they – the farmers they were there too in Dr. Ferguson's house so they was a competin' too and doctors and professors so Burns he give a toast. He says:

> You doctors and you professors all
> And now I think you're so clever
> If you can mak a cock that winna fa'
> Then I'll go on forever.[53]

Well, this is how I heard the story. You see, there was a great lady called Lady Mathilde. And as far as I heard she was a poet too. But she was very wealthy and had a big beautiful castle-hoose and plenty

o' money and everything. So – the only thing I can't tell in my story is
where she come from. But she said that she wad like to have Burns
come to her hoose and that she wad send for him. She kenned a lot
aboot him. She had heard aboot 'im bein' a great poet and she also
heard that Burns could make up poetry aboot ye by jeest lookin' at
ye. Within a few minutes he could make up a bit o' poetry aboot ye.
Especially if ye did somethin'. So she sent for Burns and Burns did
come to this big fine castle-hoose and this Lady Mathilde had it full o'
gentry, you see, and they was all settin' in the big beautiful hall, settin'
round it, but the middle o' the floor was empty. So when Burns comes
in at this door she put a drink intill his hand and he was nae dressed to
come in amangst gentry because at this time he was jeest a poor man,
he was jeest a plooman, and he was dressed like a plooman, when he
did come intill the hoose. He had his old guttery-sharney boots on –
no very weel dressed. But nevertheless it was Robbie Burns. And she
pit a drink intill his hand, you see. But all in a sudden Lady Mathilde
gathered hersel' up and Burns wondered in the name o' God what was
wrong wi' 'er, you see, because naebody in a fact kenned in the hoose
what she was goin' to dae. She was keepin' it as a kind o' a surprise.
And all in a sudden she gathered hersel' up in front o' Robbie Burns
and she gaed flyin' right frae one end o' the hall tae the other end o' the
hall, and as she was flyin' she was imitatin' the cock crowin' and flyin',
both at the same time. She imitated the cock cryin' oot 'Cock-a-loo-
ra-loo' and she was fleein' way up the hall. Now Burns lookit after
that a wee bitty surprised, you see, and when she gaes up tae the end o'
the hall where there was another door, she flew right up tae this door.
Burns lookit at her for a minute or two, and he still had his glass o'
whusky in his hand and he raised his glass o' whusky and he said:

> Mathilde tae and door she flew
> Tae imitate the cock she crew.
> She cried jeest like the little sinner
> You wad actually thocht the cock was in 'er.

So that was his wee bit o' poetry aboot Lady Mathilde.[54]

You heard tell of Rabbie Burns, I suppose. He was a Scotsman and a
poet. I mind one time, when I was workin in Scotland, about sixty
years ago. I went with a crowd to Rabbie's house. And everything was
there the very same as it was when Rabbie was livin. He was a terror
for the women and for drink. But he was at a Ball one night and there
was a lot of lassies there, toffs & lassies, and they were dyin to get in

with Rabbie and he was takin no notice of them. So some of them axed Rabbie to make a poem for them and Rabbie didn't like any of them at all and he got up and he says:

> 'Ladies, ladies, what a blessin,
> That youse can shite without undressin,
> While us poor men, poor sons o' bitches,
> We must undress or *shite our breeches*.'[55]

Jesse Lewars, daughter of John Lewars supervisor of the Excise, was nurse to Burns when he was near to death and listened to his gloom and forebodings. He scratched a toast to her on a crystal goblet:

> 'Fill me with rosy wine,
> Call a toast – a toast divine;
> Give the poet's darling flame –
> Lovely Jessie be thy name.'[56]

During a visit to Robert Ainslie's house, Burns attended church where the minister went on and on about sinners. Miss Ainslie with whom Burns was quite taken could not find the text. Burns wrote to her –

> 'Fair maid, you need not take the hint,
> Nor idle texts pursue;
> 'Twas guilty sinners that he meant,
> Not angels such as you.'[57]

Burns and a girl were having intercourse in the Meadows when a young boy came along and stopped to watch. Burns finally looked up and said

> Pass on, pass on, my bonny son
> The work of nature maun be done.[58]

Robbie Burns was once going along the road one day and there was one man and a young woman was having intercourse at the road, beside it, so he passed by and, they were having intercourse. Now about nine months after this, this lass she had a baby, and the – this man that she'd been having intercourse with would have naething to do with the baby. So she took him to court. So the, the judge, the – says to her, 'Who shall witness to prove?' So she says, she says, 'Well, there was a man passing', and she knew the man you see – the person at the time. 'And who was that?' 'That was Robert Burns.' So he was

tooken as a witness. So when the court come open, Robbie Burns was
putten up for a witness you see and the judge said, 'What did you see
Robbie?' He said, 'I saw a couple, a couple,' he says, 'fuckin' like
mad.' 'You can't use language like that in court,' he says; 'put it in
better words.' He says, 'well

> When I went past the banks of Ayr
> I saw a couple lying there
> His ass was going to and fro
> And if that's not fuckin' I don't know.'[59]

Another was after a night of debauchery, he was very sick; a passer-by
went to his assistance and asked him his name and where he lived;
Burns was supposed to have answered in the following:

> I'm Rabbie Burns frae Ayr,
> And I'm on the pier o' Leith:
> I've lost the key to my Erse,
> And I'm sh-tin' thru my teeth.[60]

A lady had been pestering Robert Burns trying to find out how to
make poetry. He told her he would teach her if she did what he told
her. He told her to strip and to put a Bible under her head. Then Burns
said:

> The word of God is under your head
> and the Son of Man is on you.
> Burns' pole is in your hole,
> And the Lord have mercy on you.
> Good bye now! That's how to make poetry.[61]

Perhaps no other facet of Burns' life has been of such persistent
interest as his relations with the opposite sex. Contemporary tradition is
filled with comments that 'he was quite a lad', 'a womaniser'. One
informant suggested that he never married Jean Armour; and to this
day, the exact number of his children remains purest speculation.
Certainly he did not lack for female companionship: contemporary
comments on this propensity continue to vacillate between envy and
criticism. He is seen as 'sex maniac', 'dirty man', 'male chauvinist pig' or
alternatively as way ahead of his time, 'either lucky or boasting', a man
with a talent worth emulating. Other accounts stress Burns' attractive-
ness, as do many extant portraits (see Plates 6, 7, 8, 9.) Some records

suggest that Burns did not pursue but was himself pursued. No matter, women have been central to the tradition. And many narratives suggest a 'takem and leavem' approach.

A young maid going to market, with a basket of eggs on her arm, meets a man, who obviously had been drinking all night, on the path. 'Who lass,' he says, 'what are you doing on the path so early?' 'Arn't you afraid of being attacked by some man?' 'I fear no man but Robert Burns Sir,' she answered. 'But I am Robbie Burns,' he says. 'Just give me time to set me eggs down first sir,' she cried.[62]

At an old age Pensioners' Burns Supper at Craigmiller some years ago, where I proposed the Immortal Memory, an elderly woman on being coaxed got up to tell this story: Robbie Burns, when he was in Edinburgh, was one day crossing The Meadows when he met a young woman carrying a basket of eggs. 'Good morning, my dear,' says Robbie. 'Good morning,' says she. 'You're a stranger here. And what's your name, Sir?' 'I'm the famous Ayrshire poet, Robbie Burns, on a visit to Auld Reekie.' 'O, is that whae ye are? I've heerd tell o' ye. I suppose I'll jeest hae to lay doon my basket o' eggs, then.'[63]

Robert Burns was coming – going along up a road, a steep brae somewhere, with a pig under one arm a – a greese – a young pig under one arm and a sack of sweet potatoes under the other more than likely. He met a woman comin' down off the common; she'd been bleachin' her linen and was bringin' down the empty tub. She'd been leavin' out to bleach you see. It was a crime of course to steal linen. You could be transported to Australia or some of those God-forsaken places if you poached, somebody touched linen. A – it was all screaming murder to steal linen bleachin' at the ring at that time. This woman sorta went round by the bank and avoided Burns comin' up the road; and he says, 'What's – what's wrong with you woman?' 'Oh,' she says, 'I thought you'd want to set tays,' that is to assault her you see. He says, 'Who in God's name could a set tays when I got a greese under yan arm and twa stane tatters under the other?' 'Oh,' says she, 'I thought maybe ye'd a put the tub over the top o the pig and put the tatties over the top of it so the pigs na getten out!'[64]

Did you know that Burns and the Pope died on the same day? Well, they did, but there was some mix-up and the Pope went to Hell and Burns to Heaven. It took a day or so to sort this out. But the exchange

of places was finally arranged and begun. At a mid-way point the
Pope and Burns passed one another and Burns, being intrigued with
the recent mistake, with the Pope, etc. wanted to stop and chat a bit.
But the Pope was in a dreadful hurry and said he couldn't, he'd just
had an urgent call from the Virgin Mary. 'Never mind,' says Burns,
'It's too late now.'[65]

Burns said to waitress, 'I wouldna mind a night out with you.' She
said, 'Ah well, you can have that any time.' So, of course, after dinner
and everything you know, he happened to be disappeared for two,
three minutes you know. So he came back in and some of his
colleagues said, 'Wher've you been?' 'Ah, well you heard the little girl
saying to me, the little waitress saying to me that to meet her outside.'
And the chaps says, 'Well – I thought you were going to see her after
dinner, after dinner.' And he says, 'Yes, I saw her, I seen her, I've seen
her after dinner.' 'Ah, have you?' 'And it was only two seconds after
that, til the cock was in her.'[66]

Burns' attitude, traditionally sanctioned, towards his many chance
encounters led in the song below to a natural connection of Burns with
raw sexuality and street language.

> 'Cottage Where Burns Was Born'
>
> On the banks of the Clyde stood an old turner ride
> And her thing was all tattered and torn
> For it was my delight for the feck her each night
> Against the cottage where Burns was born.
>
> I goosed her so hard that from sweat I drew lard
> And on her old thing turned a coin
> For the dirty old bogs, aye she slung me the pogs
> Against the cottage where Burns was born.
>
> And she took her piss and I took her kiss
> They said of her thing, give me the horn
> So I goosed her again upon the wall
> Against the cottage where Burns was born.[67]

Jean Armour was, of course, one of Burns' conquests, taken and left
and only finally acknowledged and officially wed though the lines of
marriage written much earlier and precipitously destroyed by Jean's
father – formally denoted 'irregular' – could have been legally binding.

The story, oft and many ways told, of the first meeting of Burns and Jean Armour. Some few days after Burns had been at a ball (penny reel) in Hugh Morton's ballroom at Mauchline on the race night, at which he had in the hearing of Miss Armour (Jean) expressed the wish that he 'had a lass wad lo'e him as well as his dug' (the dog tracking his master's footsteps 'through the lichtit ha'), he had occasion to pass through the Bleaching Green, when, as luck would have it, he foregathered with Miss Armour. She rallied him about his dog, which, as Robert Louis Stevenson states in his *Aspects of Burns*, 'was in its daffin staining with his four black paws the cloth she had laid out to whiten.' 'Ca' in your dog,' pertly she cried, most likely with many blushes, at the same time 'spierin' gin he had as yet gotten a lass to lo'e him as well.' So the story goes.[68]

A number of accounts have circulated about Burns and another woman – Highland Mary; they may have developed to counter the negative stories of Burns' dealings with women. Supposedly, Highland Mary was his only real love, a pure woman, and Burns was an Ayrshire Galahad rather than a 'lewd, amazing peasant of genius'.[69] This aspect of the legend, immortalised in picture, shows Burns and Highland Mary exchanging Bibles across a stream (the Water of Fail, an off-shoot of the River Ayr), a binding act, in betrothal. (See Plate 10.) Scholarly tradition suggests that Highland Mary was in fact a loose woman and one he went to on the rebound from Jean's parentally instigated rebuff.[70] Published material, based on exhumation of her tomb, suggests she died in childbirth though subsequent research indicates that the child buried with her was not hers.[71] But essentially, she remains a shadowy positive force in Burns' life and her death augured ill for his development: she could have saved him from future womanising and drink. The song 'Burns and Highland Mary' exemplifies the romanticisation of his relationship with her:

In green Caledonia there ne'er were two lovers
Sae enraptured and happy in each others arms,
As Burns, the sweet bard, and his dear Highland Mary,
And fondly and sweetly he sang o' her charms;
And lang will his sangs, sae enchanting and bonnie,
Be heard wi' delight on his own native plains,
And lang the name o' his dear Highland Mary
Be sacred to love in his heart-melting strains.

Oh, 'twas May day, and the flowers o' the summer
Were blooming in wildness a' lovely and fair,
That our twa lovers met in a grove o' green flowers
Which grew on the banks o' the clear winding Ayr.
And oh, to them baith 'twas a meeting fu' tender
And was the last ane for a while they should ha'e,
Sae love's purest raptures they tasted the gether,
Till the red setting sun showed the close of the day.

'O Mary dear Mary,' exclaimed her fond lover,
'Ye carry my heart to the Highlands with thee;'
Every burnie and bank, every grove and green bower,
May talk o' the love o' my lassie and me.
My life's sweetest treasure, my ain charming Mary,
To thee I'll be ever devoted and true;
For the heart that is beating sae fast in this bosom,
The heart that can never love any but you.

'O, dinna bide lang in the Highlands, my Mary,
O, dinna bide lang in the Highlands frae me;
For I love thee sincerely, I love thee ower dearly,
To be happy sae far, my dear Mary, frae thee.'
'I winna bide lang, my dear lad, in the Highlands,
I winna bide lang, for ye winna be there;
Although I ha'e friends I like weel in the Highlands,
The ane I love best's on the banks o' the Ayr.'

Then he kissed her red lips, they were sweeter than roses,
And he strained her lily white breast to his heart;
And her tears fell like dew-drops at e'en on his bosom,
As she said, 'My fond lover, alas, we must part.'
'Then farewell,' he said, as he flew frae his Mary;
'O, farewell,' said Mary, she could say nae mair:
O, little they kent they had parted for ever,
When they parted that night on the banks o' the Ayr.

But the green summer saw but a few summer mornings,
Till she, in the bloom of her beauty and pride,
Was laid in the grave like a bonnie young flower,
In Greenock kirkyard, on the banks o' the Clyde.
And Burns, the sweet bard o' his ain Caledonia,
Lamented his Mary in many a sad strain;

Oh, sair did he weep for his dear Highland Mary,
And ne'er did his heart love so deeply again.

Then bring me the lilies, and bring me the roses,
And bring me the daisies that grow in the vale;
And bring me the dew of a mid summer evening,
And bring me the breath of the sweet scented gale;
And bring me the sigh of a fond lover's bosom,
And bring me the tear o' a fond lover's e'e,
And I'll pour them a' doon on the grave Highland Mary,
For the sake o' thy Burns who dearly loved thee.[72]

The individual Burns has been of considerable interest, thus people have sought to record narratives depicting his outstanding qualities. These accounts give sporadic insight into the way Burns was and is perceived by his compatriots: a raconteur, Bible scholar, cause of anxiety, humanitarian 'with a burning faith that everyone was equal',[73] and as heavy drinker. Dean Ramsay provides an interesting background to the latter by discussing drinking as a generalised Scottish habit of the eighteenth century.[74] Certainly the practice continues today; and Burns' traditional consumption may provide historical precedent, if such be needed, for present consumption. Other accounts, of course, suggest that he was not a drunkard.

Burns took his own plough irons to be repaired; and during this process the story telling began. On one remarkable occasion, when a piece of iron was being welded, the man who plied the sledge hammer was so fascinated with the narrative, that he 'stood with his hammer thus' above his head immovable, till the iron cooled, and the process was effectually interrupted. 'Rab, Rab,' cried the smith, himself as much absorbed as anybody else, 'this 'ill never do; you and me man gang for a drap of yill, or deil ae steek o' graithen ill be mended this nicht!'[75]

On one occasion, Nance and the bard were sitting in the 'spence,' when the former turned the conversation on her favourite topic, religion. Burns sympathised with the matron, and quoted so much Scripture that she was fairly astonished. When she went home, she said to her husband, 'Oh, David, how they have wranged that man; for I think he has mair o' the Bible aff his tongue than Mr. Inglis himsel'.' (Mr. Inglis was the anti-burgher minister.) Burns enjoyed the compliment; and almost the first thing he communicated to his wife on her arrival was the lift he had got from auld Nance.[76]

On a beautiful summer Sabbath morn, Robert and I (says Gilbert Burns) were travelling to Ayr, and on the road overtook an old man travelling in the same direction. The old and new light doctrines about this time were causing much controversy. Robert and the old man firmly debated the question, my brother advocating the new light, this reverend sage the old light. My brother finding the old man more than his match, says 'Come away, Gibbie, I've met the apostle Paul this morning.' 'Na, na, my young friend, ye hae na met the apostle o' the Gentiles, but I hae met ane o' the wild beasts he fought wi' when in Ephesus.'[77]

Burns sometimes read books not always seen in people's hands on Sunday. Mrs. Burns checked this, when the Bard laughingly replied – 'You'll not think me so good a man as Nancy Kelly (or Cullie) is a woman?' 'Indeed, no.' 'Then I'll tell you what happened this morning. When I took a walk this morning by the banks of the Nith, I heard Nancy Kelly praying long before I came till her. I walked on, and before I returned I saw her helping herself to an armful of my fitches.' Nancy kept a cow.[78]

The following was a prophecy said to have been made about Burns by his own father when he was on his deathbed: 'Suddenly the dying man raised his voice: "There's ane o' ye," he said, "for whom my heart is wae. I hope he may na fa'." The tall, stooping figure beside the window started and trembled. "O father," he said, "is it me you mean?" For an instant their eyes met in a full deep gaze. Then slowly the father's eyelids fell, and his head sank on his breast in affirmation. He spoke no more. Shaking with sobs, Robert Burns turned to the window. As he gazed through the dim panes on the dismal world, he vowed the vow, which he did try, although he tried in vain, to keep: "Father! father on earth and Father in heaven! I will be wise." '[79]

During the American war of independence, Burns was at a party where the health of the 'heaven-born' minister, William Pitt, was proposed. The poet refused to taste the cup, and starting up, exclaimed, 'I'll give you the health of a nobler and better man, that of George Washington, one of the noblest and best of freedom's champions.'[80]

Burns himself, stimulated by his political enthusiasm, sent a present of four carronades to the French Revolutionary Government, which were intercepted by the Custom-house authorities at Dover. These guns had been purchased by him for £3, at the confiscation of a smuggler which he had himself captured on the coast.[81]

The following deals with Burns' kindness to a known drunkard Jamie Quin: 'Jamie,' said the poet one day, as he gave him a penny, 'you should pray to be turned from the evil of your ways; you are ready now to melt that penny into whisky.' 'Turn!' said Jamie, who was a wit in his way; 'I wish some ane would turn me into the worm o' Will Hyslop's whisky-still, that the drink might dribble through me for ever.' 'Weel said, Jamie', answered the poet, 'you shall have a glass of whisky once a week for that, if ye'll come sober for 't.' A friend rallied Burns for indulging such creatures. 'You don't understand the matter,' said he; 'they are poets: they have the madness of the muse, and all they want is the inspiration – a mere trifle!'[82]

Returning home to his house in the Wee Vennel, one stormy wet night after dark, he discovered a poor half-witted street-strolling beggar woman, well known about Dumfries, half-naked, drenched and shivering, huddled together almost insensible on his own door-step. In those days there was no shelter of a police-office to which such a helpless vagrant could be removed, nor was there any house open at the moment to which she could be carried, but his own. Mrs. Burns might perhaps be excused for hesitating to receive such an inmate even for the night; but remonstrance was in vain. The miserable outcast, motionless, presumably unconscious, was carefully lifted in, and housed and sheltered under the Poet's hospitable roof till morning, when, not without breakfast we may be sure, she was enabled to pursue her way. 'Then shall the King say unto them on his right hand, Come, ye blessed of my Father, inherit the Kingdom prepared for you from the foundation of the world; For I was an hungered, and ye gave me meat: I was thirsty, and ye gave me drink: I was a stranger, and naked, and sick, and ye visited and took me in.'[83]

The doctor told Burns not to drink, as the coat of his stomach was gone. He replied: he'd go on drinking 'for if the *coat* was gone, it was not worth while carrying about the *waistcoat*.'[84]

Burns died on 21 July 1796 at the age of thirty-seven, and tradition has long speculated on the cause. Today one hears of natural causes, tuberculosis, heart trouble, and drink. Drink has been one consistent explanation in the legendary tradition:

> On leaving a jovial party in the Globe Inn he was, on reaching the door, overpowered by the effects of the liquor he had drunk, fell to the ground, which was covered with snow, and lay there asleep for some hours.[85]

This event is said to have hastened his death; but death was not the end of Burns. Even while his funeral was being held, Jean was giving birth to a posthumous child and a repeated account records Burns' return to see the child he would never know and the wife he left behind:

> Soon after her husband's death, Mrs. Burns had a very remarkable dream. Her bedroom had been removed to the family parlour, when she imagined that her husband drew the curtains and said 'Are you asleep? I have been permitted to return and take one look at you and that child; but I have no time to stay.' The dream was so vivid that Mrs. B. started up, and even to this moment the scene seems to her a reality.[86]

The legendary tradition as a whole, presented above, deals with repeated aspects of Burns' life and personality – emphatically with his various occupations as farmer, excise officer, and particularly as poet and with his dealings with women. While the general topics dealt with have remained more or less constant, the particular topics stressed have changed over time as the dominant genres have changed and in fact expanded: beginning with the personal experience story, shifting to the legend in the nineteenth century and to jokes and anecdotes today. The shift from one narrative genre to another has never, of course, obliterated the previous genre, but has rather added an additional generic possibility, expanding the genres dealing with Burns. The generic distinctions are based on narrator's perspective and stance as well as expected response.

Personal experience stories about individuals' encounters with Burns undoubtedly circulated during his lifetime, especially after he had gained a reputation as a Scottish poet. His death increased the importance of accounts such as the following, for they provided a personal link with an individual deemed significant and important:

Having been requested by some of my friends to give a sketch of what occurred at the only time I had the distinguished honour, and proud satisfaction, to sit under the influence of that great man. My father proposed to make a visit to a clergyman in Dumfries-share, where I could have some hunting and fishing. On a bright autumnal day in 1795, we left my father's house, Kelvingrove, on horseback. That evening we reached Muirkirk. On the second day we rode up the Main Street of Dumfries. On approaching the George Inn, which has now been supplanted by another house, a gentleman was seen standing on the stair leading up to the entrance. My father, on seeing him, exclaimed: 'O! Burns, I am glad to see you.' The poet, who had remained motionless, now rushed down stairs, and taking my father's hand in both of his, said: 'Mr. Pattison, I am delighted to see you.' The old gentleman, though none of the party was over 40 years, asked if Dr. Maxwell was in town, and said, 'As I hope you will dine with me, may I beg you to call on Dr. Maxwell with my compliments, and beg him to join us at 4 o'clock.' 'Too happy,' replied the poet. At the appointed hour we sat down at table. My father at the head opposite Dr. Maxwell, and Burns was *vis-a-vis* to me. Both Dr. Maxwell and my father were highly-gifted, eloquent men, and Burns was in his best vein. Never can I forget the animation and glorious intelligence of his countenance. The deep tones of his musical voice, and those matchless eyes which appeared to flash fire, and stream forth living light. It was not conversation I heard, it was the outburst of noble sentiment, brilliant wit, and a flood of sympathy and good-will to fellow-men. Burns repeated many verses that had never seen the light, chiefly political. The whole three were politicians of the Fox school. No impure or obscure idea was ever uttered, or I believe thought of. It was altogether an intellectual feast. A lofty, pure, and transcendent genius alone could have made such a deep and lasting impression on a mere boy, who never before sat after dinner when he had got a glass of wine and some fruit; but under the glamour of Burns, I sat nailed to my chair some eight or nine hours.[87]

Accounts of contact with and knowledge of the deceased poet were important to many individuals, particularly the group of enthusiasts from the area of Burns' birth who began to meet, in the years immediately following his death, to recall his memory both as man and poet.

As interest in Burns moved in place further from Ayrshire and Dumfriesshire to other parts of Scotland and in time further and further from the time of Burns' life, the personal experience stories – which were local as was his early audience – gave way to less personal accounts which were primarily legends; they in turn became the basis for his national status as symbol of Scotland. The narratives given earlier are predominantly legends and emphasise positive attributes such as the following:

One day, walking down Leith Walk with a modish friend, he met an old Ayrshire acquaintance very poorly dressed, and stopped to have a crack. His dandy friend told him he was surprised he had stopped to speak to such a shabby-looking fellow. 'What!' said the manly bard, 'do you think it was the man's clothes I was speaking to – his hat, his coat, and his waistcoat? No, it was the man within the coat and waistcoat; and let me tell you, that man has more sense and worth than nine out of ten of my fine city friends.'[88]

Today, in addition to lingering family traditions of personal encounters with Burns and a continuing strong tradition of legends, there are an abundance of jokes and anecdotes, many stressing Burns' behaviour towards women or alternately utilising Burns as the central character in anecdotes which might be told about anyone, such as the following:

When Burns was in Edinburgh, he went into a restaurant one morning and ordered two eggs, scrambled. When they were served, the serving was so small that Burns suspected the cook had shortchanged him by scrambling only one egg. With typical Scotch thrift, Burns decided to double-check. The next morning, he ordered two eggs, but ordered one fried and the other scrambled, so he could check the quantity with the day before. When he was served, Burns pretended displeasure and called the waitress, saying 'I ordered two eggs, one fried and the other scrambled.' 'Well,' answered the waitress, 'isn't that what you have?' 'Yes,' agreed Burns, 'but you scrambled the wrong egg.'[89]

It is, at this late date, impossible to determine the breadth and depth of the earlier personal experience and legend traditions. And definitely ascertaining the content, distribution, and strength of contemporary tradition itself is well nigh impossible, fed as it is by such a multiplicity of oral, written, and electronic sources. Over a period of five years, during three visits to Scotland, I sought to gauge – through personal conversation with hundreds of Scots – what was known about Burns and his poetry, what was felt about him, and what his relevance might be. Certainly Burns as a man, more than his poetry, continues to dominate. Some see him as a kind of hero; a great many think of him as 'boozer and womaniser'. There is a remarkable accuracy of detail and allusion to earlier tradition, making minor inaccuracies as well as outright contradiction of facts particularly noticeable: most are amazed that Burns accomplished so much in his short life, but disagree on exactly how old he was when he died: 26, 33, 36, 38, 39. Individuals have suggested that Burns lived in various places – probable geographically – but not true in fact: Arran and Moffat. Several thought John Murdock was his private tutor, that, by extension, Burns came from monied people. One, stressing Burns' sexual irresponsibility, insisted he never married Jean Armour. All, of course, know that Burns was a poet, is, in fact, the National Poet. Many can quote chapter and verse; others have difficulty with 'Wee, sleeket, cowran, tim'rous *beastie*' from 'To a Mouse'; some attribute genuine traditional songs or songs by others to him – 'Twa Corbies', 'Annie Laurie'. But even when discussing the poet Burns, individuals often stress Burns the man, especially his nationalistic sentiments, which continue to feed national pride. A number of individuals were impressed that Burns had acquired international fame, particularly pointing out the Russian interest in him. As one informant put it, 'Scottish people are beginning to feel they're somebody now – getting a bit bolder'.[90] Thus, to many, Burns represents Scotland, the Nation, and they identify his writing in Scots as positive, though many admit they have difficulty understanding it. So as man and poet he may be hero though a variety of Scots remark that on reflection they are amazed that so 'practical a people' should praise a poet. Others admire aspects of Burns but stress their own independence and rebellion – perhaps emulating those qualities in Burns – by asserting that they do not need a hero, being content with themselves. In essence, the contemporary tradition is dominated on the one hand by anecdotes about his encounters with women, passed on almost completely in oral tradition, and on the other and more formal level, combining oral and written traditions, by the Burns Suppers to be discussed in Chapter 6.

The legendary tradition as a whole stresses Burns the man and in large measure ignores the established canon of poetry and song which initially established his reputation. Hershel Gower, in a paper called 'Burns in Limbo', deplores the traditions about the man which detract from the dignity and beauty of his poetry;[91] this view denies implicitly the very real cultural value the legendary tradition about Burns has had in fostering a sense of nationalism through Burns – as an ideal figure to emulate and as a representative Scot. It is perhaps well to remember that earlier Burns' own national feelings had been inspired by a traditional genre – folksongs: a people's oral, expressive forms may be of special importance in developing national sentiment and consciousness. For over two hundred years, the narratives about Burns have been kept alive; undoubtedly, they have helped sustain the people's pride in being Scots.

6 Tradition's Use of Burns: The Calendar Custom

Summons to Attend a Meeting of the
Burns' Anniversary Society

To William McLaren
1805

KING GEORDIE issues out his summons,
Tae ca his bairns, the Lairds an Commons,
Tae creesh the nation's moolie-heels,
An butter Commerce' rusty wheels,
An see what new, what untried tax,
Will lie the easiest on oor backs.

The priest convenes his scandal court,
Tae ken what houghmagandie sport
Has been gaun on within the parish
Since last they met, – their funds tae cherish.

But I, the servant o Apollo,
Whase mandates I am proud tae follow, –
He bids me warn you as the friend
Of Burns's fame, that ye'll attend
Neist Friday e'en, in Luckie Wricht's,
Tae spend the best – the wale o nichts;
Sae, under pain o ha'f-a-merk
Ye'll come, as signed by me, the Clerk.
                              Robert Tannahill

Perhaps the words were written facetiously and penned with 'tongue in cheek', but – nonetheless – Burns' comment about himself, sent to

117

Gavin Hamilton shortly after he arrived in Edinburgh in 1786 to arrange
another edition of his poems, is remarkably prophetic:

> For my own affairs, I am in a fair way of becoming as eminent as
> Thomas a Kempis or John Bunyan; and you may expect henceforth to
> see my birthday inserted among the wonderful events, in the Poor
> Robin's and Aberdeen Almanacks, along with the black Monday, &
> the battle of Bothwel bridge.[1]

He was right; and each year, as the calendar approaches the 25th of
January, celebrations in memory of Robert Burns fill the calendar.

The Burns Suppers in honour of Scotland's national poet are
undoubtedly Burns' most significant, albeit unwitting contribution to
Scottish traditional life: they unite Burns' poetry and songs with the
legendary traditions about him to form a remarkable event, focusing
both on the man as man and the man as poet.

This calendar custom had and continues to have nationalistic
implications for those who participate. However, like his own early
poetry and audience, the Burns Suppers were initially local and were
attended by those who had known him. Accounts of personal en-
counters with Burns, such as those discussed in Chapter 5, were
undoubtedly given. By the Centenary celebrations in memory of the
hundredth anniversary of his birth in 1859, the celebration was national
in scope and incorporated personal encounter narratives as well as
legends to project a view of Burns as a national figure, perhaps the
representative Scot – a stance Burns had himself sought after his
Edinburgh experience. Since that time, the Burns Suppers have been
smaller, more select gatherings of individuals who themselves continue
to stress Burns' national status through legends, and more recently and
less prominently, in jokes and anecdotes. The celebration is no longer
national though it occurs all over Scotland and in fact the world and is
found among many social groups and classes. There are many
detractors of the tradition who believe that it presents an out-dated
picture, that it emphasises the wrong kind of Scottishness, that it merely
offers a 'jolly good excuse for a booze up'. For the majority who have
partaken and still partake of this calendar custom, which is multigeneric
in nature, the Burns Supper is, however, a positive and affirmative event
for Burns, for Scotland, and for themselves.

Calendar customs – the habit of setting aside certain days for
particular practices – are perhaps as old as mankind; and they enable
humanity to mark off a given day as special – sometimes relieving

everyday monotony, on other occasions bringing together a community or group for specific work tasks and rituals, simultaneously uniting those present in a shared sense of interdependence before they return to the usual round of seasonal work. Calendar customs recur each year as the cycle of seasons once more recapitulates. Originally such customs reflected an organisation of life around the seasons and showed man and nature bound together in the repeated pattern of fertility, growth, and decay. The old Celtic divisions of the year – Samhain, Imbolc, Beltane, and Lughnasa – brought the people together, essentially to ensure a necessary act or ritual and at the same time to emphasise the common concerns of all so gathered. The origins of few traditional calendar customs can be historically documented for they have developed slowly through time, lasting as long as there was a reason or memory of a reason.

While the calendar custom in honour of Burns is of relatively recent origin (he died in 1796), even its history is murky and difficult to uncover as, retrospectively, many groups have claimed precedence in honouring Scotland's poet. The Burns Suppers did not spring up at one point in time full blown; rather they have developed through time in roughly five stages, incorporating the disparate traditions about Burns. Variation and change remain the hallmarks of this tradition as of all folkloric traditions; and selection has effected the current relative stability.

The complete history of the Burns Suppers – sometimes called Burns Night, a Nicht wi' Burns, Burns Anniversary, Burns Celebration, Anniversary Dinner, Anniversary Supper, Annual Festival, Annual Supper, Annual Celebration, Burns Dinner – can certainly never be written, for the custom was a spontaneous growth and its celebrants are now found all over the world though predominantly in Scotland and among the Scottish diaspora. Burns, who highly valued his own folklore, his own traditional inheritance, utilising it in his poems and songs, collecting it from himself and others to preserve it, contributed to subsequent tradition by becoming the central focus of the Burns Suppers; in both instances, Scotland has been the beneficiary.

There is some evidence of a Proto-celebration, a precedent for the Burns Supper set by Burns and his friends during his own lifetime. Many accounts of the eighteenth century mention the general predilection of groups of men to gather to share a meal, often breakfast. Burns' friend, John Richmond, writing in 1817 – some twenty-one years after Burns' death and thirty-two years after the event he described – writes of an occasion which stimulated Burns to write the poem, now an essential element in the Burns Supper meal, 'To a Haggis'[2]: he wrote that a group of friends – all males – regularly gathered to celebrate the end of harvest and frequently ate haggis – thus calling themselves the Haggis Club. On one such occasion – in 1785 – Burns is said to have used the poem as a blessing. Kinsley – differing with Richmond's account – suggests in his notes to 'To a Haggis',[3] that since the poem was published in two Edinburgh periodicals shortly after Burns arrived there in 1786, it was probably written around that time. Kinsley cites two additional traditions about the poem, one that the last verse was created by Burns extemporaneously as a grace at dinner in the home of John Morrison, a cabinet-maker in Mauchline; and the other that the poem was created to recall a dinner in Edinburgh at the home of the merchant Andrew Bruce. It is impossible to determine the accuracy or reliability of any of these accounts; conceivably, Burns could have used the poem or parts of it on all three occasions. But cumulatively, these accounts do suggest a gathering of friends to share a meal of haggis, at which Burns read or performed his poem; thus they provide a nucleus of proto-elements which later were incorporated into the Burns Suppers: a shared meal, often males only, of haggis, and the recitation of Burns' poem 'To a Haggis'.

By 1801, only five years after his death, a Burns Club had been established in Greenock, the core of which included personal friends of Burns – James Findlay, Richard Brown, Highland Mary's family, Alexander Dalziel, and Wright and Wilson of the Excise.[4] The founding of the club in Burns' memory took place on 21 July 1801 – commemorating his death date. Elizabeth Ewing suggests that it was held at Burns' birthplace in Alloway and that a meal was shared;[5] however no written account was made of this gathering until 1819, by Rev. Hamilton Paul, Assistant Minister in Ayrshire; but an account by Charles Brodie indicates that the Greenock group first met in Alloway the January after their founding, that is in 1802, to celebrate Burns' birthdate, thought to be 29 January. Nine persons were present and a supper, redolent of the proto-celebration, of sheep's head and haggis was served. It was after Greenock's 1803 festivities, again held at Alloway, that Burns' actual birthdate was discovered, thus determining the date of subsequent meetings:

On Saturday, the 29th instant, a select party of the patrons and admirers of our Ayrshire Poet, Burns, met to dinner at Alloway in the room in which he was born, to celebrate his birth day . . . ; but a doubt having arisen whether the 25th or 29th of January was his birth day, and the register of births for the parish of Ayr having been searched, it thereby appears that the 25th, and not the 29th, as has hitherto been most generally believed, was the birth day of our poet, and in the year 1759.[6]

The Greenock pattern – a core of Burns' friends and admirers gathering, either on or around his birth or death date, to do honour to his memory – proliferated. Many of the groups later became Burns Clubs and members of the Burns Federation, having at least one celebratory meeting a year, often sharing a meal of traditional Scottish fare.[7] Paisley, the second club, founded in 1805, also contained a core of Burns' acquaintances who may well have met before the offical founding of the club to remember their friend. At the first meeting, held at the Star Inn with seventy persons present, William M'Laren proposed the toast to 'The Memory of our Immortal Bard, Robert Burns'. This is the first explicit reference to the central speech and toast of the present form of celebration – The Immortal Memory. At Paisley also songs and poems in his honour, such as Tannahill's, were presented.

> Once on a time, almighty Jove
> Invited all the minor gods above
> To spend one day in social festive pleasure;
> His regal robes were laid aside,
> His crown, his sceptre, and his pride;
> And, wing'd with joy,
> The hours did fly,
> The happiest ever Time did measure.
> . . . .
> Loud, thund'ring, plaudits shook the bright abodes,
> Till Merc'ry, solemn voic'd, assail'd their ears,
> Informing that a stranger, all in tears,
> Weeping, implored an audience of the gods.
>
> Jove, ever prone to succour the distrest,
> A swell redressive glow'd within his breast,
> He pitied much the stranger's sad condition,
> And order'd his immediate admission.
>
> The stranger enter'd, bowed respect to all;
> Respectful silence reign'd throughout the hall.
> . . . .
> 'O, wouldst thou deign thy suppliant to regard,
> And grant my country one true Patriot Bard,

My sons would glory in the blessing given,
And virtuous deeds spring from the gift of heaven!'
To which the god – 'My son, cease to deplore;
Thy Name in song shall sound the world all o'er;
Thy Bard shall rise full fraught with all the fire
That Heav'n and free born nature can inspire.
. . . .'

Twas in regard to Wallace and his worth,
Jove honour'd Coila with his birth,
    And on that morn,
    When Burns was born,
    Each Muse with joy
    Did hail the boy;
And Fame, on tiptoe, fain would blown her horn,
But Fate forbade the blast, too premature,
Till Worth should sanction it beyond the critic's pow'r.

His merits proven – Fame her blast hath blown,
Now Scotia's Bard o'er all the world is known; –
But trembling doubts here check my unpolished lays,
What can they add to a whole world's praise;
Yet, while revolving Time this day returns,
Let Scotsmen glory in the name of Burns.[8]

Innumerable toasts were made.[9] Other communities (such as Kilmarnock and Ayr) followed suit; and in 1820 the Dumfries Burns Club was formally instituted, though earlier private celebrations on Burns' birthday among such personal friends of Burns as John Commelin, John Syme, and William Grierson are said to have taken place.[10] More public events to raise money for statues or monuments to Burns were also held and the one in Edinburgh, on 5 June 1819, included a formal proposal to the memory of Burns, a variety of other toasts, and the singing of some of Burns' songs. The triennial dinner in honour of Robert Burns – also held in Edinburgh in 1819 – brought together all of the leading Scots literati, including John Wilson and James Hogg, for a 'display of national enthusiasm'. The account of that event by John Gibson Lockhart in *Peter's Letters to His Kinfolk* offers a lengthy eyewitness account, complete with critical response, and provides a more personal perspective on these kinds of celebrations than other records provide.[11]

While not uniform, these early remembrances of Burns recall the

Proto-celebration of Burns and his friends over a meal of haggis and introduce elements which have continued. Initially, the celebrations were on or near either the date of death or birth – with birthdate eventually becoming dominant, undoubtedly because celebrating birth focuses on life, on the potential which death denies. And there was probably more cultural need for the friendship and conviviality of the gathering in winter than in warmer, more pleasant summer. Thus, quite early, meetings of Burns' friends and admirers to recall him took place on his birthdate, and often included a meal of haggis and other national fare – the first intimation that this occasion was in honour of both Burns and his country, Scotland. During this period the Core-celebration was developing: the toast to the Immortal Memory, the recitation of poems and songs about Burns, and the singing of Burns' own songs were introduced. The Immortal Memory given in Dumfries in 1825 by John Syme was no doubt typical and is indicative of themes subsequently reiterated: Burns as both friend and peasant poet of extraordinary genius:

> Upon the subject of Burns's works and genius, what can I possibly say or think, that has not been better expressed before? The subject, in fact, is well nigh exhausted . . . Burns was the most extraordinary man I had ever known; the lightnings of his eye, the tones of his voice, the smile that played round his lips, or the frown that occasionally shaded his brow, were all and each indicative of a mind of prodiguous power; so much so, that even the proud and titled felt themselves awed into respect by the high bearing of the peasant poet.[12]

The recitation of poems and songs about Burns – occasional and memorial pieces – reflects the strong village versifying tradition which had inspired Burns. The tendency to recite rhymes continues, if sporadically, in Burns celebrations to this day. Thus, some ten to twenty years after his death, many persons joined together each year to honour Robert Burns; and their early celebrations provided the basic core elements for many subsequent and contemporary Burns Suppers.

In 1859 – which marked the centenary of Burns' birth – the trend begun perhaps sixty years earlier for more and more celebrations in memory of Burns reached its greatest heights. Mr Colin Rae-Brown, founder and managing proprietor of the *Glasgow Daily Bulletin,* headed a campaign to encourage widespread centenary celebrations.[13] And James T. Wilson, Esq., Spittal, no doubt echoed Brown's sentiments at the King's Arms Hotel in Berwick when he said: 'There is something inexpressively grand . . . in the idea of a whole nation meeting together for special festivities in honour of a man'.[14] If John McVie is correct, the number of actual celebrations is staggering: he suggests that only 5 per cent were in any way chronicled in the tome of accounts edited by James Ballantine, whose own preface amply illustrates the extraordinary scope and magnitude of the centenary celebrations, inspired by the less public Core-celebrations:

> The celebration of the hundredth birthday of Robert Burns, on the 25th day of January, in the year 1859, presented a spectacle unprecedented in the history of the world.
>   The extent and variety of the materials necessary to chronicle the incidents of such a day may be judged of by the following analysis of the meetings herein chronicled.
>
> | | |
> |---|---:|
> | Scotland, | 676 |
> | England, | 76 |
> | Ireland, | 10 |
> | Colonies, | 48 |
> | United States, | 61 |
> | Copenhagen, | 1 |
> | Total | 872 |
>
>   The utmost enthusiasm pervaded all ranks and classes. Villages and hamlets, unnoticed in statistical reports, unrecorded in Gazetteers, had their dinners, suppers, and balls. City vied with clachan, peer with peasant, philanthropist with patriot, philosopher with statesman, orator with poet, in honouring the memory of the Ploughman Bard.[15]

These centenary celebrations, attended by as many as 3000 in New York and over 1000 in several Scottish locations, were undoubtedly the culmination of the earlier celebrations and represent a general and widespread public recognition of Burns. Many did not serve meals because the numbers of participants made it impractical, though those which did often served haggis and other national fare such as Scotch broth. Other celebrations featured public lectures or speeches, parades and processions, and in several locales enactments of his poems, especially 'Tam o' Shanter'. In Scotland the 25th of January was virtually a national holiday, with shops and businesses closing at midday.

Though it was still predominantly a male celebration, women attended many gatherings, often being admitted after the shared male meal. The central place in most meetings was given to the speech or toast to the Immortal Memory of Burns, frequently recounting the principal events of his life – built upon the legendary tradition discussed earlier – to an audience less familiar with him than those attending the earlier, smaller, more intimate celebrations. The speeches to the Immortal Memory continued the earlier focus on Burns as a friend but often broadened this to reflect his belief in the brotherhood of man: 'Burns comes amongst us almost as a friend and companion – no matter how humble or how poor we may be, he would meet us over the table, or take our arm in a country walk, and open his heart to us, and tell us of his joys and his sorrows, his hopes and his fears'.[16] In a general and abstract way, the qualities of Scotland's poet are related to those of all people:

He is allied to the greatest minds by his genius, to the gravest by his grave thoughts, to the gayest by his gay ones, to the manliest by his independence, to the frail by his frailties, to the conscientious by his regrets, to the humblest ranks by his birth, to the poorest among them by his struggles with necessity; above all, to the social by his companionship, and to the whole world by his being emphatically a human creature, 'relishing all sharply, passioned as they'.[17]

Thus Burns became, by extension, a representative of every man, and particularly the embodiment and symbol of the nation. But his humble origins were not denied.

I am sure of a hearty response to my toast, on the ground that Burns belonged to the Peasantry of Scotland. To this I ascribe much of his excellence as a poet. The sphere in which he moved was most favourable to the development of his high genius. He there conversed with nature face to face, and was able therefore more graphically to describe her beauties. He had opportunities of observing the human heart in its naked simplicity, without concealment by affectation or by the conventionalisms of polished life. Hence he could tune his harp to melodies which touch a chord in every breast. If he had been nursed in the lap of luxury, – if he had received a superior education, he might indeed have produced works of taste and elegance, but I make bold to say, we should not have had the songs of Robert Burns.[18]

And his follies and vices were admitted and dismissed: 'As the embodiment of popular genius, the champion of popular independence, and the type of popular elevation, his memory – not the memory of his faults and his follies, but the memory of his matchless genius and his noble spirit – is cherished close to the heart of every Scottish man'.[19] Thus the themes of the speeches and toasts to Burns' memory were broadened considerably during the centenary celebrations to make his life and attributes more generally known.

The list of toasts given in addition to the Immortal Memory is often staggering and shows that Burns had become the central focus for a celebration of various aspects of Scottish and national life:

Toast to the Queen
Toast to the Royal Family
Toast to their ministers
Toast to the Army & Navy
Toast the Immortal Memory of Burns (his son, James Glencairn Burns, was present and said a few words)
Toast Lord Clyde, a Glasgow man, military leader then in command in the East
Toast the poets of England
Award to the best poem written in his honour
Toast the Scottish peasantry
Toast the Poets of Scotland
Toast the city of Glasgow, its civic leaders
Toast poets of Ireland
Toast the Scottish clergy
Toast Colonel Burns and other surviving relatives
Toast centenary celebrations all over the world
Toast guests
Toast festival committee
Toast the press
Toast the lasses
Toast the chairman
Toast the croupiers[20]

Not all celebrations accompanied the toasts with hefty amounts of whisky, for a goodly number were avowedly temperance gatherings; but where whisky was served, the condition of the participants by the end of the list gave rise to such anecdotes as the one told me in 1974: A gentleman, having been asked to propose a toast far down on the programme and fearing that at the present rate of alcoholic consumption he would be in no shape to propose his appointed toast, slipped beneath the table to ensure relative sobriety when his turn came. Closing his eyes to relax, to think over his toast, he was alarmed to feel a tug at his collar. Opening his eyes he discovered that his assailant was a wee boy. 'What,' he asked, 'are you doing?' The answer, 'I'm the one that loosens the collars'.[21] The organisers of the celebration had obviously thought of everything! Another informant, illustrating the volume of alcoholic consumption, said it cost 'four times more to water than to corn'.[22] Other anecdotes suggest that, not only were there many toasts, but the length of individual proposals was inordinately long: one Immortal Memory speaker droned on and on and a listener, finally losing patience, threw an empty bottle at the speaker, unfortunately missing him but hitting the chairman. As the chairman slid under the table, he was heard to say, 'Hit me again, George; I can still hear him'. The presentation of toasts, usually accompanied by a reply from one person or representative of the person or group recognised in the toast, lengthened the programme considerably. Add the singing of selected songs written by Burns and commemorative poems in his honour and it is easy to understand how and why these celebrations often lasted far into the night.

While most earlier celebrations had predominantly included male friends and admirers of Burns, the centenary events were more catholic and public. But a link with Burns in a person or artifact seemed generally necessary to validate the meeting, indicative of a secular kind of apostolic succession. So that in Liverpool the chairman introduced to the crowd an old lady who had known Burns;[23] in Bristol 'about one hundred and twenty gentlemen sat down to dinner at the Athenaeum, under the presidency of P. F. Aiken, Esq., grandson of Robert Aiken, writer, Ayr, the early friend and patron of the poet';[24] in Thornhill the chairman, John Hastings, said: 'Then from Thornhill, gentlemen – where I daresay Robert Burns often trod, for he knew my father well and other residents in this town – let the tribute we offer this night be one that comes from the heart';[25] and from Stranraer: 'Mr. Niven proposed "The Sons and Nieces of Burns", and after a few words, stated that the Bard's uncle was my uncle; my aunty Meg was his aunty Meg; my father was Burns' bed-fellow while at the school at Kirkoswald; my grandfather was schoolmaster'.[26] Such disclosures invariably received loud applause. Where personal links with Burns were lacking, physical objects sufficed to create the necessary tie. In Boston at Revere House a wooden cup, from which the President drank to the memory of Burns, was here exhibited, and handed round as a precious relic of the Poet. It had been purchased by Mr. Thomas Cruickshanks, of Beverly Farm, Mass., at the sale of Mrs. Burns' effects at Dumfries, some time after her death. This vessel, which had been used by the poet as a stirrup-cup, and in later years by his 'bonnie Jean' as a sugar-bowl, is rendered more interesting from the fact, that the stalk had been formed of part of an old dining-table used by King Robert the Bruce.[27]

In many ways then, the centenary celebrations continued earlier elements; a tie with Burns, the singing of his songs, the recitation of poems about him, the presentation of the central toast to his Immortal Memory, and the sporadic sharing of a meal. Since these more extended 1859 events were characterised by elaboration, this period might aptly be called the Elaboration, building upon the precedents set by the Proto- and Core-celebrations.

Not only were previous trends elaborated, but new elements (which found their way into later celebrations) were introduced: a toast to the ladies or lasses, here doing honour to their presence; the verbal equation of Burns with Scotland in such statements as 'it was patriotism which brought us here to-night; it is our love for our native land, because it is our admiration of the immortal genius of a native of Scotland. It is for the purpose of still more indelibly impressing upon our minds the immortal memory of Robert Burns, the ploughboy of Ayrshire';[28] the recitation of various Burns' poems such as 'Tam o' Shanter' and 'To a Haggis', perhaps echoing Burns' reputed recitation of his own poem in the Proto-celebration; and the widespread quotation and paraphrase of lines from his poems and songs, raising them almost to the level of maxims or proverbial expression (the second reading in each instance is the authoritative reading):

> Man to man the warld o'er
>   That Man to Man the warld o'er,
> Might brithers be and a' that
>   Shall brothers be for a' that. –
>   (Kinsley, no. 482)

> Chieftain o the puddin race
>   Great Chieftan o' the Puddin-race!
>   (Kinsley, no. 136)

> Wee short hour ayont the twal
> > Some wee, short hour ayont the *twal*,
> > > (Kinsley, no. 55)

> Lad that was born in Kyle
> > There was a lad was born in Kyle,
> > > (Kinsley, no. 140)

> From Maiden Kirk to John o' Groats
> > Frae Maidenkirk to Johny Groats! –
> > > (Kinsley no. 275)

> Each took off his different way
> > An' each took off his several way,
> In hopes to meet some other day
> > Resolv'd to meet some ither day.
> > > (Kinsley, no. 71)

and the use of the song, attributed to Burns, 'Auld lang syne' as the conclusion of the event. The centenary celebration generally offered an Elaboration.

It is obvious that the elaboration and consequent length of the centenary celebrations could not and would not be sustained year after year. And in fact, never since have the celebrations been so numerous. Subsequent celebrations became smaller, less public, more homogenous gatherings of devotees of Burns, honouring him as a man, as a symbol of Scotland and, secondarily, praising his creative endeavours. The next seventy-five to one hundred years of Burns Suppers were characterised by compression, working towards a modification and stabilisation – thus this period might be called the Compression Celebration.

These gatherings were smaller, more private meetings of individuals brought together by devotion to Burns or out of shared work or other interests (PTA, Women's Institute, Burns Club for example). Still characterised by all-male meetings, some Burns Suppers began admitting women to this festivity which for many marked, and still marks, a high point of the calendar year. Because of the passage of time since his death and the death of his descendants and his friends, the personal link with Burns was no longer possible. There was a trend towards a kind of evocation of Burns himself at the Burns Suppers: as Edwin Muir said: 'When the Burnsites are assembled on the Night, they feel Burns invisibly present among them as one of themselves, a great man who by some felicitous miracle has been transformed into an ordinary man, and is the greater because of it – a man indeed more really, more universally ordinary than any mere ordinary man could ever hope to be'.[29] The meal became a dominant element of the meeting and the choice of food continued the Proto and Core stress on national foods. As the general economic situation improved, the Supper might better, as some groups recognised, be called a dinner, as haggis, once the culinary centrepiece, took, with some groups, a backseat to such dishes as roast turkey, Scotticised by calling it Roastit Bubbly Jock!

The toasts, so extended in the period of Elaboration, became fewer: and the speech and concluding toast to the Immortal Memory of Burns, first given in the Core-celebrations, became the dominant, serious presentation, continuing earlier themes found in both the Core- and Elaboration celebrations, but admitting more forthrightly his vices and follies, albeit using them to make him more human, more Everyman. F. Marian McNeill expressed this well: 'It [the Burns Supper] is the festival of the common man – in the sense of every man; for as Burns knew, no man who claims *his* [italics mine] spiritual birthright is "common" – of universal brotherhood'.[30] Increasingly, the focus shifted to Burns as an individual who supported nationalism and by extension to Burns as a symbol for the nation, for Scotland. Thus the Burns Suppers – in the food they served and in the presentation of the Immortal Memory – became more Scottish, more nationally oriented, a trend no doubt that may be even more dominant in the Suppers as Scotland works towards home rule.

While toasts to the reigning monarch and to various individuals to whom thanks were due continued in brief form, the only other central toast – balancing the Immortal Memory – became the comic or light-veined speech and toast 'To the Lasses', now often delighting in the recollection of Burns' own way with the 'fair sex', containing topical and local references, and sometimes illustrating as well the versifying and rhyming traditions earlier found in the commemorative and memorial poems and songs of the Core- and Elaboration celebrations.

The Elaboration celebrations, bringing into the circle of Burns' celebrants numbers of persons largely unfamiliar with him or with his Scots language, stressed, as had many of the Edinburgh literati in his own time, the more English poems like 'The Cotter's Saturday Night'. During the period of Compression and its overt stress on nationalism, the Scots poems received recognition, contributing to the move to reactivate or revitalise Scots, supported by such disparate factions as the Vernacular Circle of the Burns Federation, instituted in 1920, and Hugh MacDiarmid. David Murison captured Burns' centrality in this movement when he said:

By his sheer artistry he restored Scots to a place among the literary languages of the world. It would be a tragedy and a disgrace if his message should become unintelligible to his own fellow-countrymen, because they failed to cherish and preserve their linguistic inheritance. And of that there is no small danger.[31]

The re-emphasis on Burns' Scots poems during the Compression period surely supports the general nationalistic trend of the Burns Suppers.

The necessary Compression period marks the transition to the more stabilised form dominant today, which utilises elements from earlier periods of celebration to create a unified whole, generally adhered to in the majority of Burns Night gatherings. In an effort to aid organisers of Burns Suppers, various individuals have provided descriptions of the proper content, order, and tone for the celebration; these suggestions confirm my observations and represent an attempt to codify traditional practice, much as etiquette and manners' books have done over the years.[32]

The final stage to date in the development of the Burns Suppers is characterised by considerable stabilisation, adding little, save a firm sense of order – of ritual necessity – and taking from each of the earlier stages. Now the celebrations are frequently divided into two parts – the meal *and* the speeches and other performances which follow the interval at the close of the meal: this basic division is common at most banquets and formal gatherings where a meal is served. At many festivities since the late nineteenth century each celebrant has been presented with a menu card, listing the bill of fare and the order of events, often including descriptive phrases in Scots, and sometimes verses from the concluding song, 'Auld lang syne'.

Menu

'Tak' you will o't'

Sheep Heid Broth

Tattie Soup

'God bless your honours a' your days,
Wi' soups o' Kail.'

Address to the Haggis

'An' then, oh, what a glorious sight,
Warm, Reekin', Rich'

Roastit Bubbly Jocks an' Stuffin'
wi' Tatties an' Neeps

Braised Ham

'Oot wi' your blades, lads, an' dinna spare 'im!'
Tam o' Shanter Puddin'   Tipsy Puddin'
                   Fruit Salad
          Coffee   Tea

                    The Toasts
The Queen
          'In loyal true affection'
The Imperial Forces
          'The Sodger's wealth is Honor'
The Royal Burgh of Inverness
          'I'll aye ca' in by yon town'
The Immortal Memory of Robert Burns
The Lasses
          'Sweet as yon hawthorn's blossom'
Our Guests
          'Here's friends on both sides'
The Chairman
          'An' no forgetting Charlie'[33]

   The celebration begins with the meal, prefaced by a Grace chosen from
Burns' works, most typically the Selkirk Grace:

          Some hae meat and canna eat,
          And some wad eat that want it,
          But we hae meat, and we can eat.
          And sae the Lord be thankit.[34]

though others are used as alternatives.[35] The food itself is principally
chosen to reflect Scottish fare. A soup of Scotch broth, sheep's head, or
cock a' leekie may begin the meal, followed by a second course,
sometimes the main course, the haggis and mashed potatoes and mashed
turnips. This aspect of the meal is ritualised in the presentation of the
haggis, usually paraded in to the accompaniment of the pipes, by a piper
in full dress, and presented to the head table. (See Plates 11 and 12.)
Thought by purists to be an English innovation and thus spurned, the
piping in proceeds – among accepting cognoscenti – to the head table in
sunwise procession. It has become traditional at this point to address the
haggis, as Burns himself is reputed to have done in the Proto-celebration,
with Burns' poem 'To a Haggis':

Fair fa' your honest, sonsie face,
Great Chieftan o' the Puddin-race!
Aboon them a' ye tak your place,
        Painch, tripe, or thairm:
Well are ye wordy of a *grace*
        As lang's my arm.

The groaning trencher there ye fill,
Your hurdies like a distant hill,
Your *pin* wad help to mend a mill
        In time o' need,
While thro' your pores the dews distil
        Like amber bead.

His knife see Rustic-labour dight,
An' cut you up wi' ready slight,
Trenching your gushing entrails bright
        Like onie ditch;
And then, O what a glorious sight,
        Warm-reekin, rich!

Then, horn for horn they stretch an' strive,
Deil tak the hindmost, on they drive,
Till a' their weel-swall'd kytes belyve
        Are bent like drums;
Then auld Guidman, maist like to rive,
        Bethankit hums.

Is there that owre his French *ragout*,
Or *olio* that wad staw a sow,
Or *fricassee* wad mak her spew
        Wi' perfect sconner,
Looks down wi' sneering, scornfu' view
        On sic a dinner?

Poor devil! see him owre his trash,
As feckless as a wither'd rash,
His spindle shank a guid whip-lash,
        His nieve a nit;
Thro' bluidy flood or field to dash,
        O how unfit!

But mark the Rustic, *haggis-fed*,
The trembling earth resounds his tread,

Clap in his walie nieve a blade,
　　He'll mak it whissle;
An' legs, an' arms, an' heads will sned;
　　Like taps o' thrissle.

Ye Pow'rs wha mak mankind your care,
And dish them out their bill o' fare,
Auld Scotland wants nae skinking ware
　　That jaups in luggies;
But, if ye wish her gratefu' pray'r,
　　Gie her a *Haggis*![36]

The approved way of cutting the piping hot haggis is to make a St Andrews Cross, pulling back the flaps, to make serving the haggis – a pudding made of heart, liver, lights of sheep or calf, minced suet, onions, oatmeal, seasoned and then boiled in the animal's stomach – easier. Subsequent courses lack such traditional ritual, indicative of the early centrality of the haggis, but on the menu at least other dishes are often Scotticised or nationalised if only in name: the main course might feature Roastit Bubbly Jock wi chappit Tatties and Bashed Neeps and Sproots; the sweet, Edinburgh Syllabubs; and finally Oat Bannocks an' a wee bit o' the Kebbock. And for most participants, the meal and later the toasts are accompanied with generous amounts of whisky. The meal and first part of the programme are frequently concluded with the Toast to the Queen.

After a suitable interval, the celebration continues with speeches and toasts, chiefly to the Immortal Memory of Burns and to the Lasses as well as several other toasts deemed appropriate, interspersed with the singing of Burns' songs and recitations of his poems. The Speech and Toast to the Immortal Memory is the principal element of the second half of the programme and may be preceded by solo or unison singing of Burns' semi-autobiographical song, 'There was a lad', quoted earlier (see Chapter 5). Expected to praise Burns, the Immortal Memory usually does so following earlier examples; the content here is largely serious and its essential points are summarised and pointed out in the Appreciation, the reply which follows. The other set speech and toast takes second place, of course, to the Immortal Memory. 'To the Lasses' is often preceded or followed by solo or unison singing of a song in which the lasses figure prominently, like 'Green grow the Rashes. A Fragment'—

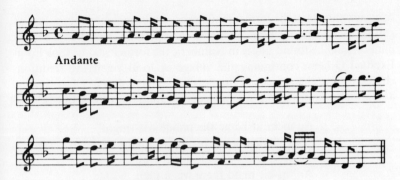

Andante

There's nought but care on ev'ry han',
    In ev'ry hour that passes, O:
What signifies the life o' man,
    An' 'twere na for the lasses, O.

Green grow the rashes, O;
Green grow the rashes, O;
The sweetest hours that e'er I spend,
Are spent among the lasses, O.

The warly race may riches chase,
    An' riches still may fly them, O;
An' tho' at last they catch them fast,
    Their hearts can ne'er enjoy them, O.

But gie me a canny hour at e'en,
    My arms about my Dearie, O;
An' warly cares, an' warly men,
    May a' gae tapsalteerie, O!

For you sae douse, ye sneer at this,
    Ye're nought but senseless asses, O:
The wisest Man the warl' saw,
    He dearly lov'd the lasses, O.

Auld Nature swears, the lovely Dears
    Her noblest work she classes, O:
Her prentice han' she try'd on man,
    An' then she made the lasses, O.[37]

Here the content is lighter, more comic, with frequent topical allusion –
recently to Women's Liberation – and jokes such as the one about two

bachelor ministers: the former minister asked the incumbent how he was getting along with his new congregation, especially the ladies. The new minister said he found safety in Numbers, the former said he took his in Exodus! Others, continuing the village or local versifying tradition, choose to give their toasts in rhyme, often referring to familiar persons and esoteric information, maybe incorporating lines from Burns.

> Ae nicht at hame the phone wis ringin'
> Afor it wis din my lugs were ringlin'
> Ye see it wis oor auld freen Dan,
> An' in his mind there wis a plan,
> says he, could you just toast the lassies,
> remember noo its no the Haggis.

> Fair fa yer honest sonsie face,
> May no be that sae oot a' place,
> Bit a'll no be that o'er hastie,
> Wi' Sleekit cow'rin tim'rous beastie.[38]

Interspersed between the two principal toasts, the Appreciation, the Reply to the Lasses, and the thanks to the Artists, organisers, and so on near the conclusion, are the performances of various songs and recitations. The centrality and essentiality of songs in the Burns Suppers pay tribute to the long recognition and appreciation of his tune/text complexes by the general public. Burns' songs most frequently heard, in addition to 'There was a lad' and 'Green Grow the Rashes' are 'Duncan Gray', 'Ae fond Kiss', 'Scots wha hae' – associated with the military – and 'Bonnie Lass o Ballochmyle'. Additionally, some groups include the singing, often by the assembled company, of songs about Burns, typically the 'Star o' Rabbie Burns'–

> There is a star whose beaming ray,
> Is shed on every clime.
> It shines by night, it shines by day,
> And ne'er grows dim, wi' time.

> It rose upon the banks o' Ayr;
> It shone on Doon's clear stream.
> A hundred years are gaen an maer,
> Yet brighter grows its beam.

> Let kings and courtiers rise an' fa',
> This world has mony turns,

But brightly beams abun them a'
The star o' Rabbie Burns.

'Tho' he was but a plo'ghman lad,
And wore the hodden grey;
Auld Scotia's bard was bred
Aneath a roof o' Strae.

Tae sweep the strings o' Scotia's Lyre,
It needs nae classic clore,
Its mither wit, and native fire
That warms the bosom's core.[39]

Recitations of especially selected poems – memorised and presented with considerable verve – are also typical. Here 'Tam o' Shanter' leads the list by far. The conclusion of the celebration is universally marked by the singing, in concert by the assembled company, of 'Auld lang syne'.

Should auld acquaintance be forgot
And never brought to mind?
Should auld acquaintance be forgot,
And auld lang syne!

For auld lang syne, my jo,
For auld lang syne,
We'll tak a cup o' kindness yet
For auld lang syne.

And surely ye'll be your pint stowp!
And surely I'll be mine!
And we'll tak a cup o' kindness yet,
For auld lang syne.

> We twa hae run about the braes,
>   And pou'd the gowans fine;
> But we've wander'd mony a weary fitt,
>   Sin auld lang syne.
>
> We twa hae paidl'd in the burn,
>   Frae morning sun till dine;
> But seas between us braid hae roar'd,
>   Sin auld lang syne.
>
> And there's a hand, my trusty fiere!
>   And gie's a hand o' thine!
> And we'll tak a right gude-willie-waught,
>   'For auld lang syne.[40]

Standing in a circle, usually holding hands, at the final verse individuals cross arms, holding hands with the persons on each side, and move their intertwined arms rhythmically up and down – thus contracting the circle and drawing all individuals closer together. This action concludes the Stabilised celebration, which has taken elements from earlier stages and moulded them to create a generally recognised pattern, adhered to, to greater or lesser extent, by most contemporary Burns Suppers.

From their earliest form to the contemporary pattern, the Burns Suppers have moved from a simple, memorial gathering of Burns' friends to a broader based celebration of individuals drawn together not merely to recall Burns but also to honour the Scotland he represents and for which he is spokesman. The singing of songs he wrote and edited as Scotland's poet, the eating of national fare, as well as listening to repeated themes, drawn from the legendary tradition, in the Immortal Memory exemplify this. But the Burns Suppers may do more for the participants than providing a night of entertainment, or supporting a generalised kind of nationalism, or fostering a nostalgic and romantic longing for the homeland when away from Scotland.

In essence the Burns Suppers are a multigeneric celebration incorporating foodways, customs, recitations, songs, not to mention the folk speech exemplified by commonplaces and maxims. And these genres are roughly structured into participatory and performance modes. The initial act of the formal structure centres on the meal, itself communal and participatory; but certain aspects of the meal are clearly performance-oriented: the grace, the piping in and address to the haggis. The primary feel of this portion of the event is obviously participatory as individuals in concert share a meal of Scottish or Scottish-esque fare. The shared Burns Supper meal not only offers a direct connection with Burns in that it includes the food he ate but it also unites the participants in its national cuisine; thus they may all symbolically partake of Scotland and her strength, renewing their own patriotism – through the food and Burns.

The second portion of the event, the performances, creates a distance between the audience and the performers who, previously, have shared the meal. The toasts and speeches, the performance of songs, and the recitation of poems are all definitely distanced from the mass of persons – usually by being delivered from the head table or from an area set aside as a stage. Occasional participatory action occurs in the response to the toasts and in the infrequent unison singing of Burns' own songs, but the thrust is performance and the spatial relationship is distance. The final act of the Burns Suppers, the communal singing of 'Auld lang syne', returns to the participatory mode which essentially frames the entire event, stressing solidarity, friendship, and unity of all, either through Burns or through Scotland or both.

One of the primary functions of the Burns Supper is thus communal and participatory, drawing together persons who recollect Burns through the shared common meal and reassert their belonging – no matter how far removed – to Scotland. Friendship and kinship draw the participants together in the name of Burns and Scotland and the convivial mood of the occasion leaves no one out. This air of belonging, indicated by the participatory emphasis of the event, may expand beyond the confines of the event itself: one belongs not only there but with Burns, a man of humble origins who achieved much, but never economically; a man of vast humanity – respecting others and allowing them the same latitude he allowed himself. It is possible that individuals affirm and see themselves in and through Burns. They – like him – can dream of infinite possibilities. Not only do participants belong at this particular event, but they belong to the race of men like Burns *and* to the Scotland which produced him and by extension them. Thus, in coming together to honour Burns, they honour themselves and Scotland and their participation in the Burns Supper may cement their relationship with both.

The Burns Suppers have developed as Burns did, beginning first at the local level and finally achieving national significance. As a calendar custom, they unite all aspects of Burns – his poems and songs, some of which were inspired by the traditional life he knew and experienced, and the legendary traditions about him, whether accounts of personal encounters with him or legends or jokes and anecdotes. Over time, these various elements have themselves been ritualised into an event which is surely the most dynamic and vital monument there is to Robert Burns.

7 Burns Today

Rabbie Burns was born in Ayr,
Noo he stauns in George's Square.
If you waant to see him there,
Tak the tram an pey yer fare.

Rhyme, learned by 'a Glasgow man' from his father

Robert Burns achieved recognition because he was a poet and songwright, but also because he was a distinct individual, a man whose own rise from obscurity gave and still gives hope to countless individuals that they too might succeed. Burns' very human traits have been stressed – traits which identify him as an ordinary human being; these characteristics are significant only because implicitly it is known that Burns became something set apart from the mass of men. The intensity of personal identification with Burns is significant: thought of as a friend, he has been referred to familiarly as Rab or Rabbie; he was relatively poor; he was not formally educated; he resisted constricting forms of authority, especially that of the church; he got into a number of difficult interpersonal situations. Burns, like those who recall him, was human, sometimes only too human. But, unlike the majority, Burns achieved fame and acclaim. In a sense he served and still serves for some as an implicit model or ideal: if he who was so like everyone else, was so human, could succeed, then potentially every man can. Identification with Burns may enable a kind of individual affirmation. It is significant that knowledge of Burns is today essentially an adult matter; as a model, he may become important only when one reaches maturity and recognises one's human limitations. Implicit identification with Burns may provide the hope for potential success which is necessary to balance a realistic assessment of oneself. The model of Burns has thus played a significant social role; by allowing identification, the model both affirms an individual's potential and counters the sometimes overwhelmingly unproductive admission of one's shortcomings and limited expectations.

On another level too, Burns as a model has been significant; by the mid- to late nineteenth century, Burns had become a symbol for Scotland. As interest in and knowledge of Burns spread beyond the region of his birth and life into the rest of Scots-speaking Scotland, the dual quality of Burns, expressed primarily in legend form, as ordinary and extraordinary, became a metaphor for Scotland; as Burns rose above his station so might Scotland, a nation practically absorbed by England with the Union of the Parliaments in 1707. Just as identification with Burns on an individual level may unconsciously affirm the status quo while holding out potential for something else, for success, identification of Burns with Scotland both accepts the present and fosters futurity – a future perhaps when Scotland may rise above the ordinary reality, becoming again a distinct and separate country. This identification of Burns with Scotland was probably first evidenced in the Burns Suppers when the national foods became an important part of the ritual honouring Burns. By extension, he became a representative Scot, a national as well as an individual model. This rise to symbolic significance probably reached its highest form in and after 1859 when thousands of celebrations were held throughout Scotland to mark the centenary of Burns' birth. At that point Burns as a symbol for Scotland had its broadest acceptance. Since that day, Burns' acceptance as a national symbol in the purest sense has diminished; however, he continues to be used as a symbol for Scotland in literary works, but especially in advertising and tourism. These uses, together with the generic shift to jokes and anecdotes, have lessened his power as a political and national symbol of the nation, still submerged, but continue to show his status as a cultural symbol with considerable economic importance.

The conscious and unconscious cultural evidences of Burns' pervasive influence are manifold. The often unrecognised conversational allusions to lines from his poems and songs indicate a culture imbued with his influence and accepting, at least in part, his sentiments. Statues of Burns pay tribute to his memory. Such public, as well as commercial and literary, uses of his name and person present explicit recognition of his symbolic power and are found both within and without Scotland.

Public recognition of Burns is best exemplified by the Clyesdale Bank's £5 note which depicts Burns on one side, with quill pen in hand, and on the other an appealing mouse, pictorially alluding to that 'wee, sleeket, cowran, tim'rous *beastie*', immortalised in the poem 'To a

Mouse, On turning her up in her Nest, with the Plough, November, 1785'. And Her Majesty's Postal Service pays tribute to Burns in one of a series of illustrated aerogrammes which shows 'Rabbie Burns' on the front panel, *the* mouse again on the end panel, and a full interior panel depicting the witches' reaching for Tam as he crosses the Brig o' Doon to safety, a picture which celebrates that famous scene from 'Tam o' Shanter'. For completeness, quotations from various Burns' pieces are printed opposite standard aerogramme directions: for example, adjacent to the advice 'To open slit here' is the appropriate, but out of context, directive, 'An' cut you up wi' ready slight' from 'To a Haggis'.

Advertising, too, has recognised the value of Burns as a promotional gimmick: Drybrough Brewery encourages drinking its Burns Extra Special by using a colourful cardboard beermat bearing the slogan, 'Make Tonight Burns Night', on one side and lines from 'Tam o' Shanter' on the other. A bakery firm urges a substitute for haggis in Haggis Pies, described as Burns described a real haggis, as 'abune them a'.[1]

Commercial uses of Burns, frequently for tourist consumption, abound – making Burns, through mass-produced artifacts, easily one of Scotland's most dominant exportable items. There are gaily coloured tea towels depicting scenes from Burns' life or sporting texts of his poems, and trivets bearing the Selkirk Grace as a silent invocation of thanks should a vocal blessing not be rendered. Ball-point pens with Burns' head, name, and birth and death dates are inexpensive and potentially useful. Pincushions in the form of his 'mouse', decked out in tartan, are perhaps less functional though equally representative of the commercial appeal of anything remotely reminiscent of the Bard. Coffee mugs depicting scenes from 'Tam o' Shanter' are a recent and attractive introduction. Less functional, but perhaps more instructive, are the heavy paper cutouts of his birthplace to be cut and pasted to create a mini replica.

Evenings of Burns' songs and performances of his poems in public readings occur throughout the peak tourist period. Most of these events are attended by many Scots, indicative of the insatiable appetite many have for Burns and Burns' related occurrences. The re-enactment of Tam o' Shanter's wild ride across the Brig o' Doon is a yearly event in Ayr. More private and serious commemorations of Burns by the Burns Federation Clubs pay tribute to his lasting literary and cultural significance and include the laying of wreaths beneath his statue in Ayr on the Sunday nearest the date of his death, 21 July 1796. The list of such contemporary references to Burns, both explicit and implicit, could go on indefinitely.

One of the most widespread uses of Burns, sometimes directly stated and at others only allusive, is in works of literature. Not all references are positive: Hugh MacDiarmid, for example recognised Burns' symbolic power while questioning its contemporary relevance:

> A' *they've* to say was aften said afore
> A lad was born in Kyle to blaw aboot.
> What unco fate mak's *him* the dumpin'-grun'
> For a' the sloppy rubbish they jaw oot?[2]

MacDiarmid and others of the contemporary literati have voiced extreme distaste – as this quotation illustrates – for the so-called Cult of Burns, for people to whom Burns remains very much alive as a man, for people who yearly recall his memory and participate in the continuation of the traditions about him. In general, however, various works of literature depict Burns and use his poetry and songs in ways similar to those already discussed, showing artistic recognition of the Burns of tradition: the legendary tradition is alluded to; lines from his poems and songs are referred to; and his works are recited. Nowhere is this more obvious than in Lewis Grassic Gibbon's *A Scots Quair*, particularly in the second book *Cloud Howe:* the Provost Hairy Hogg claimed descent from the Burns family and one character, Ake Ogilvie, a joiner, 'thought himself maybe a second Robert Burns'.[3] The Provost asserted Burns' patriotism – he was 'aye ready to shed his blood for the land' – while Ogilvie rejoined, '*Ay. He slew a fell lot of the French – with his mouth. He was better at raping a servant quean than facing the enemy with a musket*'.[4] Here Ogilvie concludes by referring to the widespread tradition of Burns' way with women. Elsewhere Gibbon has Ogilvie tell the story, reported from current oral tradition in Chapter 5, about Burns' arrival in heaven:

> Well, the creature died and he went to heaven and knocked like hell on the pearly gates. And St. Peter poked his head from a wicket, and asked *Who're you that's making a din*? And Burns said *I'm Robert Burns, my man, the National Poet of Scotland, that's who*. St. Peter took a look at the orders, pinned on the guard-room wall for the day; and he said, *I've got a note about you. You must wait outbye for a minute or so*. So Robbie sat there cooling his heels, on the top of the draughty stair to heaven, and waited and waited till he nearly was froze; syne the gates at last opened and he was let in. And Burns was fair in a rage by then, *Do you treat distinguished arrivals like this*? And

> St. Peter said *No, I wouldn't say that. But then I had special orders*
> *about you. I've been hiding the Virgin Mary away.*[5]

Jane Austen's late and unfinished novel, *Sandition*, probably alludes to
Burns' interest in women when she has the model Charlotte Heywood
respond to superficial Sir Edward's admiration of Burns by saying that,
unlike Edward, she cannot separate a 'Man's Poetry entirely from his
Character; and poor Burns's known Irregularities, greatly interrupt my
enjoyment of his Lines'.[6]

Burns' poetry and songs are not without reference in literary works:
George Douglas Brown has his Burnsomaniac Baker support
Gourlay's walking outside the village by the line from 'To William
Simson, Ochiltree':

> ⋅ The Muse nae poet ever fand her,
>   Till by himsel he learned to wander,
>   Adown some trottin burn's meander,
>   And no thick lang;
>   O sweet, to muse and pensive ponder
>   A heartfelt sang.[7]

And in Gibbon's *Sunset Song* and in *Grey Granite*, the first and final
volumes of *A Scots Quair*, 'Auld lang syne' is used as a leavetaking song:
at the end of a wedding they 'struck up the sugary surge of *Auld Lang
Syne* and they all joined hands and stood in a circle to sing it'[8] and to
conclude a New Year's Eve celebration – *'Join hands – here's New Year*:

> And here's a hand, my trusty frere,
> And here's a hand o' mine –'[9]

Within various literary works, Burns' poetry and songs are performed.
In *The House with the Green Shutters*, young John Gourlay thinks of his
favourite howff when he should have been studying, wondering, 'Will
Logan be singing "Tam Glen"?'[10] And Gibbon has Chris sing 'The Lass
that Made the Bed to Me –' at her wedding and averts the stuttering
Pooty's performance when 'he woke up then, fell keen to recite his
TIMROUS BEASTIE'.[11] All of these literary references to Burns show
his integral and perhaps sustaining role in Scots culture.

Born in 1759 to humble circumstances, he has by now touched many
through the lines he wrote or the life he lived. It is not only in Scotland
that Burns is remembered: his is a wider world. The Russians have

capitalised on his egalitarian premises, the Japanese and the Germans have found other reasons for interest. Individuals too have recognised a friend in Burns; Woody Guthrie's poem 'To That Man Robert Burns' exemplifies the easy identification many feel and have felt with Burns:

Dear Robert Burns,
You skipped the big town streets just like I done,
   you ducked the crosstown cop just like I ducked,
   you dodged behind a beanpole to beat the bigtime
   dick and you very seldom stopped off in any big
   city where the rigged corn wasn't drying nor the
   hot vine didn't help you do your talking.
Your talking was factual figures of the biggest sort,
   though. Your talking had the graphboard and the
   chart and had something else most singers seem to miss,
   the very kiss of warm dew on the stalk.
Your words turned into songs and floated upstream and then
   turned into rains and drifted down and lodged and swung
   and clung to drifts of driftwood to warm and heat and
   fertilize new seeds. Your words were of the upheath and
   the down, your words were more from heather than from
   town. Your thoughts came more from weather than from
   schoolroom and more from shifting vines than from the
   book. . . . .
   . . . .
I bought your little four-inch square book while I was a
   torpedoed seaman walking around over your clods and
   sods of Glasgow and the little book says on the outer
   cover, Fifty Songs of Burns, the price, 4d, and I read
   from page to page and found you covered a woman on
   every page. I thought as I picked the book up here at
   home that maybe the book had ought to have some kind of
   new name. Like, Fifty Pages Fifty Women, enlarged upon
   by Robert Burns . . . .
   . . . .
I'll keep you posted and brought up to date as the year
   leafs out and me and Marjorie have more kids of the kinds
   you missed out on.[12]

It seems almost extraordinary that a man born in Alloway should still be remembered at far distant parts of the earth, tempting one to say that Burns is not Scotland's but the world's. But, of course, he does belong to

Scotland and it is there that memory of his poetry and songs and recollection of his life and personality are most integral, linking the people with the past and uniting some in the present through celebration of him. Robert Burns *is* remembered: he continues to have symbolic power, being a pre-eminent export and revered native. For many, he is still a representative Scot. And that is how it should be. He came from the people, shared their traditions, used them in his work, recognised their importance to Scottish culture, and sought to speak for his fellow Scots. He succeeded so well that his own poems and songs were accepted by the people; some circulated orally; and he – as a figure – became over time the symbol for what was most valued. Robert Burns has served Scotland well – as man and poet.

Notes

1. August Angellier in *Robert Burns, La Vie, Les Oeuvres*, 2 vols (Paris, 1983) pointed to this when he said: 'But underneath this scholarly poetry there existed a popular poetry which was very abundant, very vigorous, very racy and very original'. See especially p. 14 of Jane Burgoyne's selected translation from Angellier in the *Burns Chronicle and Club Directory*, 1969. Other portions of the translation appeared in 1970, 1971, 1972, 1973.
2. J. De Lancey Ferguson (ed.) *The Letters of Robert Burns*, 2 vols (Oxford: Clarendon Press, 1931), 1: 106, no. 125. Burns adopted a superior tone here in keeping with the accepted pose of the eighteenth-century man of letters. All references to Burns' letters are to Ferguson's edition. Only letter numbers will be given when the citation appears in the text proper.
3. Most critics and students of Burns take some stance towards his relationship with previous work. Hans Hecht, *Robert Burns: The Man and His Work*, 2nd rev. ed. (London: William Hodge & Company, 1950), p. 29, suggests that Burns was the culmination of a tradition, but he speaks of a literary rather than a cultural inheritance.
4. See T. S. Eliot, *The Sacred Wood* (London: Methuen, 1950), pp. 47–59.
5. Angellier earlier suggested this division and I agree with him that Burns' work prior to Edinburgh was dominated by depiction of the world around him. After Edinburgh, Angellier indicates that Burns relied less on the specific incidents and more on general sentiments. I concur again but the significance of this move to generality is in Burns' nationalism.
6. Hecht, *Robert Burns*, p. 86 discusses the Kilmarnock poems as *Heimatkunst*.
7. For an example of Hugh MacDiarmid's view of Burns, see *Burns Today and Tomorrow* (Edinburgh: Castle Wynd Printers, 1959).
8. See John Strawhorn, 'Burns and the Bardie Clan', *Scottish Literary Journal*, 8 (1981): 5–23 for a discussion of fellow poets.
9. No. 180 'On scaring some Water-Fowl in Loch-Turit, a wild scene among the Hills of Oughtertyre' is said to have been read one evening after supper. See Robert Chambers and William Wallace (eds), *The Life and Works of Robert Burns*, 4 vols (New York: Longmans, Green, and Co., 1896), 2: 193. W. E. Henley and T. F. Henderson (eds), *The Poetry of Robert Burns*, 4 vols (Edinburgh: T. C. and E. C. Jack, 1896–7) mention several additional instances: see, for example, 1:328.
10. All references to Burns' work are to James Kinsley (ed.), *The Poems and Songs of Robert Burns*, 3 vols (Oxford: Clarendon Press, 1968). Item numbers will be given hereafter in the text. 'The Ordination' is no. 85.

11. See for example 'The Banks of Nith' (no. 229) and Burns' comment in Ferguson, *Letters*, no. 265, that it was composed as he jogged along the bank.
12. James Cameron Ewing and Davidson Cook (eds), *Robert Burns's Commonplace Book 1783–1785* (Carbondale, Illinois: Southern Illinois University Press, 1965), p. 39. In describing the inspiration for his fragment 'Altho' my bed were in you muir' (Kinsley, *Poems and Songs*, no. 22) said to be an imitation of 'a noble old Scottish Piece called McMillan's Peggy', Burns comments: 'I have even tryed to imitate, in this extempore thing, that irregularity in the rhyme which, when judiciously done, has such a fine effect on the ear. –'
13. 'Worth gaun a mile to see' is from 'The Humble Petition of Bruar Water to the Noble Duke of Athole', Kinsley, *Poems and Songs*, no. 172.
14. See 'For lake o'' from '[Lines written on a Bank-note]', ibid., no. 106.
15. See the general work on this subject by Albert Lord, *The Singer of Tales* (New York: Atheneum, 1971) and a book which presents specific application of this theory to the Scottish scene, David Buchan's *The Ballad and the Folk* (London: Routledge & Kegan Paul, 1972).
16. Ewing and Cook, *Commonplace Book*, p. 42.
17. See Kinsley, *Poems and Songs*, no. 208 – 'Musing on the roaring Ocean'.
18. Ibid., no. 306, 'The White Cockade'.
19. Ibid., no. 391, 'Here's a Health to them that's awa'.
20. It is perhaps interesting to note that this Jacobite verse is written in standard, literary English, indicative of the broad popularity of this theme.
21. For other examples, see Kinsley, *Poems and Songs*, nos 3 'I dream'd I lay', 10 'Winter, A Dirge', 66 'The Braes o' Ballochmyle', 138 'Again rejoicing Nature sees', 218 'The Winter it is Past', 316 'Lament of Mary Queen of Scots on the Approach of Spring', 336 'Gloomy December'.
22. Ferguson, *Letters*, no. 164.
23. Kinsley, *Poems and Songs*, nos 144 'On Fergusson', 160 'On the death of Sir J. Hunter Blair', 186 'On the death of the late Lord President Dundas', 233 'A Mother's Lament for the loss of her only Son', 238 'Sketch for an Elegy', 334 'Lament for James, Earl of Glencairn', 445 'Sonnet, on the Death of Robert Riddel, Esq.'
24. Ibid., no. 235 'Whistle o'er the lave o't'.
25. Ibid., no. 72 'The Cotter's Saturday Night' and also no. 71 'The Twa Dogs. A Tale'.
26. Ibid., no. 451 'Ode for General Washington's Birthday' and no. 625 'The Tree of Liberty.'
27. Ibid., no. 44 – 'A fragment – When first I came to Stewart Kyle'.
28. Ibid., no. 11, 'On Cessnock banks a lassie dwells'.
29. Ibid., no. 81, 'The Author's Earnest Cry and Prayer, to the Right Honorable and Honorable, the Scotch Representatives in the House of Commons'.
30. Ibid., no. 90, 'Letter to J—s T—t, GL—nc—r'.
31. Ibid., no. 105, 'Epistle to a Young Friend'.
32. Ibid., no. 216, 'Rattlin, roarin Willie'.
33. Ibid., no. 136, 'To a Haggis'.
34. Ibid., no. 119B, 'Robert Burns' Answer' to 'Epistle from a Taylor to *Robert Burns*'.

35. Ibid., no. 54, 'Epitaph on Holy Willie'.
36. Ibid., no. 55, 'Death and Doctor Hornbook. A True Story'.
37. Ibid., no. 120, 'The Brigs of Ayr, a Poem. Inscribed to J. B.*********, Esq; Ayr'.
38. Ibid., no. 71, 'The Twa Dogs. A Tale'.
39. Hecht, *Robert Burns*, p. 217 says, 'Burns's lyric poetry . . . clings to the clear realism of its chief sources: the Scottish popular and traditional songs'.
40. See as example Marjorie Plant, *The Domestic Life of Scotland in the Eighteenth Century* (1899; reprint ed., London: Adam & Charles Black, 1969).
41. I include Kinsley, *Poems and Songs*, nos 40 'The Ronalds of the Bennals', 57 'Epistle to J. L*****k, An Old Scotch Bard', 67 'Third Epistle to J. Lapraik', 70 'The Holy Fair', 71 'The Twa Dogs. A Tale', 72 'The Cotter's Saturday Night', 73 'Halloween', 74 'The Mauchline Wedding', 75 'The Auld Farmer's New-year-morning Salutation to his Auld Mare, Maggie', 76 'Address to the Deil', 77 'Scotch Drink', 79 'To J. S****', 86 'The Inventory', 102 'To Mr Gavin Hamilton, Mauchline', 136 'To a Haggis', 140 'There was a lad', 236 'Tam Glen', 244 'Versicles on Sign-posts', 321 'Tam o' Shanter. A Tale', 514 'Poem, Addressed to Mr. Mitchell, Collector of Excise'.
42. Ferguson, *Letters*, no. 13.
43. Ibid., no. 10.
44. Eve Blantyre Simpson, *Folk Lore in Lowland Scotland* (London: J. M. Dent, 1908), p. 14.
45. William Grant Stewart, *The Popular Superstitions and Festive Amusements of the Highlanders of Scotland* (1851: reprint ed., Hatboro, Pennsylvania: Norwood Editions, 1974), p. 161.
46. M. Macleod Banks, *British Calendar Customs: Scotland*, 3 vols (London: William Glaisher, 1937, 1939, 1941), 3: 122–4.
47. Kinsley, *Poems and Songs*, 1: 153–4.
48. See H. G. Graham, *The Social Life of Scotland in the Eighteenth Century*, 5th ed. (London: Adam & Charles Black, 1969), p. 336.
49. See Plant, *Domestic Life*, pp. 97–8.
50. R. H. Cromek, *Remains of Nithsdale and Galloway Song* (Paisley: Alexander Gardner, 1880), p. 212.
51. James Ballantine (comp. and ed.), *Chronicle of the Hundredth Birthday of Robert Burns* (Edinburgh: A. Fullarton & Co., 1859), pp. 70–1.
52. John D. Ross, *Burnsiana*, 5 vols (Paisley: Alexander Gardner, 1892), 1: 23–4.
53. See also, Kinsley, *Poems and Songs*, nos 28 'On Ja^s Grieve, Laird of Boghead, Tarbolton', 28A 'On an Innkeeper in Tarbolton', 97 'Epigram on said Occasion', 98 'Another', 146 'To M^r E——on his translation of Martial', 158 'At Roslin Inn', 159 'Epigram', 237 'To the beautiful Miss Eliza J——n', 256 'Lines written in the Kirk of Lamington', 323 'Epigram on Capt. Francis Grose, The Celebrated Antiquary', 329 'On Mr. James Gracie', 410 'On being asked why God had made Miss D—— so little and M^{rs} A—— so big', 411A 'On Maxwell of Cardoness', 411 B 'Extempore – On being shown a beautiful Country seat belonging to the same', 415 'Epigrams on Lord Galloway', 417 'On J–hn M–r–ne, laird of

L–gg–n', 426 'To Maria – Epigram – On Lord Buchan's assertion', 433 'On Captn W——R–dd–ck of C–rb–ton', 440 'On seeing Miss Fontenelle in a Favourite Character', 448 'Pinned to M^{rs} R——'s carriage', 449 'In answer to one who affirmed of D^{r} B——, that there was Falsehood in his very looks', 450 'Extempore', 455 'To Dr Maxwell, on Miss Jessy Staig's recovery', 463 'On seeing Mrs Kemble in Yarico', 464 'To the Honble Mr R. M——, of P–nm–re', 473–9 'Dumfries Epigrams', 480 'On Chloris requesting me to give her a spray of a sloe–thorn in full blosson', 487 'On Miss J. Scott, of Ayr', 511 'On Mr Pit's hair-powder tax', 512 'The Solemn League and Covenant', 519–22 'On Jessy Lewars', 523 'To a Young Lady, Miss Jessy L——, with Books', 546 'On John M'Murdo', 547 'On Gabriel Richardson', 548 'On Commissary Goldie's Brains', 552 'On Andrew Turner', 616 'The Book-Worms', 629 'Epigram on Rough Roads'.

54. Ibid., nos 31 'Epitaph on Wm Muir in Tarbolton Miln', 32 'Epitaph On a Celebrated Ruling Elder', 33 'On a Noisy Polemic', 34 'On Wee Johnie', 35 'For the Author's Father', 36 'For R. A. Esq.,' 37 'For G. H. Esq.', 50 'Lines, Wrote by Burns, while on his death-bed', 54 'Epitaph on Holy Willie', 56 'On Tam the Chapman', 76 'Address to the Deil', 104 'A Bard's Epitaph', 110 'Epitaph on John Dove, Innkeeper, Mauchline', 111 'Epitaph on a Wag in Mauchline', 117 'Tam Samson's Elegy', 142 'Epitaph. Here lies Robert Fergusson, Poet', 167 'On a Schoolmaster in Cleish Parish, Fifeshire', 184 'Epitaph for William Nicol', 221 'Epitaph on R. Muir', 239 'Elegy on Capt^{t} M—— H——', 241 'Epitaph for J. H. Writer in Ayr', 416 'On the death of Echo, a Lap-dog', 443 'Monody on Maria', 446 'On Robert Riddel', 452 'On W. R——, Esq.', 490 'Elegy on Mr William Cruikshank A.M.', 541 'Epitaph on Mr. Burton', 542 'Epitaph on D—— C——', 543 'Epitaph Extempore, On a person nicknamed the Marquis', 544 'Epitaph on J–hn B–shby', 606 'Epitaph for H—— L——, Esq., of L——', 623 'Epitaph', 631 'To the Memory of the Unfortunate Miss Burns'.
55. Peter Giles, 'Dialect in Literature', in *The Scottish Tongue*, ed. W. A. Craigie (1924; reprint ed., College Park, Maryland: McGrath Publishing Co., 1970), p. 118.
56. Hecht, *Robert Burns*, p. 88.
57. David Daiches, *The Paradox of Scottish Culture: The Eighteenth-Century Experience* (London: Oxford University Press, 1964).
58. Edward Eggleston, *The Mystery of Metropolisville* (New York: Orange Judd and Co., 1873), p. 116. I am indebted to Chris Chauvette for this reference which came out of her term study of the folklore used by Edward Eggleston in his best known work *The Hoosier School-Master* and other lesser known works, such as the novel quoted from here.
59. Robert Dewar, *Burns: Poetry and Prose* (Oxford: Claredon Press, 1929), pp. xvii–xviii.
60. Christine Keith, *The Russet Coat* (1956; reprint ed., New York: Haskell House, 1971), p. 39.
61. Thomas Crawford, *Burns: A Study of the Poems and Songs* (Edinburgh: Oliver Boyd, 1960), p. 130.
62. See David Herd, *Ancient & Modern Scottish Songs*, 2 vols (1869; reprint ed., Edinburgh: Scottish Academic Press, 1973), 2: 207 for a traditional version.
63. Ibid., 2: 32.

1. J. De Lancey Ferguson (ed.), *The Letters of Robert Burns*, 2 vols (Oxford: Clarendon Press, 1931), 1:14, no. 13. This appears in a letter to Burns' former teacher John Murdoch describing Burns' general activities and responses, before the publication of his first volume of poems some three years later.
2. The Prefaces to volumes 2, 3, 4 are undoubtedly by Burns. And the notes written on the pages of songs sent to Johnson by Burns and preserved in the Hastie Manuscript (British Library, Additional MS. 22307) enlarge the view of Burns as editor: for example, to item 19 'Tune, Niel Gow's lamentation for the death of his brother' Burns adds: 'Note – it will be proper to omit the name of the tune altogether, & only say – "A Gaelic Air" '. In the Hastie Manuscript there are at least forty-six directions of this kind out of approximately one hundred and forty-eight items in Burns' hand.
3. Examples of prods and directions to Johnson can be seen in Ferguson, *Letters*, nos. 452 and 513.
4. Ibid., 2: 118, no. 506.
5. Ibid., no. 644. Later, when Burns felt they had used all the Scottish tunes, he suggested and finally included tunes from the related Irish tradition.
6. Ibid., 1: 275, no. 288. Burns' own conception of the *Museum*, too, was a patriotic one. See also the Prefaces to the 3rd and 4th volumes of the *Museum*.
7. Robert Burns, *Notes on Scottish Song* in *The Songs of Robert Burns* and *Notes on Scottish Songs by Robert Burns* (ed.), James C. Dick (1903 and 1908; reprint ed., Hatboro, Pennsylvania: Folklore Associates, 1962), p. 24, no. 103. Unless otherwise indicated, references to Dick in the text will refer to *Notes on Scottish Songs by Robert Burns* and item numbers will be given.
8. Because Burns so consistently associated his own words with pre-existent tunes, Dick in the Preface to *The Songs of Robert Burns* calls him a 'tone-poet', p. v.
9. Ferguson, *Letters*, nos. 145, 193, 203, 598 are examples of this written collecting technique.
10. Dick, *The Songs of Robert Burns*, Preface, xi.
11. See Ferguson, *Letters*, 2: 180, no. 568 ('There was a lass, & she was fair'); 2: 266, no. 644 ('The Posie'); Dick, *Notes on Scottish Songs*, p. 54, no. 308 ('A Southland Jenny that was right bonie') for examples. From Dick, p. 37, no. 188 we additionally discover that 'this edition of the song ("Up and warn a' Willie") I got from Tom Niel of facetious fame in Edin!'. And in Ferguson, *Letters*, 2: 255, no. 636 he says that he collected 'Ca' the yowes to the knowes' from a clergyman, a Mr. Clunzie.
12. Ferguson, *Letters*, 1: 257, no. 272.
13. These latter two are included in Dick's *The Songs of Robert Burns* and *Notes on Scottish Songs by Robert Burns*. The latter, appended to the book, was edited by Davidson Cook and was first published in the *Burns Chronicle & Club Directory*, 31 (January, 1922). Any quotations, however, are from the original manuscript which will be referred to as Excise because it is written on Excise paper. Cook's edition is not entirely accurate.
14. Ferguson, *Letters*, 2: 257, no. 637. Stephen Clarke was the musical

collaborator of Burns for the *Museum* and on numerous occasions he
transcribed tunes for Burns. But there is every indication that when he was
not available – he lived in Edinburgh and Burns in or near Dumfries during
most of the collaboration – Burns was capable of notating the melodic line
himself.

15. William Stenhouse, *Illustrations of the Lyric Poetry and Music in Scotland*
   (Edinburgh: William Blackwood and Sons, 1853). Stenhouse lists 76 items
   as edited by Burns, mostly from traditional sources; 44 tunes probably
   collected but certainly communicated to Johnson (nos 157, 175, 231, 264,
   308, 326, 327, 345, 346, 348, 362, 365, 373, 377, 378, 392, 398, 400, 405, 406,
   410, 411, 412, 414, 416, 430, 434, 444, 448, 456, 461, 462, 476, 484, 486, 492,
   495, 497, 498, 499, 551, 581, 593, 597); and 36 texts sent to Johnson,
   presumably collected but not edited (nos 188, 205, 208, 233, 236, 237, 281,
   303, 320, 326, 327, 328, 345, 346, 348, 359, 361, 365, 372, 377, 384, 392, 397,
   400, 411, 416, 424, 428, 444, 459, 461, 462, 473, 484, 579, 581).

16. See the following as examples. Dick, *Notes on Scottish Songs*: nos 9, 11, 25,
   47, 85, 93, 162, 181, 182, 216, 315, 324. Excise Manuscript pp. 1, 2, 5, 6, 8, 9,
   10, 11. Ferguson, *Letters*, nos. 130, 267, 290, 586, 605, 644, 667, 684. For
   many items Burns identifies an old portion on which he based his song. Such
   fragments were either collected or remembered.

17. The following represent items probably recalled from his youth: Dick, *Notes
   on Scottish Song*: nos 7, 33, 41, 51, 158, 234, 313; Ferguson, *Letters*, nos 126,
   264, 385, 557, 567, 635, 644, 659, 667.

18. There has been much speculation about whether or not Burns met Herd in
   Edinburgh or saw his manuscript of material excluded from the published
   volumes. I do not believe he did. For a discussion, see Hans Hecht, *Songs
   from David Herd's Manuscripts* (Edinburgh: William J. Hay, 1904) and the
   same author's *Robert Burns: The Man and His Work*, 2nd rev. ed. (London:
   William Hodge & Company, 1950).

19. Ferguson, *Letters*, 2: 122, no. 507. For additional discussion of Burns' song
   library see an article in two parts by Davidson Cook, 'Burns and Old Song
   Books', *The Scottish Musical Magazine*, 8 (1 April 1927): 147–9; 8 (1 July
   1927): 207–9.

20. Ferguson, *Letters*, 2: 75, no. 452. See Dick's Preface and Bibliography
   in *The Songs of Robert Burns* for a fuller description of Burns' musical
   books.

21. This letter is found in Ferguson, *Letters*, 1: 116–17, no. 125, but is printed
   here from the original manuscript found in MS. 586, Watson Manuscript,
   National Library of Scotland. Included in this letter to Tytler are parts of six
   items, headed by the title *Fragments*: 'Rowin't in her apron', a stanza to the
   tune 'Bonie Dundee', 'Young Hynhorn', 'Willie's rare', 'The Lass o'
   Livistone', and 'Rob Roy'. Most of these have been admitted under one
   guise or another into the Burns' canon by literary students although there is
   every reason to believe that in this instance Burns simply wrote down what
   he had himself learned orally or collected.

22. David Johnson suggests that Burns' 'reintegration of oral and literary
   tradition' has assured that 'national songs have been identified with Burns,
   and no one else, ever since'. See *Music and Society in Lowland Scotland in the
   Eighteenth Century* (London: Oxford University Press, 1972), p. 149.

23. For a discussion of Burns' musical aptitude, see Dick's Introduction to *Notes on Scottish Songs by Robert Burns.*
24. Hastie Manuscript, British Library, Additional Manuscript 22307, item 19.
25. Burns' work for Thomson, coming after the initial work with Johnson, is less influenced by collecting and involves much editorial work, especially on book-derived texts.
26. See Ferguson, *Letters,* 2: 103, no. 488. Gershon Legman (ed.), *The Merry Muses of Caledonia, Collected and in Part Written by Robert Burns* (New Hyde Park, New York: University Books, 1965) suggests that Burns often added verses to the end of bawdy songs and fragments he collected. And many of these songs were the 'indelicate' verses he rewrote or discarded completely in his work for the Museum.
27. Legman, *Merry Muses,* Introduction, pp. liv–v. See also Gershon Legman, *The Horn Book: Studies in Erotic Folklore and Bibliography* (New Hyde Park, New York: University Books, 1964) and James Kinsley, 'Burns and the Merry Muses', *Renaissance and Modern Studies* 9 (1965): 5–21.
28. As an example, see Ferguson, *Letters,* 1: 125, no. 137.
29. James Cameron Ewing and Davidson Cook (eds), *Robert Burns's Commonplace Book 1783–1785* (Carbondale, Illinois: Southern Illinois University Press, 1965), 37–8.
30. For examples of attribution of authorship from the Interleaved Museum alone, see Dick, *Notes on Scottish Songs,* nos 8, 20, 36, 37, 46, 49, 69, 91, 97, 102, 104, 120, 121, 126, 133, 141, 162, 166, 176, 184, 186, 190, 197, 201, 205, 208, 218, 228, 246, 269, 278, 285, 289, 293, 330, 340.
31. Dick, *Notes on Scottish Songs,* nos 9, 93; Excise Manuscript, pp. 6, 7, 9, 10.
32. See as examples, Dick, *Notes on Scottish Songs,* nos 16, 18, 25, 47, 51, 68, 96, 103, 107, 140, 162, 216, 231, 258, 290, 323; Ferguson, *Letters,* no. 646; Excise, pp. 1, 2, 11, 12.
33. See Dick, *Notes on Scottish Songs,* nos 151, 176, 209, 247, 278, 312, 315, 323, 324, 337, 338; Ferguson, no. 557. In the Hastie Manuscript, B. L. Add. MS. 22307, Burns says in his note to item no. 142 'Auld King Coul' 'I have met with many different sets of the tune & words but these appear to be the best'.
34. Dick, *Notes on Scottish Songs,* no. 85. This verse from Child 237 is another example of collected or recollected material.
35. For examples see Dick, *Notes on Scottish Songs,* nos 35, 102, 201.
36. Ibid., no. 174. Also see no. 188.
37. For a discussion of the relationship between text and tune in Burns' songs, see Catarina Ericson-Roos, *The Songs of Robert Burns: A Study of the Unity of Poetry and Music,* Acta Universitatis Upsaliensis, Studia Anglistica Upsaliensia no. 30 (Uppsala, 1977).
38. Henry George Farmer, 'Foreword', in Dick, *The Songs of Robert Burns* and *Notes on Scottish Songs,* p. vi.
39. Preface dated 1 March 1788, vol. 2, *The Scots Musical Museum.*
40. Preface dated 2 February 1790, vol. 3, *The Scots Musical Museum.*
41. During Burns' lifetime volumes of the *Museum* did not name him as author of many items he could have claimed. He did have a letter code, several letters of which referred the initiated to his works. See Ferguson, *Letters,* 1: 267, no. 280.
42. Ferguson, *Letters,* 2: 129, no. 513. This portion of the letter has perished and

is published by Ferguson on the authority of Cromek who had printed it and who may have seen the original.

43. Joseph Ritson (ed.), *Scottish Songs*, 2 vols (London: J. Johnson & J. Egerton, 1794), 1: lxxv and footnote 69.

44. Sir Walter Scott, 'Art. II *Reliques of Robert Burns, consisting chiefly of original Letters, Poems, and Critical Observations on Scottish Songs.* Collected and published by R. H. Cromek. 8 vo. pp. 453. London, Cadell and Davies. 1808', *Quarterly Review*, 1 (1809): 30.

45. Legman, *Merry Muses*, p. lxv. Parenthetically, following Legman's suggestion, one can surely say that Burns would undoubtedly have been an excellent informant. And perhaps in a certain sense he should be viewed as such, as a remarkably original yet tradition-bound redactor of oral material.

46. See Farmer, 'Foreword', in Dick, *Songs and Notes on Scottish Songs*, p. viii: 'We must not forget that it was his flair for and apperception of the old and neglected melodies, that prevented the loss of much of Scotland's proud heritage from her social and cultural past which otherwise would certainly have fallen into desuetude'.

47. James Kinsley (ed.), *The Poems and Songs of Robert Burns*, 3 vols (Oxford: Clarendon Press, 1968), 1: 494, no. 275.

CHAPTER 3   THE ANTIQUARIAN AND NATIONALISTIC IMPULSE: THE LATER SONGS AND POEMS

1. For discussion of this point see W. E. Henley and T. F. Henderson (eds), *The Poetry of Robert Burns*, 4 vols (Edinburgh: T. C. and E. C. Jack, 1896–7), 4: 73, 332.

2. David Buchan's valuable book *The Ballad and the Folk* (London: Routledge & Kegan Paul, 1972) does much to redress this balance, describing the general possessors of the ballad and the songs' role in the social and economic matrix.

3. See James C. Dick (ed.), *The Songs of Robert Burns* and *Notes on Scottish Songs by Robert Burns* (1903 and 1908; reprint ed., Hatboro, Pennsylvania: Folklore Associates, 1962).

4. In a paper called 'Some Uses of the Past: The Traditional Song Repertoire of Robert Burns', in *Folklore Today*, eds. Dégh, Glassie, Oinas (Bloomington: Research Center for Language and Semiotic Studies, 1976), pp. 324–33, I (see, Lewis, in Bibliography) hypothetically created a traditional song repertoire for Robert Burns and suggested that he knew 111 items (primarily lyric) as a passive member of the oral culture. But the unavailability of comparative material makes recovery of these texts – often referred to elliptically by Burns – presently extraordinarily difficult. The list produced, however, may well be of help should a study of traditional Scottish lyric songs in English or Scots be undertaken. For another treatment which identifies 25 items Burns knew, see John Strawhorn, 'Burns and the Bardie Clan', *Scottish Literary Journal*, 8 (1981), 8–10. For a discussion of Burns' debt to traditional vernacular song, see Henley and Henderson, *Poetry*, 4: 321–34.

5. James Kinsley (ed.), *The Poems and Songs of Robert Burns*, 3 vols (Oxford:

Clarendon Press, 1968), 2: 541–2, no. 313 takes this as title and in subject matter deals with the battle.

6. David Herd, *Ancient & Modern Scottish Songs*, 2 vols (1776; reprint ed., Edinburgh: Scottish Academic Press, 1973), 2: 122–4.
7. See Dick, *Notes on Scottish Songs*, p. 37.
8. For a discussion of the necessity of establishing a new category of Burns' material, see M. E. B. Lewis, 'What to Do With "a red, red rose": A New Category of Burns' Songs', *Scottish Literary Journal*, 3 (1976): 62–75.
9. Herd, *Ancient and Modern*, 2: 122.
10. Kinsley, *Poems and Songs*, 3: 1514.
11. Ibid., 3: 1510.
12. Dick, *Notes on Scottish Songs*, p. 55.
13. Henley and Henderson, *Poetry*, 3: 319.
14. Hans Hecht (ed.), *Songs From David Herd's Manuscripts* (London: William Hodge & Company, 1950), pp. 183, 308.
15. John Ord, *The Bothy Songs & Ballads of Aberdeen, Banff & Moray, Angus and the Mearns* (Edinburgh: John Donald, 1930), p. 215.
16. Gershon Legman (ed.), *The Merry Muses of Caledonia, Collected and in Part Written by Robert Burns* (New Hyde Park, New York: University Books, 1965), p. xxx.
17. Sydney Goodsir Smith, 'Robert Burns and "The Merry Muses of Caledonia"', *Arena*, 4 (1950): 4.
18. James Kinsley, 'Burns & the Merry Muses', *Nottingham: Renaissance & Modern Studies* (1964–7): 10.
19. Kinsley, *Poems and Songs*, 3: 1135 describes no. 78, 'Brose and Butter' as 'the earliest surviving specimen of work [by Burns] as a collector of folk-songs'.
20. Christina Keith, *The Russet Coat* (1956; reprint ed., New York: Haskell House, 1971), p. 143.
21. Kinsley, *Poems and Songs*, nos 17 'O raging Fortune's withering blast', 21 'Remorse', 107 'Highland Lassie O', 124 'A Fragment', 215 'An I'll kiss thee yet, yet', 313 'Killiecrankie', 368 'Johnie Blunt', 378 'The Slave's Lament', 403 'Open the door to me Oh', 564 'We'll hide the Couper behint the door', 586 'The Taylor'.
22. Frances Grose, *Antiquities of Scotland*, 2 vols (London: Hooper & Wigstead, 1797), 2: 199–201.
23. Ibid., 1: xxi. Grose also provided a general description of the church:

> This church stands by the river, a small distance from the bridge of Doon, on the road leading from Maybole to Ayr. About a century ago it was united to the parish of Ayr; since which time it has fallen to ruins. It is one of the eldest parishes in Scotland, and still retains these privileges: the minister of Ayr is obliged to marry and baptise in it, and also here to hold his parochial catechisings. The magistrates attempted, some time ago, to take away the bell; but were repulsed by the *Alloites vi & armes*.

He followed this by a specific introduction to the tale:

> This church is also famous for being the place wherein the witches and warlocks used to hold their infernal meetings, or sabbaths, and prepare

their magical unctions: here too they used to amuse themselves with dancing to the pipes of the muckle-horned Deil. Diverse stories of these horrid rites are still current: one of which my worthy friend Mr. Burns has here favored me with in verse.

24. J. De Lancey Ferguson (ed.), *The Letters of Robert Burns*, 2 vols (Oxford: Clarendon Press, 1931), 2: 22–4. This is letter no. 401.
25. Reidar Th. Christiansen, *The Migratory Legends* (Helsinki: Folklore Fellows Communication no. 175, 1958), p. 61.
26. Katharine M. Briggs, *A Dictionary of British Folk-Tales*, 2 parts, 4 vols (Bloomington, Indiana: Indiana University Press, 1971), A, 1: 70.
27. H. L. Gee, *Folk Tales of Yorkshire* (London: Thomas Nelson and Sons, 1952), pp. 67–8. I am indebted to Katherine M. Briggs for this reference to Gee.
28. Kinsley, *Poems and Songs*, 3: 1364.
29. Burns footnotes this belief at line 206: 'It is a well known fact that witches, or any evil spirits, have no power to follow a poor wight any farther than the middle of the next running stream. – It may be proper likewise to mention to the benighted traveller, that when he falls in with *bogles*, whatever danger may be in his going forward, there is much more hazard in turning back.'
30. Margaret Alice Murray, *The Witch-Cult in Western Europe* (Oxford: Clarendon Press, 1921), pp. 111–12.
31. Thomas Davidson, *Rowan Tree and Red Thread* (Edinburgh: Oliver and Boyd, 1949), p. 6.
32. Ibid., p. 10.
33. Murray, *Witch-Cult*, p. 173.
34. Ibid., p. 68.
35. Ibid., p. 61.
36. Ibid., p. 112.
37. Ibid., p. 67.
38. Ibid., p. 158.
39. Ibid., p. 157.
40. My debt here and throughout this discussion is to Linda Dégh and Andrew Vazsonyi, 'Legend and Belief', *Genre*, 4 (1971): 281–304.
41. Kinsley, *Poems and Songs*, 3: 1354–5. See also Henley and Henderson, *Poetry*, 1: 437.
42. David Daiches, *Robert Burns* (London: Andre Deutsch, 1966), p. 256.
43. For a discussion of metanarrational devices, see Barbara Babcock-Abrahams, 'The Story in the Story: Metanarration in Folk Narrative', *Studia Fennica: Review of Finnish Linguistics and Ethnology*, 20 (1976): 177–84.
44. Ferguson, *Letters*, 2: 24.

CHAPTER 4   TRADITION'S USE OF BURNS: THE SONGS AND POEMS

1. 'Heron's Memoir of Burns' in Hans Hecht, *Robert Burns: The Man and His Work*, 2nd rev. ed. (Edinburgh: William Hodge & Company, 1950), p. 266.

2. James Ballantine (comp. and ed.), *Hundredth Birthday of Robert Burns* (Edinburgh: A Fullarton & Co., 1859), p. 287.
3. Personal tape, 1976, no. 8.
4. James Kinsley (ed.), *The Poems and Songs of Robert Burns*, 3 vols (Oxford: Clarendon Press, 1968), 2: 557–64, no. 321 'Tam o' Shanter. A Tale'.
5. See Kinsley, *Poems and Songs*, no. 55 'Death and Doctor Hornbook. A True Story'.
6. Ibid., no. 482 'Song – For a' that and a' that'.
7. Ibid., no. 64 'Man was Made to Mourn, A Dirge'.
8. Ibid., no. 83 'To a Louse, On Seeing one on a Lady's Bonnet at Church'.
9. Ballantine, *Hundredth Birthday*, p. 107.
10. See Kinsley, *Poems and Songs*, no. 53 'Holy Willie's Prayer'
11. See the introductory material to Gershon Legman (ed.), *The Merry Muses of Caledonia, Collected and in part written by Robert Burns* (New Hyde Park, New York: University Books, 1965).
12. Kinsley, *Poems and Songs*, 3: 1455. See also the notes to 'A Red, Red Rose' in W. E. Henley and T. F. Henderson (eds.), *The Poetry of Robert Burns*, 4 vols (Edinburgh: T. C. and E. C. Jack, 1896–7), 3: 402–6.
13. Ibid., 2: 917.
14. J. De Lancey Ferguson (ed.), *The Letters of Robert Burns*, 2 vols (Oxford: Clarendon Press, 1931), 1: 116–17, no. 126. This transcription differs slightly from the version printed in Ferguson: it is taken from Manuscript 586, the Watson Manuscript, National Library of Scotland.
15. Fletcher of Saltoun did not, however, necessarily agree with this sentiment. See *The Dictionary of National Biography* (London: Oxford University Press, since 1917), 8: 295.
16. David Daiches, *Robert Burns* (London: Andre Deutsch, 1966), p. 233.
17. Kinsley, *Poems and Songs*, 2: 642.
18. MS 2181, Aberdeen University Library, Ballads from Glenbuchat, Vol. 1, no. 13, pp. 25–6.
19. Henley and Henderson, *Poetry*, 3: 389–90.
20. Personal tape, 1972.
21. Personal tape, no. 15, 1976. I participated as instigator in a revealing conversation with several leaders of the Traditional Music and Song Association of Scotland during the Folk Music Festival in Keith on just this subject. The issue hinged on what was traditional and my friends and willing discussants reflected the ambiguity and confusion often attendant on the subject.
22. Roger D. Abrahams and George Foss, *Anglo-American Folksong Style* (Englewood Cliffs, New Jersey: Prentice-Hall, 1968), pp.171–2.
23. Kinsley, *Poems and Songs*, no. 257 'Afton Water'.
24. School of Scottish Studies Archive, University of Edinburgh, SA 1962/25.
25. Kinsley, *Poems and Songs*, 3: 1301; 1:461.
26. I am indebted to Jacob Love for advice on this transcription.
27. School of Scottish Studies Archive, University of Edinburgh, SA 1962/25.
28. Ferguson, *Letters*, no. 586.
29. Henley and Henderson, *Poetry*, 3: 407–10.
30. School of Scottish Studies Archives, University of Edinburgh, SA 1952/15/A9.

31. School of Scottish Studies Archives, University of Edinburgh, SA 1960/167/A15. Also see Almeda Riddle's version in Roger Abrahams, *A Singer and Her Songs: Almeda Riddle's Book of Ballads* (Baton Rouge: Louisiana State University Press, 1970), p. 61:

> Should old acquaintance be forgot,
> And never brought to mind
> The blooming cook fell overboard,
> Now he's forty leagues behind.

Also see George Carey, 'A Further Note on the Singing-Stammering Seaman', *Western Folklore*, 35 (1976): 160–1. I am indebted to Bob Blackman for pointing out this latter reference to me.

CHAPTER 5 TRADITION'S USE OF BURNS: THE LEGENDARY TRADITION

1. Personal tape, 1976, no. 10.
2. Personal tape, 1976, no. 10.
3. Personal tape, 1976, no. 9.
4. James Scotland, *The History of Scottish Education*, vol. 1 (London: London University Press, 1969), 1: 44.
5. See M. Mackintosh, *Education in Scotland* (Glasgow: Robert Gibson & Sons, 1962) for further material on the history of Scottish education.
6. Robert Chambers and William Wallace (eds.), *The Life and Works of Robert Burns*, 4 vols (New York: Longmans, Green, and Co., 1896), 2: 9–10.
7. See James Barke's five-volume work, called in totality, *Immortal Memory* (*The Wind that Shakes the Barley*; *The Song in the Green Thorn Tree*; *The Wonder of All the Gay World*; *The Crest of the Broken Wave*; *The Well of the Silent Harp*) (London: Collins, 1946–59).
8. Sir John Sinclair, *The Statistical Account of Scotland*, 21 vols (Edinburgh: William Creech, 1792), 3: 598–600.
9. Robert Burns, *Poems, Chiefly in the Scottish Dialect* (Kilmarnock: John Wilson, 1786), Preface.
10. James Kinsley (ed.), *The Poems and Songs of Robert Burns*, 3 vols (Oxford: Clarendon Press, 1968), 1: 86, no. 57.
11. Kinsley, *Poems and Songs*, no. 140.
12. See Donald A. Low (ed.), *Robert Burns: The Critical Heritage* (London: Routledge & Kegan Paul, 1974) for examples of early critical comment about Burns.
13. See Robert Fitzhugh, *Robert Burns, His Associates and Contemporaries* (Chapel Hill: University of North Carolina Press, 1943).
14. Ibid., pp. 42–3 – for an account told of Drummond and of Burns: 'Burns looked into a room where some persons was enjoying themselves & and was retiring when one of them called come in Johnny Bopeep. After it was proposed that he who wrote the best verse should be kept free when Burns wrote:

> Here I am Johnny Bopeep
> I saw three sheep

> And those three sheep saw me
> Half a crown apiece
> Will pay for their fleece
> And so Johnny Bopeep gets free.'

These lines are also said to have been by Drummond, who on a similar occasion said

> 'I bopeep
> Saw your four sheep
> And each of you his fleece
> The reckning is five shilling
> If each of you is willing
> Tis fifteen pence a piece.'

Similarly, see Dean Ramsay's account in his *Reminiscences of Scottish Life and Character* (Edinburgh: T. N. Foulis, 1924), pp. 78–9 related to the account in Chapter 6.

15. James Ballantine (comp. and ed.), *Hundredth Birthday of Robert Burns* (Edinburgh: A. Fullarton & Co., 1859), p. 325.
16. Ibid., p. 159.
17. P. Hately Waddell, *Life and Works of Robert Burns* (Glasgow: David Wilson, 1867), Appendix xxiii.
18. Robert Burns, *Poems, Chiefly in the Scottish Dialect* (Edinburgh: William Creech, 1787), Preface.
19. A. M. Kinghorn, 'The Literary and Historical Origins of the Burns Myth', *Dalhousie Review*, 39 (1959): 77.
20. John D. Ross, *Burnsiana*, 5 vols (Paisley: Alexander Gardiner, 1892), 1: 24.
21. See notes 23–5 below. Most other excise or gauging narratives show the exciseman being duped. See especially *Tocher*, published by the School of Scottish Studies, University of Edinburgh, 2 (1971): 62–8 and 3 (1971) 71–7.
22. J. De Lancey Ferguson (ed.), *The Letters of Robert Burns* 2 vols (Oxford: Clarendon Press, 1931), 2: 41, no. 419.
23. Ballantine, *Hundredth Birthday*, p. 230. See also Alexander Hislop, *The Book of Scottish Anecdote* (Edinburgh: The Edinburgh Publishing Co., 1874), p. 67 and Charles S. Dougall, *The Burns Country* (London: Adam and Charles Black, 1904), pp. 259–60.
24. Ballantine, *Hundredth Birthday*, p. 230.
25. Hislop, *Scottish Anecdote*, pp. 264–5; see also Ballantine, *Hundredth Birthday*, p. 230.
26. Fitzhugh, *Robert Burns*, p. 33.
27. Ibid., p. 31.
28. Ibid., p. 33.
29. Ibid., p. 29.
30. Manuscript Book, Robert Burns, authored by W. W. 1886, xerox in my possession, pp. 24–5.
31. Thomas Carlyle, 'Review of Lockhart's *The Life of Robert Burns*',

Edinburgh Review, 1828, as reprinted in *Essays* (London: Chapman and Hall, 1883), p. 6.

32. Collected by questionnaire, January 1973 from MBB of Dearborn, Michigan, a member of the Detroit Burns Club.

33. Dougall, *Burns Country*, pp. 156–7. See also J. Taylor Gibb, *The Land of Burns: Mauchline Town & District* (Glasgow: Carson & Nicol, 1911), pp. 62–3.

34. Dougall, *Burns Country*, pp. 196–7.

35. James Cameron Ewing and Davidson Cook (eds), *Robert Burns's Commonplace Book 1783–1785* (Carbondale, Illinois: Southern Illinois University Press, 1965), p. 3.

36. Personal tape, 1976, no. 1.

37. Ferguson, *Letters*, no. 52.

38. Personal tape, 1976, no. 16.

39. R. Jamieson (ed.), *Burt's Letters* or *Letters from a Gentleman in the North of Scotland to His Friend in London*, 2 vols (London: Ogle, Duncan, and Co., 1822), 1: lxxi.

40. Fitzhugh, *Robert Burns*, p. 66.

41. Ibid., p. 76.

42. Ibid., p. 85.

43. Collected July 1972 from FM, Edinburgh. Personal tape, 1972.

44. Hislop, *Scottish Anecdote*, p. 305.

45. Ross, *Burnsiana*, 1: 87.

46. Ibid.

47. Ibid.

48. Collected July 1972 from FM, Edinburgh. Personal tape, 1972.

49. Ross, *Burnsiana*, 2: 66–7.

50. Ibid., 3: 52.

51. Herschel Gower, 'Jeannie Robertson: Portrait of a Traditional Singer', *Scottish Studies*, 12 (1968): 121–2. Also collected July 1972 from JR, Aberdeen. Personal tape, 1972. See also School of Scottish Studies Archive, University of Edinburgh, SA 1953/195.

52. Ms. 1803: 133, Department of Irish Folklore, University College, Dublin.

53. School of Scottish Studies Archive, University of Edinburgh, SA 1953/195. Herschel Gower prints a related version in 'Burns in Limbo', *Studies in Scottish Literature* 5 (1967–8): 234.

54. Gower, 'Jeannie Robertson', 122–3; also Gower, 'Burns', 229–37. Also collected July 1972 from JR, Aberdeen. Personal tape, 1972. Additional version collected July 1972 from LS, Fetterangus, Aberdeenshire. Personal tape, 1972. For a related version see School of Scottish Studies Archive, University of Edinburgh, SA 1960/229. An additional version was collected by questionnaire, January 1973 from SRD of Dearborn, Michigan, a member of the Detroit Burns Club.

55. Ms. 1486:536, Department of Irish Folklore, University College, Dublin.

56. Ross, *Burnsiana*, 3: 53.

57. Ibid., 3: 51–2.

58. Collected July 1972 from FM, Edinburgh. Personal tape, 1972. See also Herschel Gower, 'Burns', 229–37.

59. Collected from LS, Fetterangus, Aberdeenshire, in July 1972 and from her nephew. Personal tape, 1972.

60. Collected by questionnaire in January 1973 from SR of Dearborn, Michigan. See also Ms. 1480: 9, Department of Irish Folklore, University College, Dublin.

61. Collected in April 1974 by Department of Irish Folklore.

62. Collected by questionnaire, January 1973 from EJVT, Atlanta, Georgia.

63. Herschel Gower, 'Burns', 235. Also collected in July 1972 from FM, Edinburgh and from a questionnaire in January 1973 from SRD, Dearborn, Michigan.

64. Collected in July 1972 from FM, Edinburgh.

65. Collected in October 1973 from WS at the School of Scottish Studies *Ceilidh*. Also collected in March 1974 from JLB, Edinburgh.

66. Personal tape, 1976, no. 6.

67. Transcribed from the School of Scottish Studies Archive, University of Edinburgh, SA 1960/229.

68. Gibb, *The Land of Burns*, p. 25. See also Dougall, *Burns Country*, p. 152 and Waddell, *Life and Works*, Appendix xxv and Yvonne Helen Stevenson, *Burns and His Bonnie Jean* (Sidney, British Columbia: Gray's Publishing, 1967), pp. 10–11; Maurice Lindsay, *Burns: the man, his work, the legend* (London: MacGibbon & Kee, 1971), p. 96; 'Burns's Unpublished Common-Place Book', ed. William Jack in *Macmillan's Magazine* 29 (1879): Part IV, 251.

69. Ferguson, *Letters*, p. xxxviii.

70. Fitzhugh, *Robert Burns*, pp. 54–5.

71. Lindsay, *Burns*, pp. 111ff. Also see Fitzhugh, *Robert Burns*, pp. 440–2.

72. This version was collected by questionnaire in January 1973.

73. Personal tape, 1976, no. 11.

74. Ramsay, *Reminiscences*, pp. 81–3.

75. John Ingram, *Anecdotes of Burns* (Glasgow: Thomas D. Morison, 1893), p. 42.

76. Hislop, *Scottish Anecdotes*, p. 716. See also Waddell, *Life and Works*, Appendix xxi.

77. Ballantine, *Hundredth Birthday*, p. 240. See also Ross, *Burnsiana*, 5: 67.

78. Ingram, *Anecdotes*, p. 79. See also Hislop, *Scottish Anecdotes*, p. 716 and Waddell, *Life and Works*, Appendix xxi.

79. Dougall, *Burns Country*, p. 140.

80. Ballantine, *Hundredth Birthday*, p. 84. See also p. 568.

81. Waddell, *Life and Works*, Appendix xxxv. See also Lindsay, *Burns*, pp. 280–1. This has often been treated as apocryphal, but there is some documentary evidence to support portions of the account. See Fitzhugh, *Robert Burns*, pp. 218–19.

82. Hislop, *Scottish Anecdotes*, p. 31.

83. Waddell, *Life and Works*, Appendix xxxix.

84. Ross, *Burnsiana*, 5: 67.

85. Alan Dent, *Burns in his time* (London: Thomas Nelson and Sons, 1966), p. 26. Scholars themselves have continued the debate about the cause of Burns' death: James Currie in 1800 suggested that drink was the cause: *The Life of*

Robert Burns, with a Criticism on His Writings (Edinburgh: William and Robert Chambers, 1838). For more contemporary discussions, see R. D. Thornton, *James Currie: The Entire Stranger and Robert Burns* (Edinburgh: Oliver & Boyd, 1963) and Robert Fitzhugh, *Robert Burns: The Man and The Poet* (Boston: Houghton Mifflin, 1970).

86. Waddell, *Life and Works*, Appendix xxiv–xxv. See also Stevenson, *Burns and Jean*, p. 107.
87. Ballantine, *Hundredth Birthday*, pp. 319–20.
88. Ibid., p. 33.
89. Collected by questionnaire in January 1973 from HN of Detroit, Michigan.
90. Personal tape, 1976, no. 1.
91. See Gower, 'Burns', 229–37.

CHAPTER 6   TRADITION'S USE OF BURNS: THE CALENDAR CUSTOM

1. J. De Lancey Ferguson (ed.). *The Letters of Robert Burns*, 2 vols (Oxford: Clarendon Press, 1931), 1: 55, no. 62.
2. This letter from Richmond is given in Robert Fitzhugh (ed.), *Robert Burns, His Associates and Contemporaries* (Chapel Hill: University of North Carolina Press, 1943), pp. 37–8.
3. James Kinsley (ed.), *The Poems and Songs of Robert Burns*, 3 vols (Oxford: Clarendon Press, 1968), 3: 1221.
4. Charles L. Brodie, 'Greenock Burns Club: A Sketch of Its History', *Burns Chronicle* (1927): 124–30.
5. Elizabeth Ewing, 'The First "Burns Nicht" (Alloway) and the First Burns Club (Greenock)', *Burns Chronicle* (1948): 38–42.
6. Ibid., 41. Quoted by Ewing from *Glasgow Courier*, 3 February 1803.
7. J. B. Morrison, 'Greenock Burns Club', *Burns Chronicle* (1893): 115–22.
8. David Semple (ed.), *The Poems and Songs and Correspondence of Robert Tannahill with Life and Notes* (Paisley: Alexander Gardner, 1876), pp. 45–9.
9. Robert Brown, *Paisley Burns Clubs 1805–1893* (Paisley: Alexander Gardner, 1893).
10. 'Dumfries Burns Club Centenary Celebration', *Burns Chronicle* (1921): 109–16.
11. John Gibson Lockhart, *Peter's Letters to His Kinfolk*, ed. William Ruddick (Edinburgh: Scottish Academic Press, 1977), pp. 29–47.
12. From *Dumfries Courier*, 1825, in Bi-centenary Paper Clippings.
13. John McVie, *The Burns Federation: A Bicentenary Review* (Kilmarnock, 1959).
14. James Ballantine (comp. and ed.), *Chronicle of the Hundredth Birthday of Robert Burns* (Edinburgh: A. Fullarton & Co., 1859), p. 430.
15. Ibid., p. v.
16. Ibid., p. 82.
17. Ibid., p. 66.
18. Ibid., p. 364.
19. Ibid., p. 4.
20. Ibid., pp. 39–59.

21. Dean Ramsay, *Reminiscences of Scottish Life* (Edinburgh: T. N. Foulis, 1924), pp. 78–9 provides another version of the narrative.
22. Personal tape, 1976, no. 8.
23. Ballantine, *Hundredth Birthday*, p. 464.
24. Ibid., p. 438.
25. Ibid., p. 403.
26. Ibid., p. 399.
27. Ibid., p. 557.
28. Ibid., p. 36.
29. Edwin Muir, 'The Burns Myth', in William Montgomerie, ed. *New Judgements: Robert Burns* (Glasgow: William Maclellan, 1947), p. 7.
30. F. Marian McNeill, *The Silver Bough*, 4 vols (Glasgow: William Maclellan, 1957–1961), 3: 142.
31. David Murison, 'The Language of Burns', *Burns Chronicle* (1950): 47.
32. See J. F. T. Thomson, 'Suggested lines for organising a Burns Supper', *Burns Chronicle* (1979): 31–2 and Hugh Douglas, *Johnnie Walker's Burns Supper Companion* (Ayr: Alloway Publishing, 1981).
33. Taken from a menu card among those kindly loaned me in 1974 by Robert Dinwiddie & Co. Ltd., Dumfries, Scotland.
34. Kinsley, *Poems and Songs*, no. 531. I have not given the text as printed in Kinsley, but as it is traditionally performed and reproduced on menus, napkins, etc.
35. See Kinsley, *Poems and Songs*, nos 266, 267, 532 for several frequently used graces.
36. Ibid., no. 136.
37. Ibid., no. 45.
38. Taken from a toast 'To the Lassies', given at a Burns Dinner, Edinburgh Ayrshire Association, 18 January 1974, by G. Henderson Laing.
39. This version was sent to me by Sanuel Dickey, Dearborn, Michigan, in 1972.
40. Kinsley, *Poems and Songs*, no. 240.

CHAPTER 7   BURNS TODAY

1. James Kinsley (ed.), *The Poems and Songs of Robert Burns*, 3 vols (Oxford, Clarendon Press, 1968), 1: 310–2, no. 136. In Burns' poem 'To a Haggis' the line reads 'Aboon them a' ye tak your place'.
2. Hugh MacDiarmid, *A Drunk Man Looks at the Thistle* (Edinburgh: William Blackwood & Sons, 1926), p. 3.
3. Lewis Grassic Gibbon, *Cloud Howe* (London: Jarrolds, 1933), p. 96.
4. Ibid., p. 133.
5. Ibid., p. 173.
6. Jane Austen, *Sandition, The Watsons, Lady Susan and Other Miscellanea* (New York: E. P. Dutton, 1934), p. 45.
7. George Douglas Brown, *The House with the Green Shutters* (London: John MacQueen, 1901), p. 36.
8. Lewis Grassic Gibbon, *Sunset Song* (London: Jarrolds, 1932), p. 190.
9. Lewis Grassic Gibbon, *Grey Granite* (London: Jarrolds, 1934), p. 159.

10. Brown, *Green Shutters*, p. 238.
11. Gibbon, *Sunset Song*, p. 189.
12. Woody Guthrie, *Born to Win*, ed. Robert Shelton (New York: Macmillan, 1965), pp. 213–15. I am indebted to Bob Blackman for calling this poem to my attention.

Bibliography of Principal Works Cited and Examined

Aberdeen, University Library. MS. 2181. 'Ballads From Glenbuchat'.

Abrahams, Roger D., 'A Rhetorical Theory of Folklore', *Journal of American Folklore*, 81 (1968): 143–58.

—— (ed.), *A Singer and Her Songs: Almeda Riddle's Book of Ballads* (Baton Rouge: Louisiana State University, 1970).

——, 'Folklore and Literature as Performance', *Journal of the Folklore Institute*, 9 (1972): 75–94.

——, 'Some Varieties of Heroes in America', *Journal of the Folklore Institute*, 3 (1966): 341–62.

Angellier, August, *Robert Burns, La Vie, Les Oeuvres* (Paris, 1893). Translated selectively by Jane Burgoyne, *Burns Chronicle and Club Directory*, 1969–73.

Austen, Jane, *Sandition, The Watsons, Lady Susan and other Miscellanea* (New York: E. P. Dutton, 1934).

Babcock–Abrahams, Barbara, 'The Novel and the Carnival World: an Essay in Memory of Joe Doherty', *Modern Language Notes*, 89 (1974): 911–37.

——, 'The Story in the Story: Metanarration in Folk-Narrative' *Studia Fennica: Review of Finnish Linguistics and Ethnology*, 20 (1976): 177–84.

Ballantine, James (comp. and ed.), *Chronicle of the Hundredth Birthday of Robert Burns* (Edinburgh: A. Fullarton & Co., 1859).

Banks, M. Macleod, *British Calendar Customs: Scotland*, 3 vols (London: William Glaisher, 1937–41).

Barke, James, *Immortal Memory*, 5 vols (London: Collins, 1946–59).

Barnes, Daniel, 'The Bosom Serpent: A Legend in American Literature and Culture', *Journal of American Folklore*, 85 (1972): 111–22.

Baughman, Ernest W., *Type and Motif Index of the Folktales of England and North America* (The Hague: Mouton, 1966).

Boyd, William, *Education in Ayrshire through Seven Centuries* (London: University of London Press, 1961).

Briggs, Katharine M., *A Dictionary of British Folk-Tales*, 4 vols (Bloomington: Indiana University Press, 1970).

Brodie, Charles L., 'Greenock Burns Club: A Sketch of Its History', *Burns Chronicle*, 2 (1927): 124–30.

166   *Burns and Tradition*

Brown, George Douglas, *The House with the Green Shutters* (London: John MacQueen, 1901).

Brown, Mary Ellen, 'But you, or me will never see, another Robbie Burns: The Social Significance of the Burns' Legend', *Arv: Scandinavian Yearbook of Folklore*, 37 (1981).

——, 'That Bards are Second Sighted is Nae Joke: The Orality of Burns' World and Work', *Studies in Scottish Literature*, 16 (1981): 208–16.

Brown, Robert, *Paisley Burns Clubs 1805–1893* (Paisley: Alexander Gardner, 1893).

Buchan, David, *The Ballad and the Folk* (London: Routledge & Kegan Paul, 1972).

Burns Chronicle and Club Directory (Kilmarnock: The Burns Federation, 1892–).

Burns, Robert, *Poems, Chiefly in the Scottish Dialect* (Edinburgh: William Creech, 1787).

——, *Poems, Chiefly in the Scottish Dialect* (Kilmarnock: John Wilson, 1786).

Campbell, Joseph, *The Hero with a Thousand Faces* (Cleveland: The World Publishing Co., 1962).

Carey, George, 'A Further Note on the Singing-Stammering Seaman', *Western Folklore*, 35 (1976): 160–1.

Carlyle, Thomas, *Essays* (London: Chapman and Hall, 1883).

Catalogue of the Lauriston Castle Chapbooks, National Library of Scotland, Edinburgh (Boston: G. K. Hall & Co., 1964).

Chambers, Robert and Wallace, William (eds), *The Life and Works of Robert Burns*, 4 vols (New York: Longmans, Green, and Co., 1896).

Christiansen, Reidar Th., *The Migratory Legends* (Helsinki: Folklore Fellows Communication no. 175, 1958).

Collinson, Francis, *The Traditional and National Music of Scotland* (London: Routledge & Kegan Paul, 1966).

Cook, Davidson, 'Burns and old Song Books', *The Scottish Musical Magazine*, 3 (1927): 147–9, 207–9.

Crawford, Thomas, *Burns: a study of the poems & songs* (Edinburgh: Oliver & Boyd, 1960).

Cromek, R. H., *Remains of Nithsdale and Galloway Song* (Paisley: Alexander Gardner, 1880).

Cunningham, Allan, *The Works of Robert Burns; with his Life*, 8 vols (London: James Cochrane and Co., 1834).

Currie, James, *The Life of Robert Burns, with a Criticism on His Writings* (Edinburgh: William and Robert Chambers, 1838).

Daiches, David, *Robert Burns*, revised ed. (London: Andre Deutsch, 1966).

——, *The Paradox of Scottish Culture: The Eighteenth-Century Experience* (London: Oxford University Press, 1964).

Davidson, Thomas, *Rowan Tree and Red Thread* (Edinburgh: Oliver and Boyd, 1949).

Dégh, Linda and Andrew Vázsonyi, '*The Crack on the Red Goblet or Truth and Modern Legend*' in *Folklore in the Modern World*, ed. Richard M. Dorson (The Hague: Mouton, 1978).

——, 'The Hypothesis of the Multi-Conduit Transmission in Folklore', in *Folklore: Performance and Communication*, eds Dan Ben–Amos and Kenneth Goldstein (The Hague: Mouton, 1975).

Dégh, 'Legend and Belief', *Genre*, 4 (1971): 281–304.

Dent, Alan, *Burns in his Time* (London: Thomas Nelson and Sons, 1966).

Dewar, Robert, *Burns: Poetry and Prose* (Oxford: Clarendon Press, 1929).

Dick, James C., *The Songs of Robert Burns* and *Notes on Scottish Songs by Robert Burns*, 1903 and 1908 (reprint. Hatboro, Pennsylvania: Folklore Associates, 1962).

The Dictionary of National Biography (London: Oxford University Press, since 1917).

Dougall, Charles S., *The Burns Country* (London: Adam and Charles Black, 1904).

Douglas, Hugh, *Johnnie Walker's Burns Supper Companion* (Ayr: Alloway Publishing, 1981).

'Dumfries Burns Club Centenary Celebration', *Burns Chronicle*, 30 (1921): 109–16.

Dundes, Alan, 'The Study of Folklore in Literature and Culture', *Journal of American Folklore*, 78 (1965): 136–42.

Dundes, Alan and Alessandro Falassi, *La Terra in Piazza: An Interpretation of the Palio of Siena* (Berkeley: University of California Press, 1975).

Dunn, Charles W., 'The Cultural Status of Scottish Gaelic: A Humanistic Interpretation', *Modern Language Quarterly*, 22 (1961): 3–11.

Eggleston, Edward, *The Mystery of Metropolisville* (New York: Orange Judd and Company, 1873).

Eliot, T. S., *The Sacred Wood* (London: Methuen, 1950).

Ericson–Roos, Catarina, *The Songs of Robert Burns: A Study of the Unity of Poetry and Music* (Acta Universitatis Upsaliensis, Studia Anglistica Upsaliensia. Uppsala, 1977).

Ewing, Elizabeth, 'The First "Burns Nicht" (Alloway) and the First Burns Club (Greenock)'. *Burns Chronicle* (1948): 38–42.

Ewing, James Cameron and Davidson Cook (eds), *Robert Burns's Commonplace Book 1783–1785* (Carbondale, Illinois: Southern Illinois University Press, 1965, and London: Centaur Press, 1965).

Ferguson, J. De Lancey (ed.), *The Letters of Robert Burns*, 2 vols (Oxford: Clarendon Press, 1931).

——, *Pride and Passion* (New York: Oxford University Press, 1939).

Fergusson, Robert, *The Works of Robert Fergusson* (Edinburgh: The Mercat Press, 1970).

Finnegan, Ruth, *Oral Poetry: Its nature, significance and social context* (Cambridge: Cambridge University Press, 1977).

Fitzhugh, Robert, *Robert Burns, His Associates and Contemporaries* (Chapel Hill: University of North Carolina Press, 1943).

——, *Robert Burns: The Man and The Poet* (Boston: Houghton Mifflin, 1970).

Gee, H. L., *Folk Tales of Yorkshire* (London: Thomas Nelson and Sons, 1952).

Gibb, J. Taylor, *The Land of Burns: Mauchline Town and District* (Glasgow: Carson & Nicol, 1911).

Gibbon, Lewis Grassic, *Cloud Howe* (London: Jarrolds, 1933).

——, *Grey Granite* (London: Jarrolds, 1934).

——, *Sunset Song* (London: Jarrolds, 1932).

Giles, Peter, 'Dialect in Literature', in *The Scottish Tongue*, ed. William Alexander Craigie, 1924 (reprint. College Park, Maryland: McGrath Publishing Company, 1970).

Gower, Herschel, 'Burns in Limbo', *Studies in Scottish Literature*, 5 (1967–8): 229–37.

——, 'Jeannie Robertson: Portrait of a Traditional Singer', *Scottish Studies*, 12 (1968): 113–26.

Graham, H. G., *The Social Life of Scotland in the Eighteenth Century*, 5th ed. (London: Adam & Charles Black, 1969).

Granger, Byrd Howell, 'Folklore in Robert Burns' "Tam o' Shanter"', in *Folklore International: Essays in Traditional Literature, Belief, and Custom in Honor of Wayland Debs Hand*, ed. D. K. Wilgus (Hatboro, Pennsylvania: Folklore Associates, 1967).

Grose, Francis, *Antiquities of Scotland*, 2 vols (London: Hooper & Wigstead, 1797).

Guthrie, Woody, *Born to Win* (New York: Macmillan, 1965).

Hecht, Hans, *Robert Burns: The Man and His Work*, 2d rev. ed. (London: William Hodge & Co, 1950).

—— (ed.), *Songs from David Herd's Manuscripts* (William J. Hay, 1904).

Henley, W. E. and Henderson, T. F. (eds), *The Poetry of Robert Burns*, 4 vols (Edinburgh: T. C. and E. C. Jack, 1896–7).

Herd, David, *Ancient & Modern Scottish Songs*, 2 vols, 1869 (reprint. Edinburgh: Scottish Academic Press, 1973).

Hislop, Alexander, *The Book of Scottish Anecdote* (Edinburgh: The Edinburgh Publishing Company, 1874).

Ingram, John, *Anecdotes of Burns* (Glasgow: Thomas D. Morison, 1893).

Jack, William (ed.), 'Burns's Unpublished Common-Place Book', *Macmillan's Magazine*, 39 (1879): 448–60, 560–72; 40 (1880): 32–43, 124–32, 250–61.

Jamieson, R. (ed.), *Burt's Letters* or *Letters from a Gentleman in the North of Scotland to His Friend in London* (London: Ogle, Duncan, and Co., 1822).

Johnson, David, *Music and Society in Lowland Scotland in the Eighteenth Century* (London: Oxford University Press, 1972).

Johnson, James, *The Scots Musical Museum*, 6 vols (Edinburgh: 1787–1803).

Keith, Alexander, *Burns and Folk-Song* (Aberdeen: D. Wyllie & Son, 1922).

Keith, Christina, *The Russet Coat*, 1956 (reprint. New York: Haskell House, 1971).

Kinghorn, A. M., 'The Literary and Historical Origins of the Burns Myth', *Dalhousie Review*, 39 (1959).

Kinsley, James, 'Burns and the Merry Muses', *Renaissance and Modern Studies*, 9 (1965): 5–21.

——, (ed.), *The Poems and Songs of Robert Burns*, 3 vols (Oxford: Clarendon Press, 1968).

Klapp, Orrin E., *Heroes, Villains, and Fools* (Englewood Cliffs, N. J.: Prentice-Hall, 1962).

Kluckholm, Clyde, 'Recurrent Themes in Myths and Mythmaking', in *The Study of Folklore*, ed. Alan Dundes (Englewood Cliffs, N.J.: Prentice-Hall, 1965).

Legman, Gershon, *The Horn Book: Studies in Erotic Folklore and Bibliography* (New Hyde Park, New York: University Books, 1964).

—— (ed.), *The Merry Muses of Caledonia, collected and in Part written by Robert Burns* (New Hyde Park, New York: University Books, 1965).

Lewis, Mary Ellen B., 'Burns' "tale o' truth": A Meeting of Folklore and

Literature', *Journal of the Folklore Institute*, 13 (1976): 241–62.

Lewis, Mary Ellen B., 'Some Uses of the Past: The Traditional Song Repertoire of Robert Burns', in *Folklore Today*, eds L. Dégh, H. Glassie, F. Oinas (Bloomington: Research Center for Language and Semiotic Studies, 1976).

——, ' "The Joy of my heart": Robert Burns as Folklorist', *Scottish Studies*, 20 (1976): 45–67.

——, 'The Progress of "Lady Mary Ann" ', *Philological Quarterly*, 52 (1973): 97–107.

——, 'The Study of Folklore in Literature,' *Southern Folklore Quarterly*, 40 (1976): 343–51.

——, 'What To Do With "a red, red rose": A New Category of Burns' Songs', *Scottish Literary Journal*, 3 (1976): 62–75.

Lindsay, Maurice, *Burns: the man, his work, the legend* (London: MacGibbon & Kee, 1971).

——, *The Burns Encyclopedia*, 3rd rev. ed. (New York: St. Martin's Press, 1980).

Lockhart, John Gibson, *The Life of Robert Burns* (Edinburgh: Constable & Co., 1828).

——, *Peter's Letters to His Kinfolk*, ed. William Ruddick (Edinburgh: Scottish Academic Press, 1977).

Lord, Albert, *The Singer of Tales* (New York: Atheneum, 1971).

Low, Donald A. (ed.), *Critical Essays on Robert Burns* (London: Routledge & Kegan Paul, 1975).

——, *Robert Burns: The Critical Heritage* (London: Routledge & Kegan Paul, 1974).

Lyle, E. B., 'The Burns Text of *Tam Lin*', *Scottish Studies* 15 (1971): 53–65.

MacDiarmid, Hugh, *Burns Today and Tomorrow* (Edinburgh: Castle Wynd Printers, 1959).

——, *A Drunk Man Looks at the Thistle* (Edinburgh: William Blackwood & Sons, 1926).

Mackie, Albert, *Scottish Pageantry* (London: Hutchinson & Co., 1967).

Mackintosh, M., *Education in Scotland* (Glasgow: Robert Gibson & Sons, 1962).

MacLean, Calum, 'Traditional Belief in Scotland', *Scottish Studies*, 3 (1959): 189–200.

McNeill, F. Marian, *The Silver Bough*, 4 vols (Glasgow: William Maclellan, 1957–61).

McVie, John, *The Burns Federation: A Bicentenary Review* (Kilmarnock, 1959).

Meletinsky, E. M., 'The "Low" Hero of the Fairy Tale', in *The Study of Russian Folklore*, eds F. Oinas and S. Soudakoff (The Hague: Mouton, 1976).

Mitchell, John, D. D., 'Memories of Ayrshire about 1780', *Scottish Historical Society Miscellany*, 6 (1939).

Montgomerie, William (ed.), *New Judgements: Robert Burns* (Glasgow: William MacLellan, 1947).

Morison, J. B., 'Greenock Burns Club', *Burns Chronicle*, 2 (1893): 115–22.

Morton, Richard, 'Narrative Irony in Robert Burns's *Tam o' Shanter*', *Criticism*, 1 (1961): 12–20.

Muir, Edwin, *Essays on Literature and Society*, enl. and rev. ed. (London: Hogarth Press, 1965).

Murison, David, 'The Language of Burns', *Burns Chronicle* 25 (1950): 39–47.

Murray, Margaret Alice, *The Witch-Cult in Western Europe* (Oxford: Clarendon Press, 1921).

Ord, John, *The Bothy Songs & Ballads of Aberdeen, Banff & Moray, Angus and the Mearns* (Paisley, 1930; reprint. Edinburgh: John Donald).

Plant, Marjorie, *The Domestic Life of Scotland in the Eighteenth Century* (Edinburgh: University Press, 1952).

Priestley, J. B., *Literature and Western Man* (New York: Harper & Brothers, 1960).

Ramsay, Dean, *Reminiscences of Scottish Life and Character* (Edinburgh: T. N. Foulis, 1924).

Ritson, Joseph (ed.), *Scottish Songs* (London: J. Johnson & J. Egerton, 1794).

Ross, John D., *Burnsiana*, 5 vols (Paisley: Alexander Gardner, 1892).

Roy, G. Ross., 'The Merry Muses of Caledonia', *Studies in Scottish Literature*, 2 (1964–5): 211–12.

Schipper, Jakob, *A History of English Versification* (Oxford: Clarendon Press, 1910).

Scotland, James, *The History of Scottish Education* (London: London University Press, 1969).

Scott, R. E., 'The Pin that mended a Mill', *Burns Chronicle* 13 (1964): 31–2.

Scott, Sir Walter, 'Art. II. *Reliques of Robert Burns, consisting chiefly of original Letters, Poems, and Critical observations on Scottish Songs*. Collected and published by R. H. Cromek. 8 vo. pp. 453. London, Cadell Davies, 1808', *Quarterly Review*, 1 (1809).

Semple, David (ed.), *The Poems and Songs and Correspondence of Robert Tannahill with Life and Notes* (Paisley: Alexander Gardner, 1876).

Simpson, Eve Blantyre, *Folk Lore in Lowland Scotland* (London: J. M. Dent, 1908).

Sinclair, Sir John, *The Statistical Account of Scotland*, 21 vols (Edinburgh: William Creech, 1791–99).

Smith, Sydney Goodsir, 'Robert Burns and "the Merry Muses of Caledonia"', *Arena*, 4 (1950): 4–26.

Stenhouse, William, *Illustrations of the Lyric Poetry and Music of Scotland* (Edinburgh: William Blackwood and Sons, 1853).

Stevenson, Yvonne Helen, *Burns and His Bonnie Jean* (Sidney, British Columbia: Gray's Publishing, 1967).

Stewart, William Grant, *The Popular Superstitions and Festive Amusements of the Highlanders of Scotland*, 1851 (reprint. Hatboro, Pennsylvania: Norwood Editions, 1974).

Strawhorn, John, 'Burns and the Bardie Clan', *Scottish Literary Journal*, 8 (1981): 5–23.

Taylor, Archer, 'The Biographical Pattern in Traditional Narrative', *Journal of the Folklore Institute*, 1 (1964): 114–29.

Thompson, Harold William (ed.), *The Anecdotes and Egotisms of Henry Mackenzie 1745–1831* (London: Oxford University Press, 1927).

Thompson, Stith, *Motif-Index of Folk-Literature*, 6 vols (Bloomington: Indiana University Press, 1955–7).

Thomson, George, *A Select Collection* (London: Preston & Son, 1793–1818).

Thomson, J. F. T., 'Suggested lines for organising a Burns Supper', *Burns Chronicle* (1979): 31–2.

Thornton, R. D., *James Currie: The Entire Stranger and Robert Burns* (Edinburgh: Oliver & Boyd, 1963).

——, *The Tuneful Flame: Songs of Robert Burns as He Sang Them* (Lawrence, Kansas: University of Kansas Press, 1957).

Tocher (Edinburgh: School of Scottish Studies, Edinburgh University, 1971–).

Van Gennep, Arnold, *The Rites of Passage* (Chicago: University of Chicago Press, 1972).

Waddell, P. Hateley, *Life and Works of Robert Burns* (Glasgow: David Wilson, 1867).

Index